THE PATHOLOGY OF PLENTY

This open access book critically examines the role international law plays in post-colonial countries, which primarily rely on the exploitation of their natural resources for economic and human development.

Since the 1990s, expressions such as the 'resource curse' and 'paradox of plenty' have been associated with unequal patterns of power and wealth distribution in post-colonial and neo-colonial countries. They have also been applied to the ecological and social costs of natural resources exploitation, and the planetary costs of mineral resources-based production and consumption patterns.

Taking various resource-curse and paradox-of-plenty theories as a starting point, the book illustrates how the law's role in resource-cursed countries is at once constitutive, preventive, remedial and punitive. It does so by engaging with various fields of public international law. The book revisits how rights and principles such as sovereignty over natural resources and economic self-determination were applied in decolonisation processes; studies the proliferation of international treaties protecting foreign property rights; and zooms in on various contract models used in the mineral resources sector to evaluate the distributional choices of cost and revenue.

This will be important reading for scholars in the fields of international law and international development.

Volume 98 in the series Studies in International Law

Studies in International Law

Recent titles in this series

Truth and Transitional Justice: Localising the International Legal Framework in Muslim Majority Legal Systems
Alice Panepinto

State Responsibility for Non-State Actors: Past, Present and Prospects for the Future
Richard Mackenzie-Gray Scott

International Agreements between Non-State Actors as a Source of International Law
Melissa Loja

Judicial Decisions in International Law Argumentation: Between Entrapment and Creativity
Letizia Lo Giacco

South-South Migrations and the Law from Below: Case Studies on China and Nigeria
Oreva Olakpe

Territorial Status in International Law
Jure Vidmar

Marine Bioprospecting, Biodiversity and Novel Uses of Ocean Resources: New Approaches in International Law
Edited by Niels Krabbe and David Langlet

The Standard of Review Before the International Court of Justice: Between Principle and Pragmatism
Felix Fouchard

Global Lawmaking and Social Change: The Varieties of Customary International Law
Gregor Novak

The Effectiveness of the Inter-American Court of Human Rights: The Case of Indigenous Territorial Rights
Gabriela CB Navarro

Individuals in International Humanitarian Law: A Historical Analysis
Sarina Landefeld

The Pathology of Plenty: Natural Resources in International Law
Lys Kulamadayil

For a complete list of titles in this series
see www.bloomsbury.com/uk/series/studies-in-international-law/

The Pathology of Plenty

Natural Resources in International Law

Lys Kulamadayil

•HART•
OXFORD • LONDON • NEW YORK • NEW DELHI • SYDNEY

HART PUBLISHING

Bloomsbury Publishing Plc

Kemp House, Chawley Park, Cumnor Hill, Oxford, OX2 9PH, UK

1385 Broadway, New York, NY 10018, USA

Bloomsbury Publishing Ireland Limited, 29 Earlsfort Terrace, Dublin 2, D02 AY28, Ireland

HART PUBLISHING, the Hart/Stag logo, BLOOMSBURY and the Diana logo are trademarks of Bloomsbury Publishing Plc

First published in Great Britain 2025

A catalogue record for this book is available from the British Library.

A catalogue record for this book is available from the Library of Congress.

Library of Congress Control Number: 2025905173

ISBN: HB: 978-1-50996-962-3
ePDF: 978-1-50996-964-7
ePub: 978-1-50996-963-0

Typeset by Compuscript Ltd, Shannon

For product safety related questions contact productsafety@bloomsbury.com

To find out more about our authors and books visit www.hartpublishing.co.uk. Here you will find extracts, author information, details of forthcoming events and the option to sign up for our newsletters.

To Mathew and Sosamma

Acknowledgements

THE PUBLICATION OF *The Pathology of Plenty* coincides with turbulent times for international law and the global order. Security alliances are evaporating, and instead, military assistance is traded for access to natural resources, while intentions of imperial land grabs – through forced resettlement and ethnic cleansing – are openly discussed. While I certainly did not write this book with these developments in mind, my hope is that it will nonetheless offer explanatory value for the present moment. It unpacks international law's role in preserving colonial structures of domination and exploitation at the moment of decolonisation, exposes double standards in how law has been applied, and reflects on which legal regimes gain traction and which do not. Hopefully, it therefore provides insights not only into how international law governs the exploitation of natural resources but also into how natural resources have shaped international law. The project behind *The Pathology of Plenty* has been with me for more than a decade. During that time, it has been my primary portal into the field of international law. As I engaged with the project, the manuscript that eventually became this monograph took on many different shapes and forms, each reflecting encounters with the work and ideas of cherished colleagues, new legal material, and various theoretical and methodological approaches. With this book, I extend an invitation to you, the reader, to think with me, as I have thought with others.

There are countless people who have inspired, guided, and supported me throughout this project. I thank my colleagues at the Geneva Graduate Institute, where the project first took shape – particularly Martine Basset – the Institute of Human Sciences in Vienna, and Amsterdam Law School, which hosted me for periods of time. I am also grateful to Sigrid Boysen and Helmut Schmidt University, whose generous support enabled me to complete this book, as well as to the networks of the Institute for Global Law and Policy, Transregional Academy (2016), and the Global South Workshop (2017), which provided me with valuable feedback on various chapters. I would also like to acknowledge the generous support of the Swiss National Science Foundation, which has awarded me an open access grant for this book (grant no. 232566). Material from this book was published in the form of two journal articles in the *London Review of International Law* and the *Journal of the History of International Law*.

I am deeply grateful to Fred Kimonge, Baby Matabishi, Nicole Mandesi, and all my colleagues at the Carter Center in Lubumbashi for their inspiration and guidance during my stay with them in 2015, and to Ratna Kapur and Duncan Kennedy for giving me the confidence that my project could indeed one day become a book. I also thank María Victoria Cabrera, María Consuelo Velasco,

Robi Rado, Kevin Crow, Martin Clark, Dimitri Van Den Meerssche, Marie Petersmann, and Love Rönnelid for their generous engagement with my book. I am equally grateful to Sulekha Agarwal, Praggya Surana, and Anne Bevan for their editorial work. This book would not exist without my friendship with Danny Mulé and James Douglas, whose exceptional passion for critical praxis and unfailing kindness to others have always inspired me – and always will.

Finally, let me turn to those to whom I owe my deepest gratitude: my family. To Kiyana, Nayra, Eliyo, and Timaya, who never fail to remind me that real meaning lies in the smaller things; to Nidhi and Holger, exemplary role models of everyday life; and above all, to my parents, Mathew and Sosamma. In light of all the social identity markers of its author, this book is a statistical anomaly willed into existence by their (mostly) quiet resolve, unshakable confidence, and unwavering support. It is to them that I dedicate this book.

Contents

1

Introduction

SHORTLY BEFORE HIS assassination by Belgian and Congolese soldiers, Patrice Lumumba, the first prime minister of the Republic of Congo, wrote a letter to his wife Pauline from Thysville Prison near Lubumbashi. Likely knowing that his days were numbered, Lumumba looked back at his struggle for independence and observed:

> But what we wanted for our country – its right to an honourable life, to perfect dignity, to independence with no restrictions – was never wanted by Belgian colonialism and its Western allies, who found direct and indirect, intentional and unintentional support among certain high officials of the United Nations, that body in which we placed all our trust when we called on it for help. They have corrupted some of our countrymen; they have bought others; they have done their part to distort the truth and defile our independence.[1]

Lumumba knew not to look to the West, nor the United Nations (UN) for support in his country's efforts to overcome the shackles of colonialism, which had left the Congolese soil drenched in the blood of its people, who had been exploited and brutalised in the merciless efforts of its colonisers to extract value from the country's nature and its people. He understood that while formal colonialism may have ended, what followed in its wake was an equally treacherous form of oppression, one which recruited the country's political leadership in the subjugation of its people, one which replaced white men with guns, whips and machetes with Black men wielding the same weapons. Yet, even as he endured torture and faced his death, Lumumba remained hopeful for his country's future:

> I know and feel in my very heart of hearts that sooner or later my people will rid themselves of all their enemies, foreign and domestic, that they will rise up as one to say no to the shame and degradation of colonialism and regain their dignity in the pure light of day. We are not alone. Africa, Asia, and the free and liberated peoples in every corner of the globe will ever remain at the side of the millions of Congolese who will not abandon the struggle until the day when there will be no more colonizers and no more of their mercenaries in our country.[2]

[1] P Lumumba, 'Letter to Pauline Lumumba (December 1960)' in J van Lierde (ed), *Lumumba Speaks: The Speeches and Writings of Patrice Lumumba, 1958–1961* (Boston, Little, Brown and Company, 1972) 421.

[2] ibid, 422.

History has proven him wrong. To this day, Congolese people, like many other peoples of the Global South, continue to be haunted, not only by the darkness of their colonial past but also by the riches beneath their feet. Copper, cobalt, lithium, petroleum, uranium, gold, silver and gemstones – there are no minerals or ores that the Congo does not have in abundance. Yet, the country's riches have been its people's curse. While the rest of the world depends on Congolese minerals to produce the technologies that have become indispensable for modern ways of living, the Congolese, like many other people of postcolonial resource-wealthy countries, have not benefited, but suffered from the insatiable demand for their country's minerals. Under Belgian colonial rule, King Leopold's mercenaries and then Belgian state forces enslaved the Congolese population to extract value from them and their lands, for example by harvesting rubber or hunting and killing elephants for their ivory. Punishments given out for not meeting certain quotas included whipping, torture, mutilation, or killing either the workers themselves or their families.[3]

Today in the mines of the central African copper belt, soldiers of the Forces armées de la république démocratique du Congo (FARDC), the Mai-Mai militia and other organised armed groups extort artisanal miners for a share of their meagre daily income, which they earn through the hazardous labour of pit and tunnel mining, employing the very same means once used by their colonisers. Both debt bondage and child labour are rampant in the sector and video footage, as well as survivor testimonies, offer ample evidence that the practices of whipping, sexual assault and exemplary executions are still administered in Congolese mining communities today as a deliberate strategy for disciplining the labour force and ensuring their participation in the continued destruction of their lands and looting of its riches. Their terrorisers too, however, are merely pawns, fulfilling assigned roles in the lowest segments of global mineral supply chains that sustain the hallmarks of modern development and civilisation.

The crushing of countless Black bodies crippled and dreaded in tunnel collapses, at the bottom of global lithium, cobalt and copper supply chains, has merely been collateral damage in unrelenting corporate pursuits of maximising profit. When turning magnificent forests and farm lands into barren wastelands, global corporations and their agents are knowingly creating sacrifice zones which are kept from view of those whose ways of living the sacrifice was made for. Greed knows no colour or creed, which is why Lumumba's hope for the solidarity of other Asian and African people was in vain. Even worse, as global manufacturing of electronics has shifted from the West to the East, in Congo, white masters have been replaced with brown and Black ones.[4]

[3] See, eg: J Marchal, *Lord Leverhulme's Ghosts: Colonial Exploitation in the Congo* (London, Verso, 2017); J Marchal, *Forced Labor in the Gold & Copper Mines: A History of Congo under Belgian rule, 1910–1945* (San Francisco, Per Ankh Publishers, 2005).

[4] See generally: S Kara, *Cobalt Red: How the Blood of the Congo Powers Our Lives* (New York, St Martin's Press, 2023).

In another letter written on 4 January 1961 to the Special Delegate of the UN Secretary-General in Kinshasa, Lumumba described the conditions of his arrest and imprisonment concluding accurately that both were in blatant violation of the Congolese penal code and international humanitarian law. He pleaded with the Special Delegate to take his cause to the UN Secretary-General, but his plea was not heard.[5] The institution, which he had mistrusted to defend the cause of the people of Congo, sealed his fate, and with it the fate of the country he loved. Despite Lumumba having international law on his side, the United Nations did not intervene on his behalf, so only a few days later Lumumba was not only killed, but all evidence of his bodily existence, except a tooth, was dissolved.

Did the hope for a better future for his country and, for that matter, for all former colonies plundered for their earth's riches dissolve with him? Will he forever be right in his views of Western states and the United Nations, and will law's failure to save him be in perpetuity also be law's failure to save everything he stood for? This book seeks to answer some of these questions.

I. 'RESOURCE CURSE' AND 'PARADOX OF PLENTY'

Awareness for the challenges that countries with significant mineral resources wealth often face dates back to the age of colonialism, but it was the gruesome images of mutilated and tortured bodies from resources-fuelled conflicts in Cambodia, Liberia and Sierra Leone which led to broader interest in questions of mineral resources governance, exemplified in the founding of designated civil society organisations such as Global Witness and Transparency International.[6] In the late 1990s and early 2000s, the terms 'resource curse' and 'paradox of plenty' became synonymous with the negative economic, social and political effects of mineral resource extraction. Today, these terms are used interchangeably to refer to different models that seek to explain why the presence and exploitation of mineral resources do not lead to better development outcomes for postcolonial resource-wealthy countries, oftentimes creating instead significant ecological devastation, economic turmoil and social frictions.

Commonly associated with the resource curse is the political economy of states heavily reliant on the export of mineral resources, which are sometimes also referred to as 'Rentier states'.[7] To the World Bank, the resource curse is

[5] P Lumumba, 'Letter to Dayal (4 January 1961)' in J van Lierde (ed), *Lumumba Speaks: The Speeches and Writings of Patrice Lumumba, 1958–1961* (Boston, Little, Brown and Company, 1972).

[6] 'An Inside Job: Zimbabwe: The State, the Security Forces, and a Decade of Disappearing Diamonds' (Global Witness, 11 September 2017); 'A Rough Trade: The Role of Companies and Governments in the Angolan Conflict' (Global Witness, 1 December 1998); 'The Ogoni Crisis – A Case-Study Of Military Repression in Southeastern Nigeria' (Global Witness, 1 July 1995).

[7] H Mahdavy, 'The Pattern and Problems of Economic Development in Rentier States: The Case of Iran' in MA Cook (ed), *Studies in the Economic History of the Middle East* (Oxford, Oxford University Press, 1970).

caused by the inability of institutional contexts to properly manage public revenues earned through the export of natural resources, reduce fiscal volatility, and promote a macroeconomic environment conducive to long-term investment, suggesting that it can be avoided by the implementation of the 'right' economic and fiscal policies.[8] Others equate the resource curse with the 'Dutch disease', which refers to the crowding out of labour-intensive economic sectors, and the resulting rise in unemployment, which has often followed the commencement of large mineral resources export operations.[9] Some political scientists use the term paradox of plenty to describe kleptocratic public institutions and significant income disparities among the peoples of resource-wealthy countries. Such work originally related to 'petro-states', ie, states which rely heavily on the export of petroleum and natural gas to generate public revenue.[10] Others identify the sudden political and economic empowerment of domestic political elites that came with decolonisation and the high demand of mineral resources in post-war recovery efforts' energy demand, as the reason for the disproportionately high number of authoritarian and corruption-riddled regimes ruling such states.[11] Yet others are concerned with how the positive effects of resource extraction, namely revenue opposed to its adverse effects and ecological harm, have been distributed among domestic constituencies.[12] Finally, the presence and exploitation of mineral resources as well as ores and gemstones have been linked to the creation and reinforcement of cultural, religious and political frictions to explain the disproportionately high occurrence of armed conflict in resource-wealthy states, as opposed to states without such resources.[13]

What all the different interpretations of the resource curse have in common is the acknowledgement that all problems described as resource curse or paradox of plenty do not arise from the mere presence of mineral resources, but from the value attributed to them by humankind. In other words, it is understood that

[8] 'World Development Report 2017: Governance and the Law' (Washington DC, World Bank, 2017) 3.

[9] 'The Dutch Disease' *The Economist* (26 November 1977); JD Sachs and AM Warner, 'The Big Push, Natural Resource Booms and Growth' (1999) 59 *Journal of Development Economics* 43.

[10] TL Karl, *The Paradox of the Plenty: Oil Booms and Pedro States* (Berkeley, University of California Press, 1997); I Gary and L Karl, 'Bottom of the Barrel, Africa's Oil Boom and the Poor' (Catholic Relief Services, 2003). See also: V Menaldo, *The Institutions Curse, Natural Resources, Politics, and Development* (Cambridge, Cambridge University Press, 2016); M Shafer, *Winners and Losers: How Sectors Shape the Developmental Prospects of States* (Ithaca, NY, Cornell University Press, 1994).

[11] T Mitchell, *Carbon Democracy: Political Power in the Age of Oil* (New York, Verso, 2011); CRW Dietrich, *Oil Revolution* (New York, Cambridge University Press, 2017).

[12] M Watts, 'Resource Curse? Governmentality, Oil and Power in the Niger Delta, Nigeria' (2004) 9 *Geopolitics* 50. See also: E Kashi, *Curse of the Black Gold: 50 Years of Oil in the Niger Delta* (New York, Powerhouse Books, 2008); R Nixon, *Slow Violence and the Environmentalism of the Poor* (Cambridge, MA, Harvard University Press, 2011).

[13] See generally: P Le Billon, *The Geopolitics of Resource Wars* (London, Routledge, 2017); P Le Billon, *Wars of Plunder: Conflicts, Profits and the Politics of Resources* (London, Hurst, 2012). For relevant NGO reports, see also: 'Well Oiled' (Human Rights Watch, 9 July 2009); 'African Progress Report: Equity in Extractives' (African Progress Panel, 2013); 'An Inside Job: Zimbabwe: The State, the Security Forces, and a Decade of Disappearing Diamonds' (Global Witness, 11 September 2017).

resource curse and paradox of plenty phenomena are first and foremost a matter of social relations among humankind. And, while planetary costs of mineral resource extraction are of course material, the problems that particularly post-colonial countries that are wealthy in mineral resources face – the pathology of plenty as I call it – is structured entirely by human relations with nature, and among humans. All of these relations in one way or another fall under the preview of law, a fact regularly acknowledged by 'resource curse' and 'pathology of plenty' scholars, but never fully unpacked. Unfortunately, this book also neither can nor wants to offer a comprehensive picture of the legal structures that uphold the pathology of plenty. Rather, it attempts to offer impressions of different ways in which law, more specifically international law, relates to the pathology of plenty. Just as paradox of plenty and resource curse scholars have done previously, the goal is to offer explanatory paradigms of the role of international law in governing mineral resources, and their extraction in postcolonial resource-wealthy countries. This will not only shed more light on the pathology of plenty, but also on international law and its understanding of nature, resources and justice.

II. WHY AN INTERNATIONAL LAW PERSPECTIVE?

Mineral resources and their governance have of course long been a subject of interest for international law scholarship. Broadly speaking, this scholarship falls into three different categories. The first category is work accompanying the early years of the San Francisco legal order, which firmly established mineral resources as a regulatory object of international law, due to their centrality in decolonisation processes.[14] Such work is preoccupied with how the political sovereignty of newly independent states relates to their economic entanglements with their former colonisers, most notably in various forms of property rights.[15] The second category of scholarship reflects back on international law's role in decolonisation processes and its effect on the governance of natural resources, through concepts such as self-determination, sovereignty and

[14] I Brownlie, 'The Legal Status of Natural Resources in International Law (Some Aspects)' in Hague Academy of International Law (eds), *Collected Courses of the Hague Academy of International Law* (Leiden, Brill, 1979); I Brownlie, *Loaves and Fishes: Access to Natural Resources and International Law* (London, London School of Economics and Political Science, 1978).

[15] M Bedjaoui, *Towards a New International Economic Order* (New York, Holmes and Meier, 1979); G Abi-Saab, 'Le droit au développement' (1988) 44 *Annuaire Suisse de Droit International* 9; G Abi-Saab, 'The Role of Law in the Process of Development: with Special Reference to the Transfer of Technology to Underdeveloped Countries' in S Antonius, C Nader and A Zahlan (eds), *Science and Technology in Developing Countries: Proceedings of a Conference held at the American University of Beirut* (Cambridge, Cambridge University Press, 1969); 'Institutional Change and the International Legal Order: A Third World Perspective' (Ecumenical Institute Bossey World Council of Churches, 1970).

development.[16] The third category of scholarship addresses specific aspects of mineral resources governance, such as studies on mineral resources in armed conflict and post-conflict situations,[17] corporate social responsibility and corporate self-regulation,[18] and the possibilities of holding transnational corporations domiciled in Western countries accountable for their conduct abroad.[19]

This book builds on these three categories of scholarship, but rather than taking mineral resources or decolonisation as its starting point, it starts with the puzzles, which have moved resource curse and pathology of plenty scholars. Why is it that countries with extraordinary mineral resources wealth often do so poorly in terms of economic and human development? Why is it that the economic benefits of resource extraction are frequently enjoyed by shareholders far removed from those who suffer from its ecological costs? And, what is it that international law has to say about this? How may law be implicated in the distributional dynamics of mineral resources wealth? Do its underlying conceptions of justice support the pathology of plenty, or offer ideas which permit exposing its problems? May international law even offer tools and techniques to bring about structural change? These broad questions inform the different chapters of this book, with each one of them offering an impression of the paradoxical ways in which international law's promise of universality stands diagonally opposed to the role it plays in the pathology of plenty. As a result, this book is not one grand theory of the pathology of plenty, but rather an effort to expose the ways in which international law is simultaneously constitutive of, and responsive to, the pathology of plenty.

[16] A Anghie, Imperialism, *Sovereignty and the Making of International Law* (Cambridge, Cambridge University Press, 2005); S Pahuja, *Decolonising International Law Development, Economic Growth and the Politics of Universality* (Cambridge, Cambridge University Press, 2011); A Becker-Lorca, *Mestizo International Law* (Cambridge, Cambridge University Press, 2014); M Fakhri, *Sugar and the Making of International Trade Law* (Cambridge, Cambridge University Press, 2017).

[17] D Dam-de Jong, *International Law and Governance of Natural Resources in Conflict and Post-Conflict Situations* (Cambridge, Cambridge University Press, 2015); M Pertile, *La relazione tra risorse naturali e conflitti armati nel diritto internazionale* (CEDAM, 2013). See generally: E Morgera and K Kulovesi, *Research Handbook on International Law and Natural Resources* (Cheltenham, Edward Elgar, 2016).

[18] JA Zerk, *Multinationals and Corporate Social Responsibility: Limitations and Opportunities in International Law* (Cambridge, Cambridge University Press, 2006); G Teubner, 'Globale Bukowina, Zur Emergenz eines transnationalen Rechtspluralismus'(1996) 15 *Rechtshistorisches Journal* 255; G Teubner, 'Globale Zivilverfassungen: Alternativen zur staatszentrierten Verfassungstheorie' in M Neves and R Voigt (eds), *Die Staaten der Weltgesellschaft: Niklas Luhmanns Staatsverständnis* (Baden-Baden, Nomos, 2007).

[19] B Stephens, 'Translating Filartiga: A Comparative and International Law Analysis of Domestic Remedies for International Human Rights Violations' (2002) 27 *Yale Journal of International Law* 1; LJ Dhooge, 'Aguinda v Chevrontexaco: Mandatory Grounds for the Non-Recognition of Foreign Judgments for Environmental Injury in the United States' (2009) 19 *Journal of Transnational Law & Policy* 1; J Kimberling, 'Indigenous Peoples and the Oil Frontier in Amazonia: The Case of Ecuador, Chevrontexaco, and Aguinda v Texaco' (2006) 38 *New York University Journal of International Law and Politics* 413.

III. STRUCTURE OF THE BOOK

The book is structured as follows: The next chapter, chapter two, offers a brief overview of what this book refers to as the pathology of plenty, the point not being to validate or critique any of the existing paradox of plenty and resource curse theories, but rather to use them to illustrate the issues that postcolonial resource-wealthy countries face. The next two chapters, chapters three and four, offer accounts of the role international law played in state formation processes and the emancipatory efforts of postcolonial resource-wealthy countries. Chapter three explores how international law was implicated in producing unequal patterns of wealth and power distribution that are so characteristic for the pathology of plenty. It does so by revisiting the role played by the principles of economic self-determination, *uti possidetis* and permanent sovereignty over natural resources in state-formation processes. It argues that the interplay of these principles sets the course for developing and cementing these unequal patterns of wealth and power distribution. In exploring how prominent economic theorists conceived of the ways in which mineral resources wealth may affect political and economic conditions in postcolonial countries, the chapter reflects on the distributive intentionality with which certain legal principles were applied. Chapter four highlights the marks left on international law by Iran's and Algeria's early, and mid-twentieth century paths to reclaiming sovereignty over their petroleum reserves. It shows that Iran has significantly affected the contractual model of petroleum operations, whereas Algeria has championed the international law turn of Third World Internationalism. It thus hopes to shift attention from the frequently cited non-consequentialism of key moments in Third World Internationalism, such as Bandung and the the New International Economic Order (NIEO) to the significance of these domestic and transnational processes. While doing so, it is careful to point to the extraordinary bargaining power given to petro-states by the fossil-fuel dependent global economy, which elevated their influence in global affairs over that of other states in the Global South.

The subsequent chapters, chapters five, six and seven, engage with various legal responses to the resource curse under international corruption and anti-money laundering law, international humanitarian and criminal law and international human rights law. Commonly subsumed under the legal concepts of corruption and money laundering, the theft of public wealth on a massive scale with the aid of transnational financial institutions has, so far, largely been neglected by legal scholarship and legal practice. Drawing on two grand theft cases, the objectives of chapter five are threefold. First, it explains the concept of grand theft by illustrating how it operates. Secondly, it retraces legal responses to grand theft in jurisdictions of countries, which are home to key financial markets places, to highlight the strengths and weaknesses of this legal regime in practice. Thirdly, it reflects on the obstacles to researching grand theft. Chapter six then explores how international law governs questions of property and sovereignty in resource wars. In doing so it hopes to show how, in such wars, international law's moralist aspirations decisively clash with its deference to hegemony and capitalism. It pays particular attention to the ways in which normative progress has been achieved and undone, not only by mere power politics, but also by the ways in which occupying powers' law and legal reasoning is absorbed into national and international law in ways which deprive people of their right to their natural resources, while simultaneously forcefully imposing market liberalisation on the mineral resources sector. By zooming in on four such instances, the chapter hopes to show how capitalism intersects with the victor's justice when it concerns questions of mineral resources property rights and legal authority over their governance. Chapter seven is dedicated to human rights responses. Scholars have famously pointed out that human rights were, among other things, sanctifying planned misery,[20] that their movement was 'part of the problem',[21] that they were 'powerless companions'[22] and 'not enough' or 'fellow travelers'[23] to neoliberalism, or that they simply came in 'too late'.[24] To make sense of this work in the context of the pathology of plenty, this chapter takes neo-extractivism, one important cause for the pain of plenty, ie, devastating human misery in the presence of immeasurable extractive value, as a starting point, in order to escape the public–private divide, which informs so many reflections on human rights and their potential to remedy the social costs of global capitalism. The chapter illustrates the ineffectiveness of welfarist efforts, which are premised on extractivism. It does however also show how human rights have been shaped, mobilised and developed as a strategy and language of contestation. Chapter eight concludes.

IV. PURPOSE AND DEFINITIONS

Some definitions are in order. 'Mineral resources' refers to non-renewable resources that are either labour, or capital-intensive to exploit, such as crude oil, copper, cobalt, lithium etc. This book uses the words resource-cursed states, and postcolonial resource-wealthy countries interchangeably to refer to postcolonial states which exhibit some symptoms of the pathology of plenty. The book recognises that states which were formally never colonised can also be 'resource-cursed' so to speak, the most prominent example for this being of

[20] S Marks, 'Human Rights and Root Causes' (2011) 74 *Modern Law Review* 57.

[21] D Kennedy, 'International Human Rights Movement: Part of the Problem?' (2002) 15 *Harvard Human Rights Journal* 101.

[22] S Moyn, 'A Powerless Companion: Human Rights in the Age of Neoliberalism' (2014) 77 *Law and Contemporary Problems* 147.

[23] J Whyte, *The Morals of the Market: Human Rights and the Rise of Neoliberalism* (London, Verso, 2019).

[24] I Venzke, 'The Law of the Global Economy and the Spectre of Inequality' (2021) 9 *London Review of International Law* 111.

course the Dutch experience of the 1970s. Yet it contends that the path dependencies as it concerns international law's role in former colonial, as opposed to former imperial countries, is quite distinct. This is due to the vastly different ways in which international law governed moments of decolonisation as well as the ways in which colonisation permitted the establishment of a distinct set of property regimes.

This book is an exercise in the sense-making of an international lawyer. Such an exercise is twofold. On the one hand, in applying doctrinal methods, analysing legal material and using the codes of the discipline, this book seeks to understand how international law relates to social and material conditions which have come to be associated with resource wealth in postcolonial countries. On the other hand, by undertaking this very exercise one inevitably learns more about international law, as a technique, a normative commitment, an ideology and a means of contestation. In other words, this book is as much about better understanding international law as it is about understanding the pathology of plenty.

2

The Pathology of Plenty

I. INTRODUCTION

WHY REFER TO the 'pathology of plenty' to describe the state in which many postcolonial countries wealthy in terms of mineral resources find themselves in? The *Oxford English Dictionary* defines 'pathology' as the 'science of the causes and effects of diseases'.[1] Thinking of postcolonial resource-wealthy countries as diseased implies, on the one hand, that they could, or rather should be doing better on various good governance, and human and economic development indicators, and, on the other hand, that mineral resources are linked to this detected underperformance. This is of course not an unproblematic assertion, as those ways of thinking about national development trajectories are typically associated with liberal and neoliberal thought, which postulate that progress achieved through economic growth is the 'normal'.[2] This is explicitly not the point this book seeks to make. Instead, it seeks to expose how the internalising of predetermined paradigms of achieving progress and development in the law and governance of the global political economy has set the foundations for the pathology of plenty to fester. The baseline expectation is that the presence and exploitation of mineral resources should not have any detrimental effects on a country's people, or its political economy. By recounting findings from the 'resource curse' and 'paradox of plenty' literature, this chapter will offer a brief overview of how this baseline expectation is not met. Because these findings cannot be presented in complete abstraction from the theories they have inspired, these will also be sketched briefly as a way of introducing the scholarship, which this book seeks to complement.

II. THE ECONOMIC DIMENSION

The pathbreaking study coining the term 'resource curse' was published by Auty in 1994. It found that the growth performance of mineral-exporting countries

[1] 'Pathology' in A Stevenson (ed), *Oxford Dictionary of English* (Oxford, Oxford University Press, 2010).

[2] WW Rostow, *The Stages of Economic Growth: A Non-Communist Manifesto* (Cambridge, Cambridge University Press, 1960).

was significantly lower than that of other countries. Oil-exporting countries averaged 2.2 per cent GDP growth compared with 5.1 per cent GDP growth for manufacturing countries.[3] Since his study was published, the growth trajectory of economies built on the exploitation of mineral resources has inspired various economic theories, which focus, among other things, on the different impacts of foreign resources trade in co-relation to other variables such as the size of their economy, varying durations, market value variations and collapses, the presence of other economic sectors, and human development indicators.[4] In addition, the advantages and disadvantages of managing mineral resources through state-owned enterprises as opposed to transnational ones have been the subject of much debate.[5] Two prominent strands of economic theories explaining why mineral resources wealth may adversely affect a country's economy are referred to as the 'Dutch disease' as well as one built on the nature, structure and volatility of mineral resources revenues.[6] Both will now briefly be outlined.

In 1959, Europe's largest natural gas reserves were discovered in the Netherlands, which turned the country into a major exporter of natural gas in Europe. The revenues generated from these exports boosted the Dutch government's budget significantly and it seemed that the natural gas discoveries benefited the thriving Dutch economy and its strong manufacturing sector.[7] Additionally, national energy security was achieved. Despite this seemingly forward-moving growth, after some years the Dutch economy took a downward turn that the *Economist* eventually labelled as the 'Dutch disease'.

In the 1970s, Dutch industrial production stagnated and the unemployment rate rose from 1.1 per cent in 1970 to 5.1 per cent in 1977, with employment in the manufacturing sector falling by 16 per cent. At the same time, the Dutch currency guilder grew strong, and over six years, its value rose by 16.4 per cent in trade-weighted terms.[8] While the Netherlands had been a recipient of foreign direct investment (FDI) during the period from 1967 to 1971, it turned into an exporter of FDI in the years that followed. It is this disparity between the boost

[3] R Auty, 'Trade and Industrial Policy for Sustainable Resource-based Development: Policy Issues, Achievements and Prospects' (UNCTAD, 1994) 7.

[4] CS Hendrix and M Noland, *Confronting the Curse: The Economics and Geopolitics of Natural Resource Governance* (New York, Columbia University Press, 2014) 9–26.

[5] See generally: P Heidrich, 'The Regional Context of Latin-American Resource Nationalism' in PA Haslam and P Heidrich (eds), *The Political Economy of Natural Resources and Development: From Neoliberalism to Resource Nationalism* (London, Routledge, 2016).

[6] 'The Resource Curse: The Political and Economic Challenges of Natural Resource Wealth' (Natural Resource Governance Institute, 2015).

[7] During the same period, the Nigerian economy underwent similar developments. As oil revenues poured in, peanut and cocoa production – Nigeria's main export goods at the time – declined and the basis for economic subsistence of thousands of farmers vanished. The exploitation of oil in Nigeria therefore had a detrimental effect on the agricultural sector. The sudden large-scale inflow of revenues from extractive sectors therefore has a negative impact on labour-intensive sectors. The sudden large-scale inflow of external resource rents crowded out labour-intensive sectors such as manufacturing and agriculture.

[8] 'The Dutch Disease' *Economist* (26 November 1977).

in the country's export capital and the loss of domestic production, which led to a redistribution of wealth from the poorer segments of society to the richer ones, that the *Economist* described as 'Dutch disease'.[9] Around the same time, the Netherlands implemented policy measures aimed at increasing the social security of workers, which, in turn, led to an increase in the costs of labour. Coupled with the effects of inflation, the costs for manufacturing in the Netherlands rose rapidly in a short period, suddenly placing the Netherlands, as a place for labour-intensive production at a competitive disadvantage, explaining the withdrawal of foreign capital, and the resulting loss of domestic employment.[10] In addition, the Dutch government committed the resources generated by natural gas in ways which did little to counter-balance the adverse effects they had on other economic sectors.[11]

While the term 'Dutch disease' is associated with the Dutch case, and an important reminder that adverse effects of mineral resources wealth are not a 'Third World problem', related dynamics could be observed in other parts of the world as well. In the 1970s and early 1980s following the nationalisation of mineral resources and production sites, international institutions such as the International Monetary Fund (IMF) and the World Bank were happy to grant countries large loans based on the prospect of their increased future earnings through the export of mineral resources. For various reasons, including the fact that petroleum prices during the 1980s stagnated and even fell, many borrowing countries struggled to meet the terms of the loans. The economic austerity and privatisation measures that followed, often mandated by their creditors as part of structural adjustment programmes, have in many cases amplified domestic inequality levels.[12]

III. VOLATILITY OF RESOURCE REVENUES

Even before Auty's resource curse theory, economists were preoccupied with the detrimental effects of revenue volatility.[13] They observed that oftentimes governments that relied heavily on mineral resources revenues eventually struggled with

[9] ibid.

[10] ibid.

[11] ibid.

[12] M Humphreys, JD Sachs and JE Stiglitz, 'What is the Problem with Natural Resource Wealth?' in M Humphreys, JD Sachs and JE Stiglitz (eds), *Escaping the Resources Curse* (New York, Columbia University Press, 2007) 8; JD Sachs, 'How to Handle the Macroeconomics of Oil Wealth' in M Humphreys, JD Sachs and JE Stiglitz (eds), *Escaping the Resource Curse* (Columbia University Press, 2007); For instance, in 1999 the IMF estimated that Angola's oil-backed loans amounted to 33% of the country's total external debt. See I Gary and L Karl, 'Bottom of the Barrel, Africa's Oil Boom and the Poor' (Catholic Relief Services, 2003) 33; EA Cardoso and A Fishlow, 'The Macroeconomics of the Brazilian External Debt' in JD Sachs (ed), *Developing Country Debt and the World Economy* (Chicago, IL, University of Chicago Press, 1989).

[13] Humphreys, Sachs and Stiglitz, 'What is the Problem with Natural Resource Wealth?' (n 12) 6.

fiscal and solvency problems, induced often by their inability to adjust to what is referred to as economic 'boom-bust cycles'. Two factors affecting the volatility of resource revenues are extraction rate variations and market value variations. Generally speaking, factors affecting extraction levels include the state of production infrastructure, technical issues, weather conditions, resource discovery or depletion, armed conflict,[14] and unexpected turmoil in global markets.[15]

Similarly, market value fluctuations have various causes. While price theory suggests that the relationship between supply and demand dictates the price of any good, how mineral resources are valued by the market does not necessarily operate according to this logic. This is due to the highly financialised nature of global commodities markets, which respond to any news which may affect mineral resources, such as the invasion of Ukraine by Russia, or the fear of the effects of the COVID-19 pandemic on the global economy. Furthermore, the mineral resources sector being dominated by a limited group of actors who control global supply is more easily affected by the coordinated actions of certain actors such as the Organization of Petroleum Exporting Countries (OPEC).[16]

IV. THE POLITICAL DIMENSION

What is the political dimension of the pathology of plenty, or more specifically, how do mineral resources relate to power? These questions are complex, with much of the scholarship addressing them having a strong liberal bias. This is in part due to Karl's foundational work on this issue, on petro-states, that is to say, states which generate more than half of their public revenue through the export of petroleum, which finds the 'paradox of plenty' to be a 'primarily political and not an economic phenomenon'.[17] She notes that the presence of petroleum leads

[14] Gary and Karl (n 12) 21–23; TL Karl, 'The Case for a Transparent Fiscal Social Contract' in M Humphreys, JD Sachs and JE Stiglitz (eds), *Escaping the Resource Curse* (New York, Columbia University Press, 2007); Humphreys, Sachs and Stiglitz, 'What is the Problem with Natural Resource Wealth?' (n 12) 6, 8; ML Ross, *The Oil Curse: How Petroleum Wealth Shapes the Development of Nations* (Princeton, NJ, Princeton University Press, 2012) 50, 170; L Hosman, 'Dividing the Oils: Dynamic Bargaining as Policy Formation in the Nigerian Petroleum Industry'(2009) 26 *Review of Policy Research* 617; 'Regional Economic Outlook, Sub-Saharan Africa – Fostering Durable and Inclusive Growth' (IMF, 2014) 8.

[15] Cameroon was one of the countries that saw an opportunity in the 1970s oil revolution and began extracting its oil reserves at a fast pace. As a result, its production peaked in 1991, only 14 years after production had begun. B Gauthier and A Zeufack, 'Cameroon's Oil Wealth: Transparency Matters' in B Akitoby and S Coorey (eds), *Oil Wealth in Central Africa: Policies for Inclusive Growth* (IMF, 2012) 156; 'Cameroon' 2014, available at: www.eia.gov/countries/country-data.cfm?fips=cms.

[16] J Hummel, 'Diamonds are a Smuggler's Best Friend: Regulation, Economics, and Enforcement in the Global Effort to Curd the Trade in Conflict Diamonds' (2007) 41 *International Lawyer* 1145, 1147.

[17] Karl (n 14) 257.

to extraordinarily high levels of intervention and revenue capture by foreign states and companies. However, rather than identifying foreign interference in and of itself as the problem, she instead points to countries such as Norway, to argue that the adverse effects of mineral resources wealth were the result of unfortunate sequencing, namely when resource extraction began before domestic institutions in postcolonial countries were 'mature enough' to withstand the political challenges of governing resources wealth.[18] She also notes that since the public income generated by petroleum involved only a very small part of the constituency, there was less scrutiny on how this income was spent, and not enough pressure to put effective control mechanisms in place.[19] Others have built on Karl's work to put forward variants of her arguments.[20] In sum, this strand of scholarship implies that postcolonial and post-Soviet countries are more prone to suffer from the adverse effects of resource wealth than liberal ones.[21] For example, Sachs has argued that the effects that mineral resources wealth would have on a country's political economy were a matter of choosing the 'right investment strategy'.[22] This should include promoting economic growth by investing in a country's infrastructure and creating improved conditions for the private sector to flourish.[23] Others have turned their attention to how mineral resources revenues are contractually structured and the problems for oversight that such structures pose. For instance, in the petroleum sector, production-sharing agreements have become the most common contract type regulating the relationship between the agencies of the host state and extraction operators, typically a consortium of several petroleum companies.[24] Such contracts, also referred to as host government contracts, are frequently supplemented by auxiliary contracts which include contracts of association between the different companies involved, amendments to the host-government contracts, as well

[18] ibid 272.

[19] ibid 262.

[20] Gary and Karl (n 12) 322; P Collier, *The Bottom Billion: Why the Poorest Countries are Failing and What Can Be Done About It* (Oxford, Oxford University Press, 2007) 42; C Leite and J Weidmann, 'Does Mother Nature Corrupt? Natural Resources, Corruption, and Economic Growth' (1999) IMF Working Paper 30.

[21] PJ Luong and E Weinthal, *Oil is not a Curse: Ownership Structure and Institutions in Soviet Successor States* (Cambridge, Cambridge University Press, 2010) 2; D Acemoglu and J Robinson, *Why Nations Fail: The Origins of Power, Prosperity, and Poverty* (New York, Crown Business, 2012) 96.

[22] Sachs, 'How to Handle the Macroeconomics of Oil Wealth' (n 12).

[23] T Gylfason, 'Natural Resources, Education, and Economic Development'(2001) 45 *European Economic Review* 847.

[24] 'Oil Contracts – How to Read and Understand them' (*OpenOil*, 2012) 16; See also: J Calder, 'Resource Tax Administration: Functions, Procedures and Institutions' in D Philip, M Keen and C McPherson (eds), *The Taxation of Petroleum and Minerals: Principles, Problems and Practice* (London, Routledge, 2010); C Nakhle, 'Petroleum Fiscal Regimes: Evolution and Challenges' in D Philip, M Keen and C McPherson (eds), *The Taxation of Petroleum and Minerals: Principles, Problems and Practice* (London, Routledge, 2010).

as agreements on social, environmental, or technical investments.[25] The problem with these contracts is that even when they are publicly available – which they are frequently not – they are notoriously difficult to monitor. For example, despite the Democratic Republic of the Congo's transparency laws requiring all contracts concerning mining oil and forestry to be published, many remain inaccessible.[26] In instances in which they are available, their complex fiscal regimes, the volatility of extraction rates, and oil market value make it very difficult to keep track of the profitability of any given extraction project without access to the extraction data, which the operators of the project are often reluctant to share. To return to the example of the production-sharing agreement, the difficulty in accounting for profit begins with the fact that its provisions designate how the product, rather than the profit, is shared between the government and the operators of the extraction site at different stages of the extraction cycle.[27]

This begins with the extraction of crude oil of which a share, referred to as royalty, is due to the government. The royalty is due without the subtraction of any costs of the operators and can vary from a share of zero to 35 per cent. How much public revenue royalties yield depends on several variables including volume.[28] The counterpart to royalty is called cost oil. It designates the share of petroleum allocated to the operators – before taxes – to recover their costs. Recoverable costs may include the costs of production, transport and storage, sometimes, as signature bonuses, with most petroleum contracts having a cost limit to guarantee a minimum share of profit, even in the first years of the production phase.[29] Cost oil and royalties only make up one portion of crude oil produced. The other portion is referred to as profit oil. Profit oil is divided between the government and the operators of an extraction site, with the size of the shares typically varying throughout the project's production cycle. In the initial years of the project, operators' profit shares tend to be higher. This is again to account for the high investment costs of operators. In the later stages of a project cycle, however, operators' proportionate profit shares typically decrease in favour of government shares. In any event, unlike in the case for cost oil, operators' profit oil shares are subject to taxes.[30]

What complicates monitoring the profitability of a petroleum project in general – and the revenues it generates for a host state in particular even further – is that different payment types fall under the competence of different government

[25] JE Stiglitz, 'What is the Role of the State?' in M Humphreys, JD Sachs and JE Stiglitz (eds), *Escaping the Resource Curse* (New York, Columbia University Press, 2007) 23.

[26] Décret Nr 011/26 du 20 Mai 2011 portant obligation de publier tout contrat ayant pour objet les ressources naturelles.

[27] D Johnson, 'How the Evaluate the Fiscal Terms of Oil Contracts' in M Humphreys, JD Sachs and JE Stiglitz (eds), *Escaping the Resource Curse* (New York, Columbia University Press, 2007).

[28] 'Oil Contracts' (n 24) 51.

[29] ibid 128.

[30] ibid 54.

agencies, including state-owned companies.[31] As a result, public income and spending in petro-states can be less transparent than in other states.[32] This makes it prone to grand theft, that is to say, revenue capture by elites.[33] For example, 54 per cent of all petroleum revenues that the government of Cameroon ought to have received between 1977 and 2006, could not be accounted for.[34] Another example of such grand theft is Equatorial Guinea, where President Teodoro Obiang and his family have clung to power for decades, using the revenues of their oil-wealthy country for personal gain. The extravagant escapades of his son Teodorin Obiang are well documented, as is the fact that his expenses were partly paid for by international commodities traders.[35] Meanwhile, the life expectancy in Equatorial Guinea is as low as 56 years for men and 59 years for women, and child mortality has risen, rather than decreased, since oil production began in the early 2000s while 76.8 per cent of the population continues to live below the national poverty line.[36]

A contentious debate among resource curse and paradox of plenty scholars is whether the likelihood of grand theft occurring is affected by whether or not petroleum operations are carried out by state-owned companies or by transnational ones. The problem with transnational corporations, being relied on to operate a country's extraction projects is that such companies, due to their transnational corporate structure, are notoriously hard to oversee for domestic institutions and, at the same time, exercise an extraordinarily high level of control over public revenue generation.[37] In contrast, those favouring the involvement of transnational corporations have argued that their involvement provides an extra level of accountability. Michael Ross, for instance, argues that the resource curse is a result of the nationalisation of oil and gas industries and the emergence of national companies in the 1970s, and that since then resource wealth has led to bad policy choices.[38] The higher the share of oil income per capita in an authoritarian country or a low-level democracy, the less the likelihood of such a country transitioning into a democracy.[39]

[31] Only few countries have centralised oversight bodies that control and reconcile all payments: M Katz et al, 'Lifting the Oil Curse, Improving Petroleum Revenue Management in Sub-Saharan Africa' (IMF, 2004) 46.

[32] Ross (n 14) 59.

[33] Leite and Weidmann (n 20).

[34] Gauthier and Zeufack (n 15).

[35] For a detailed exposée, see: K Silverstein, *The Secret World of Oil* (New York, Verso, 2015).

[36] 'Equatorial Guinea country profile', *BBC News* (20 September 2017); 'Equatorial Guinea', 10 February 2023, available at: data.worldbank.org/country/equatorial-guinea.

[37] Stiglitz (n 25).

[38] Ross (n 14) 1–25.

[39] To underpin this finding, he points to the Arab Spring where regimes in oil-poor countries such as Tunisia and Egypt were overthrown more quickly than regimes in oil-rich countries such as Libya, Bahrain and Saudi Arabia: ibid 63, 94.

V. THE GEO-POLITICAL DIMENSION

A less well-known strand of scholarship studies the pathology of plenty from the perspective of political geography. Development economists have argued that geographical conditions in Sub-Saharan Africa have impeded its economic and human development.[40] This thinking goes back to Adam Smith for whom the development of a country depended on whether it was landlocked or had access to the sea, whether it had navigable rivers to facilitate domestic trade, and, whether it was integrated into the international trading system.[41] Among contemporary scholars, Sachs and Collier are the most prominent proponents of what is referred to as the 'co-relation argument' with Collier arguing that the stage of economic development of neighbouring countries is as important as domestic infrastructure and regional economic integration and that it is not the actual distance from international or navigable waters, but infrastructural investments of neighbouring countries, which affect landlocked countries' development prospects.[42] Sachs by contrast points to the success of the Asian Tigers, to attribute the importance of location to a country's ability to import and diffuse technology.[43] Such liberal theories about the role of geography stand in stark contrast to Marxist-environmentalist accounts such as that of historian Mike Davis who found that colonial integration into imperial markets has increased rather than decreased poverty in countries wealthy in natural resources.[44] What is not in dispute, however, is that the location of resources affects where humans settle.[45] For example, the discovery of resources suited for artisanal mining typically leads to an influx of persons. In contrast, when resource extraction causes

[40] JD Sachs and AM Warner, 'The Curse of Natural Resources' (2001) 45 *European Economic Review* 827; JD Sachs, 'Government, Geography, and Growth: The True Drivers of Economic Development' (2012) 91 *Foreign Affairs* 142.

[41] 'All the inland parts of Africa and all the part of Asia which lies any considerable way north of the Equine and Caspian Sea, as the ancient Scythia's, the modern Tartars and Siberia seem in all ages of the world to have been in the same barbarous and uncivilized state in which we find them at present … There are in Africa none of those great inlets, such as the Baltic and Adriatic seas in Europe, the Mediterranean and Equine seas in both Europe and Asia and the gulfs of Arabia, Persia, India, Bengal and Siam in Asia to carry maritime commerce into the interior parts of that great continent: and the great rivers of Africa are at too great distance from one another to give occasion to any considerable inland navigation. The commerce beside which any nation can carry out by means of a river which does not break itself into any great number of branches or canals, and which runs into another territory before it reaches the sea, can never be very considerable; because it is always in the power of the nations who possess that other territory to obstruct the communication between the upper country and the sea': A Smith, *An Inquiry of the Nature and Causes of the Wealth of Nations* (Harriman House, 2009).

[42] Collier (n 20) 54.

[43] Sachs, 'Government, Geography, and Growth: The True Drivers of Economic Development' (n 40).

[44] M Davis, *Late Victorian Holocausts: El Niño Famines and the Making of the Third World* (London Verso Books, 2002).

[45] AJ Venables and P Collier, *Plundered Nations? Successes and Failures in Natural Resource Extraction* (London, Palgrave, 2011); Sachs, 'Government, Geography, and Growth: The True Drivers of Economic Development' (n 40).

severe ecological harm, this will eventually result in migration away from extraction sites. How the discovery of natural resources affects armed conflict has been examined by Ross, who found that while countries with offshore resources had lower conflict rates than countries without resources, countries with onshore resources or onshore and offshore resources were significantly more frequently affected by armed conflict.[46]

Le Billon in his typology of resources conflict, ie, conflicts triggered, aggravated, or substantiated by natural resources, found that small countries having concentrated and proximate resources were associated with competition over state control or coup d'états because these resources were easily a subject of contestation since their exploitation was capital-intensive.[47] In contrast, large countries having concentrated and distant resources were associated with secessions as the region where resources were located had a financial incentive to secede to avoid the redistribution of its revenues across the country.[48] And, in countries with diffused and distant resources, conflicts among different communities were the most likely type of conflict to occur, as such resources could be exploited with little technology and capital once control over the territory was secured. Finally, countries with diffused and proximate resources involving a large number of producers tend to be more prone to riots and rebellions.

Of course, armed violence and conflict are sometimes also strategically deployed to crush opposition against extraction protests or clear lands suitable for mining. This was famously the experience of the Ogoni people in Nigeria and of the inhabitants of Kilwa, a town in the Democratic Republic of the Congo.

VI. THE ECOLOGICAL AND HUMAN DIMENSIONS

Finally, let us turn to the everyday effects of mineral resource extraction on local communities and ecosystems.[49] Such effects are frequently neglected in resource curse and pathology of plenty theories, and when they are acknowledged they

[46] Ross (n 14) 145–79; See also: P Collier and A Hoefler 'The Political Economy of Secession' in EF BAbbitt and H Hannum (eds), *Negotiating Self-Determination* (Development Research Group, World Bank, 2006) 117.

[47] P Le Billon, *Wars of Plunder: Conflicts, Profits and the Politics of Resources* (London, Hurst, 2012).

[48] ibid 79; Nigeria and Sudan are examples of this and even in the 2014 Scottish Referendum on secession in the United Kingdom, the idea of guarding the Scottish resources wealth for the Scottish people was an important argument: 'Agenda for Independence', available at: www.snp.org/vision/better-scotland/independence.

[49] 'An ecosystem is an ecological community – the living organisms inhabiting an area – and its associated physical (nonliving) environment. Ecosystems perform two basic functions, capturing and processing energy, and cycling and regenerating nutrients. Each function involves interactions between the ecological community (biotic component) and the physical environment (abiotic component). Performing these functions requires an interacting group of organisms including producers (autotrophs) who capture energy, and consumers/decomposers (heterotrophs), WHO degrade wastes and regenerate nutrients. Because no single species does both, ecosystems are the

are almost always framed as a side-effect of resource extraction, which can at most be mitigated, but not entirely avoided. The question of whether these effects are such that they upset any perceived economic or political advantage of resource extraction is rarely asked. Yet, from a political economy perspective these questions are pressing, as this book hopes to show. By contrast, on a granular level, the ecological and social costs of resource extraction are better understood. For instance, in artisanal gold mining, mercury is used to separate gold from ore. This process is estimated to account for 37 per cent of global mercury emissions.[50] In some cases, 95 per cent of the mercury used in artisanal mining is released into the local environment.[51] The vaporised mercury eventually settles on the soil and surface water and transforms into methyl mercury. In water bodies, it gets absorbed by living organisms and subsequently enters and contaminates the food chain, endangering the health of coastal and artisanal communities.[52] Children, particularly child workers, are most vulnerable.[53] They make up a significant proportion of the artisanal mining workforce, which exposes them not only to health risks, including psychological abuse, chronic diseases and disabling injuries, but also prevents them from receiving an education and contributes to locking them in a life of low-skill labour.[54] Yet, the health risks of resource extraction are not just limited to artisanal forms. Highly industrialised extraction processes have severe health implications as well. For instance, if earth formations are too dense for oil drilling, the porosity is increased by introducing hydrochloric acid.[55] And, to increase the viscosity of crude oil, methods such as steam injection or on-site burning are used. Such processes contaminate water and soil.[56]

The effects that extraction activities have on eco and water systems not only depends on the environmental safeguards taken, but also on the climate zone and geological conditions. For example, Sub-Saharan Africa has tropical or sub-tropical weather, which means that it experiences high-intensity precipitation, resulting in natural flooding, which affects the ways in which pollutants

smallest ecological units capable of sustaining life': MR Walbridge, 'Ecosystems' in D Cuff and A Goudle (eds), *The Oxford Companion to Global Change* (Oxford University Press, 2008).

[50] H Rehani and J Kippenberg, 'Mercury Rising: Gold Mining's Toxic Side Effect' (Human Rights Watch, 27 September 2017), available at: www.hrw.org/news/2017/09/27/mercury-rising-gold-minings-toxic-side-effect.

[51] United Nations, Human Rights Council, *Report of the Special Rapporteur on the human rights obligations related to environmentally sound management and disposal of hazardous substances and waste*, C Georgescu, A/HRC/21/48, 2 July 2012, para 34; WHO, 'Children's exposure to mercury compounds' (2010) 4.

[52] H Gibb and KG O'Leary, 'Mercury Exposure and Health Impacts among Individuals in the Artisanal and Small-Scale Gold Mining Community: A Comprehensive Review' (2014) 122 *Environmental Health Perspectives* 667, 687; 'Mercury – Time to Act' (UNEP, 2013) 23.

[53] See generally: WHO (n 51) 1; A/HRC/21/48 (n 51) para 28; Gibb and O'Leary (n 52) 671.

[54] *Address of the Special Rapporteur on Hazardous Substances and Waste to the Human Rights Council*, C Georgescu (18th session, Human Right Council, 14 September 2011).

[55] T Haller et al, *Fossil Fuels, Oil Companies, and Indigenous Peoples* (Zurich, LIT, 2007) 32.

[56] 'Environmental Assessment of Ogoniland – Executive Summary' (UNEP, 2011).

are spread. To build the facilities and infrastructure necessary for oil extraction, the extractive site needs to be cleared of trees and greenery, which exposes these areas to soil erosion. Combined with the oil and gas spills and unsound waste management this results in the loss of biodiversity and puts entire ecosystems at risk.[57]

In Ogoniland even years after the production activities ended, layers of oil still float through the creeks of the Niger Delta, killing fish and destroying wetlands.[58] In the Unity Region in South Sudan, a study conducted by German and South Sudanese geologists in the Thar Jath, Mala and Unity oilfields found that the oil operations contaminated groundwater with heavy metals and salt.[59] They found that the contamination caused by lead, aluminium and chrome was two to five times higher and water four times saltier than the permissible WHO and German standards.[60] Another very serious issue linked to the production of fossil energy sources is the one of gas flaring. Nigeria for instance flares 75 per cent of the gas it produces.[61] Flaring releases soot and CO^2 as well as sulphur dioxide into the atmosphere. Sulphur dioxide combines with water to form sulfuric acid. Sulfuric acid then becomes a component of acid rain. Soot is known to bind very toxic substances such as heavy metals, which reduce soil productivity. In addition, black smoke filters light, which causes temperatures to fall thereby slowing the growth of vegetation.[62]

[57] Haller et al (n 55) 28.

[58] 'Environmental Assessment of Ogoniland' (n 56).

[59] H Rueskamp et al, 'Effect of Oil Exploration and Production on the Salinity of a Marginally Permeable Aquifer System in the Thar Jath-, Mala- and Unity Oilfields, Southern Sudan' (2014) 1 *Zentralblatt für Geologie und Paläontologie* 95.

[60] ibid 113.

[61] In 2004, Nigeria flared close to 2.5 billion cubic feet daily, amounting to about 70 million tons of carbon dioxide yearly. Nigerian gas flaring has contributed more greenhouse gas emissions than all other sources in Sub-Saharan Africa combined: 'Environmental Assessment of Ogoniland – Executive Summary' (n 56) 25.

[62] Haller et al (n 55) 29.

3

The Foundation of Plenty

I. INTRODUCTION

WHILE MOST EFFECTS of the pathology of plenty in postcolonial states are localised, its causes are not. They are the result of structural systems of global exploitation beginning with colonisation and culminating in today's hyper-financialised global political economy, which is not only heavily dependent on mineral resources, but also premised on the distribution of their value from the periphery to the core. Historically, this meant that wealth was shifted from colony to empire. Today, distributional shifts are marked by national borders, by identity markers such as class, caste, gender, religion, race and ability, and by the redistribution from humans to corporate entities. What began with the quasi-sovereign rule of colonial companies such as the British, Dutch and Portuguese East India Companies, is continued today in some parts of the world by that of transnational corporations like Shell, ExxonMobil, Total, British Petroleum, but also state-owned companies like PDVSA and Saudi Aramco.

This chapter is interested in how such continuities were made possible from a legal perspective. It argues that this was among other things, due to the ways in which international law governed the transition of property and possession of mineral resources from colonial to postcolonial times, through different legal principles including permanent sovereignty over natural resources, economic self-determination, *pacta sunt servanda*, *rebus sic standibus* and *uti possidetis*. They were implicated in ensuring the continuity of, rather than the rupture from, corporate and imperial claims to the natural riches of the Global South throughout processes of decolonisation.[1]

Because of norms such as the principle of permanent sovereignty over natural resources and the principle of economic self-determination, which emphasise the importance of the domestic government in governing mineral resources, many scholars foreground possibilities of improving mineral resources

[1] See generally: T McCreary and V Lamb, 'Reflections on a Political Ecology of Sovereignty: Engaging International Law and 'the Map' in J Dehm and U Natarajan (eds), *Locating Nature: Making and Unmaking International Law* (Cambridge: Cambridge University Press, 2022); S Boysen, *Die postkoloniale Konstellation: Natürliche Ressourcen und das Völkerrecht der Moderne* (Tübingen, Mohr Siebeck, 2021).

governance through domestic law.[2] This focus however neglects the colonial and neo-colonial legacies of mineral resource regimes, particularly in international economic law.[3]

Two enquiries represent liberal and cosmopolitan views on how to address the resource curse. Wenar argues that the primary cause of the resource curse is what he refers to as the 'principle of effectiveness'. Whoever had effective control over a population also controlled resources in legal terms ('might makes right').[4] In turn, once control over natural resources was established, the revenues generated with their international trade fuelled the means to sustain unchecked power.[5] Wenar proposes to break this vicious cycle, using the market, as counter-power, namely by asking end-consumers not to purchase petroleum from tyrannic or authoritarian regimes. He refers to this power as 'popular resource sovereignty'.[6] Whereas Wenar puts his faith in the market, Pogge turns to international institutions, to explore their potential in curtailing excesses of power, and protect the global poor. Concerning wealth distribution between countries, he observes that international rules favoured wealth production in already wealthy countries, pointing for example to the rules of the World Trade Organization (WTO).[7] He further argues that international law and governance also intensify domestic wealth disparities, and 'democratic deficits'. This was because in the global order, groups exercising effective control over a country, even if by using coercion, were by default recognised as having the right to act for their people, sell their mineral resources, and dispose of their proceeds.[8]

> The *resource privilege* we confer upon *de facto* rulers includes the power to effect legally valid transfers of ownership rights over resources. A corporation that has purchased resources from a tyrant thereby becomes entitled to be – and actually is – recognized anywhere as their legitimate owner. This is a remarkable feature of our global order.[9]

[2] J Radon and G Soros, 'How to Negotiate an Oil Agreement' in M Humphreys, JD Sachs and JE Stiglitz (eds), *Escaping the Resource Curse* (New York, Columbia University Press, 2007); D Johnson, 'How the Evaluate the Fiscal Terms of Oil Contracts' in ibid.

[3] M Chi, 'Resource Sovereignty in the WTO Dispute Settlement: Implications in China – Raw Materials and China – Rare Earths' (2015) 12(1) *Manchester Journal of International Economic Law* 2; B Gu, 'Mineral Export Restraints and Sustainable Development – Are Rare Earths Testing the WTO's Loopholes?' (2011) 14 *Journal of International Economic Law* 765; JE Viñuales, 'International Investment Law and Natural Resource Governance' in E Morgera and K Kulovesi (eds), *Research Handbook on International Law and Natural Resources* (Cheltenham, Edward Elgar, 2016).

[4] Similarly: P Okowa, 'Sovereignty Contests and the Protection of Natural Resources in Conflict Zones' (2013) 66(1) *Current Legal Problems* 33.

[5] L Wenar, *Blood Oil: Tyrants, Violence, and the Rules that Run the World* (Oxford, Oxford University Press, 2016) xlv.

[6] ibid, lii.

[7] T Pogge, 'The Role of International Law in Reproducing Massive Poverty' in S Besson and J Tasioulas (eds), *The Philosophy of International Law* (Oxford, Oxford University Press, 2010) 421.

[8] ibid, 428.

[9] ibid.

Wenar and Pogge in some ways are quite perceptive in their assessments, whereas in others, they are not fully grappling with the imperatives of the global political economy. Wenar is right in pointing to the market as a source of power for petro-tyrants, but he grossly overestimates its potential as a source of counterpower that consumers can mobilise effectively. The transnational and financialised structure of global petroleum markets, but also just the sheer overwhelming centrality of petroleum in the everyday life of most persons, and the absence of available alternatives, limits the extent to which consumers are even put in the position to make deliberate choices about the petroleum they consume.[10] By contrast, Pogge makes a valuable point by insisting on the effects of global institutions' interference on domestic wealth distribution and social hierarchies. At the same time, with his arguments on the creation of democratic deficits which global interventions amplify, he, like the liberal paradox of plenty theorists, insinuates that stronger, or more mature democratic institutions could offset interventions by global institutions. This may not necessarily be true as phenomena such as the 'Dutch disease', which was introduced earlier, show.

While agreeing with both Wenar and Pogge in their concern about the effects of global markets and institutions on the pathology of plenty, particularly when it comes to its distributive effects in the domestic context, this chapter is concerned with how international law predetermines economic and political structures in postcolonial countries. For this purpose, it will not only retrace how international law structured the transition from colonial regimes of property to permanent sovereignty over natural resources in a formal sense, but also grapple with the economic philosophies that underpin the choice for such structuring, in light of imaginable alternatives. For this purpose, this chapter exams two cardinal legal principles of natural resources law governing the decolonisation of natural resources in the former colonies, namely the principle of permanent sovereignty over natural resources that now forms part of customary international law, and the principle of economic self-determination.[11]

II. THE DOUBLE-EDGED NATURE OF SELF-DETERMINATION

At the end of the Second World War, much of the world was economically devastated, deeply divided, and marked by tensions between the Allied forces

[10] C Cutler, *Private Power and Global Authority: Transnational Merchant Law in the Global Political Economy* (Cambridge, Cambridge University Press, 2003); IGLP, 'The role of law in global value chains: a research manifesto' (2016) 4 *London Review of International Law* 57.

[11] UN, General Assembly, Resolution 1803 (XVII) Permanent Sovereignty over Natural Resources, A/RES/1803(XVII), 14 December 1962; UN, General Assembly, Resolution 3201 (S-VI) Declaration on the Establishment of a New International Economic Order, 1 May 1974; United Nations, General Assembly, Resolution 3281 (XXIX) Charter of Economic Rights and Duties of States, 12 December 1974; International Court of Justice, *Case Concerning Armed Activities on the Territory of the Congo (Democratic Republic of the Congo v Uganda)*, Judgment of 19 December 2005, ICJ Reports 2005, 168.

and the Soviet Union. On 26 June 1945, at the San Francisco conference, just six weeks after Germany's surrender, and while the war in Asia was still ongoing, 50 states signed the UN Charter. One year earlier, some states at the Bretton Woods conference had agreed on a post-war currency system and the institution of international financial organisations to lay down the basis for a stable and robust decolonised global economy. The institutional separation between international economic organisations on the one side, and organisations of the United Nations (UN) family thought of as primarily political on the other, was thereby cemented.[12] Placed in between this separation was the governance of postcolonial nature and resources.[13] Eventually, the United Nations took on the task of developing general principles for the governance of natural resources in newly independent states.[14] After one decade of consultations, the General Assembly adopted Resolution 1803 which conceptualised sovereignty over natural resources as an expression of self-determination, which had emerged as the cardinal principle of the UN Charter even if its precise meaning was contested at the time, and has remained so ever since.[15]

The different meanings of self-determination can be traced back to its prominent roles in Western political thought, namely the 1776 American Declaration of Independence, which directed it against colonial rules, and the 1789 French Declaration of the Rights of Man and of the Citizen, in which it served political emancipation from feudal rule.[16] The internationalisation of self-determination, or rather the idea that it should be applicable among sovereign nation-states, is credited to Wladimir Lenin and Woodrow Wilson, albeit for very different reasons.[17] Both considered self-determination to mean that those in power ought to be elected by the people, but when it came to the application of the principle for state formation, their views significantly diverged. Wilson advocated for it to be the governing principle for re-drawing the map of Central and Eastern

[12] For more on the split between economic and political matters in the global order by means of international law, see S Pahuja, *Decolonising International Law Development, Economic Growth and the Politics of Universality* (Cambridge, Cambridge University Press, 2011) 22.

[13] Boysen (n 1) 15–18; L Kulamadayil, 'Placed in between: the natural environment in international law' (2022) 13(4) *Transnational Legal Theory* 466.

[14] The first international treaty recognising this importance is presumed to be the Atlantic Charter, point five; see N Schrijver, *Sovereignty over Natural Resources: Balancing Rights and Duties* (Cambridge, Cambridge University Press, 1997) 37; A Anghie, *Imperialism, Sovereignty and the Making of International Law* (Cambridge, Cambridge University Press, 2005) 212.

[15] See generally: T Sparks, *Self-Determination in the International Legal System: Whose Claim, to What Right?* (Oxford, Hart Publishing, 2023); M Bak Mckenna, *Reckoning with Empire: Self-Determination in International Law* (Leiden, Brill, 2022); A Getachew, *Worldmaking after Empire: The Rise and Fall of Self-Determination* (Princeton, NJ, Princeton University Press, 2019).

[16] R Redslob, *Völkerrechtliche Ideen der Französischen Revolution* (Mohr Siebeck, 1916); F Ermacora, 'Ursprung und Wesen des Selbstbestimmungsrechts der Völker und seine Entwicklung bis zum Zweiten Weltkrieg' [1964] *Rabl, Kurt* 50.

[17] For more detail, see A Cassese, *Self-Determination of Peoples: A Legal Reappraisal* (Cambridge, Cambridge University Press, 1995) 14–23.

Europe after the First World War,[18] yet he was very cautious not to embrace it when Caribbean peoples mobilised it for demands of their independence from colonial rule.[19] In contrast, Lenin saw self-determination as a means of political separation 'from foreign rule and the pathway to the formation of independent national states'.[20] Drawing on the work of Hilferding, he described that in the context of colonialism, nationalism was a natural response to imperialism, which in turn was the highest stage of capitalism.[21]

Self-determination's ability to accommodate both liberal and socialist world views likely led to its centrality in the UN Charter. After all, international law-making processes at the time had to reconcile the interests of hegemons looking to cement their power, with those of dwindling empires and newly independent states.[22] In Tunkin's words:

> The concept that the basis of law is community, particularly a common ideology, is completely unfounded. Of course, in the absence of a specific community between people, the existence of human society, and consequently of laws, is inconceivable, but it still does not follow that the community is the reason for the formation of law, or is reflected in law. The history of human society shows completely the opposite.[23]

[18] 'Peoples are not to be handed about from one sovereignty to another by an international conference or an understanding between rivals and antagonists. National aspirations must be respected; peoples may now be dominated and governed only by their own consent. "Self-determination" is not a mere phrase. It is an imperative principle of action, which statesmen will henceforth ignore at their peril', Woodrow Wilson, 'Address to Congress on International Order' (11 February 1918).

[19] 'When we actually fulfilled to the letter our promise that we would set helpless Cuba up as an independent government and guarantee her independence – when we carried out that great policy we astounded and converted the world. Then began … the confidence of the world in America. We … were frightened by it, because we knew that they were expecting things of us that we could not accomplish; we knew that they were hoping for some miracle of justice which would set them forward the same hundred years that we have travelled on the progress toward free government; and we knew that it was a slow road; we knew that you could not suddenly transform a people from a people of subjects into a people of self-governing units' 'Address at the Opera House (Marlow Theater) in Helena, Montana' (11 September 1919); See generally M Pomerance, 'The United States and Self-Determination: Perspectives on the Wilsonian Conception' (1976) 70 *American Journal of International Law* 1.

[20] V Lenin, *The Right of Nations to Self-Determination* (3rd edn, Collected Works vol 20, Progress Publishers 1977).

[21] 'In the newly opened-up countries the capital imported into them intensifies antagonisms and excites against the intruders the constantly growing resistance of the peoples who are awakening to national consciousness; this resistance can easily develop into dangerous measures against foreign capital. The old social relations become completely revolutionised, the age-long agrarian isolation of "nations without history" is destroyed and they are drawn into the capitalist whirlpool. Capitalism itself gradually provides the subjugated with the means and resources for their emancipation and they set out to achieve the goal which once seemed highest to the European nations: the creation of a united national state as a means to economic and cultural freedom', R Hilferding, *Das Finanzkapital: Eine Studie über die jüngste Entwicklung des Kapitalismus* (Vienna, Wiener Volksbuchhandlung, 1910) cited after Vladimir Lenin, *Imperialism: The Highest Stage of Capitalism* (London, Resistance Books, 1999) 117.

[22] G Simpson, *Great Powers and Outlaw States: Unequal Sovereigns in the International Legal Order* (Cambridge, Cambridge University Press, 2004) 165.

[23] GI Tunkin, *Theory of international law* (Cambridge, MA, Harvard University Press, 1974) 27.

In other words, not shared values, but rather the need to bridge divisions gave rise to the adoption of the UN Charter.[24] One concrete effect of this was that its drafters could not agree on the precise meaning of self-determination and instead opted to specify, what they did not mean to become part of the principle's normative content, namely not the right to secession or democratic governance, and not the right of colonial peoples to independence (opposed to their right to self-government).[25] In the years since its adoption, these negative definitions of the principle were challenged, and in part overcome. Whereas the existence of the rights to secession, and democratic governance[26] remain contested, self-determination went on to occupy a central role in formal decolonisation processes.[27] It was in these processes that self-determination became entangled with sovereign statehood even though it was never a precondition to it.[28] This is for instance made explicit in the 1975 Final Act of the Conference on Security and Co-operation in Europe which separates the rights inherent in sovereignty (Article I) from the rights associated with people's self-determination (Article VII), construing the former as a prerequisite for the latter.

In the expansion of Westphalian sovereign statehood to the colonial world, self-determination entered into a norm conflict with the principle of *uti possidetis*, which had been applied to the decolonisation processes in Latin America in the early nineteenth century to mean that in the process of decolonisation, the territory of newly independent states should remain delimited by the former colonial boundaries.[29] Or, in the words of the ICJ:

> The essence of the principle [of *uti possidetis*] lies in its primary aim of securing respect for the territorial boundaries at the moment when independence is achieved. Such territorial boundaries might be no more than delimitations between different administrative divisions or colonies all subject to the same sovereign. In that case, the

[24] For a different perspective, see G Abi-Saab, 'Whither the International Community? (1998) 9 *European Journal of International Law* 248.

[25] Cassese (n 17) 42.

[26] On democratic governance: see T Franck, 'The Emerging Right to Democratic Governance' (1992) 86 *American Journal of International Law* 46; S Marks, *The Riddle of all Constitutions: International Law, Democracy, and the Critique of Ideology* (Oxford, Oxford University Press, 2000); on secession, see M Kohen, *Secession: International Law Perspectives* (Cambridge, Cambridge University Press, 2006).

[27] UN, General Assembly, Resolution 1314 (XIII) Recommendations concerning International Respect for the Right of Peoples and Nations to Self-Determination, 12 December 1958; International Court of Justice, *Legal Consequences of the Separation of the Chagos Archipelago from Mauritius in 1965*, Advisory Opinion of 25 February 2019, ICJ Reports 2019, 95; International Court of Justice, *East Timor (Portugal v Australia)*, Judgment of 30 June 1995, ICJ Reports 1995, 90; International Court of Justice, *Legal Consequences for States of the Continued Presence of South Africa in Namibia (South West Africa) Notwithstanding Security Council Resolution 276 (1970)*, Advisory Opinion of 21 June 1971, ICJ Reports 1971, 16.

[28] Against: J Fisch, 'State Power and the Will of the People' in B Fassbender and A Peters (eds), *The Oxford Handbook of the History of International Law* (Oxford, Oxford University Press, 2012) 32–33.

[29] M Kohen, 'Titles and *effectivités* in territorial disputes' in M Kohen and M Hébié (eds), *Research Handbook on Territorial Disputes in International Law* (Cheltenham, Edward Elgar, 2018) 156–57.

> application of the principle of *uti possidetis* resulted in administrative boundaries being transformed into international frontiers in the full sense of the term.[30]

And, in discussing its relationship with self-determination, the ICJ further held:

> At first sight this principle conflicts outright with another one, the right of peoples to self-determination. In fact, however, the maintenance of the territorial status quo in Africa is often seen as the wisest course, to preserve what has been achieved by peoples who have struggled for their independence, and to avoid a disruption which would deprive the continent of the gains achieved by much sacrifice.[31]

The application of the principle of *uti possidetis* in decolonisation processes has been a highly controversial issue. Some commentators, siding with the ICJ's position, have observed that the principle's 'obvious purpose is to prevent the independence and stability of new States being endangered by fratricidal struggles provoked by the challenging of frontiers following the withdrawal of the administering power'.[32] They maintain that it is politically agnostic.[33] Others are more sceptical, pointing to the dynamics of inclusion and exclusion in the naturalisation of colonially drawn territorial borders that the use of this principle brings about.[34] Yet others are also concerned about how the principle legitimises and naturalises not only territorial boundaries drawn by colonial masters, but also their legal concepts, namely that of bounded territory, as one of the prerequisites of statehood.[35]

III. THE MAKING OF RESOURCE SOVEREIGNTY

Whereas the relationship between self-determination on the one side, and sovereignty and territory on the other remained diffuse, what the transition from colonial to postcolonial states without alterations to territorial boundaries permitted was the seamless transferral of existing concessionary and contractual regimes. As Mutua points out, 'the West decolonized the colonial state,

[30] International Court of Justice, *Case Concerning the Frontier Dispute (Burkina Faso/Republic of Mali)*, Judgment of 22 December 1986, ICJ Reports 1986, 554, para 23.

[31] ibid, para 25.

[32] ibid, para 565.

[33] M Kohen, 'Uti Possidetis, Prescription et Pratique Subsequente a un Traite dans l'Affaire de l'Ile de Kasikili/Sedudu Devant la Cour Internationale de Justice' (2000) 43 *German Yearbook of International Law* 253. A Peters, 'The Principle of Uti Possidetis Juris, How Relevant Is It for Issues of Secession?' in C Walter et al (eds), *Self-Determination and Secession in International Law* (Oxford, Oxford University Press, 2014) 114.

[34] M Koskenniemi, 'National Self-Determination Today: Problems of Legal Theory and Practice' (1994) 43 *International & Comparative Law Quarterly* 241.

[35] V Nesiah, 'Placing International Law: White Spaces on a Map' (2003) 16 *Leiden Journal of International Law* 1; see also NM Rajkovic, 'The Visual Conquest of International Law: Brute Boundaries, the Map, and the Legacy of Cartogenesis' (2018) 31 *Leiden Journal of International Law* 267.

not the African peoples subject to it', noting that 'dependence continued under the post-colonial state, the instrument of narrow elites and their international backers'.[36]

Whereas the contentions between self-determination, sovereignty and territory were squarely identified as questions of the political order, the relationship between self-determination, sovereignty and mineral resources in postcolonial states was initially thought of as an economic one. Mineral resources were of course part of states' territory and its nature, but they were also indispensable for global carbon capitalism, which is why former imperial powers had a strong interest in framing natural resources, or rather the contractual regimes that governed them, as a purely economic matter. It was the application of *uti possidetis* in the transition of colonies to postcolonial sovereign states within the boundaries of the former, which permitted legal continuities, including the inheritance of legal and contractual obligations. This in turn was significant for the continued access of former empires to colonial nature and her resources. Due to the widening use of the combustion engine throughout the 1930s and 1940s, industrial economies had become heavily dependent on petroleum. Whereas the United States had significant reserves of her own, decolonisation meant that European states, many of whom were still economically devastated from the Second World War, were at risk of losing access to petroleum reserves.[37] In light of this, decisions such as that by Iranian Prime Minister Dr Mossadegh to nationalise assets of the foreign Anglo-Iranian Oil Company and annul its concession agreement on the exploitation of Iranian petroleum reserves, were perceived as a threat to post-war recovery efforts in Europe.

In this context, all recognised that natural resources had become a pertinent issue for international law and international institutions, particularly as it concerned questions of possession and ownership.[38] This was not only because decolonisation ended formal imperial rule over colonial resources, but also because the San Francisco global order was premised on the concept of Westphalian sovereignty which introduced a new variable to the relationship between global extractive companies and the communities living at sites of extraction. As two studies commissioned by the United Nations revealed, no universally shared principles governing competences and property relations on mineral resources between the nation-state, regional districts or sub-states, local communities and individual households existed.[39] This is why the United

[36] MW Mutua, 'Why Redraw the Map of Africa: A Moral and Legal Inquiry' (1994) 4 *Michigan Journal of International Law* 1113, 1116–19.

[37] For more detail, see T Mitchell, *Carbon Democracy: Political Power in the Age of Oil* (New York, Verso, 2011) 109–43.

[38] For a detailed analysis of the emergence of natural resources law from a distributive-moralist perspective, see O Schachter, *Sharing the World's Resources* (New York, Columbia University Press, 1972).

[39] UN, Commission on Permanent Sovereignty over Natural Resources, The Status of Permanent Sovereignty over Natural Wealth and Resources – Preliminary Study by the Secretariat, A/AC.97/5,

Nations took it upon itself to develop two distinct and novel principles to govern such relationships. First, it affirmed the rights of all states, with the postcolonial ones in mind, to permanent sovereignty over their natural resources.[40] Secondly, it proclaimed the right of all peoples to freely dispose of their natural resources.[41]

The 1952 General Assembly Resolution 523 was the first significant step towards resource sovereignty. It was the first resolution to contain a conditional right of 'underdeveloped countries' to freely determine the use of their natural resources, though only for stimulating their national development and in pursuance of their national interests, and to further the expansion of the world economy.[42] Noting that varying demand for raw materials had led to resource price fluctuations, causing economic difficulties for 'underdeveloped' countries, this resolution also foresaw the possibility for the General Assembly to facilitate the negotiation of international commercial agreements.[43] In parallel, equally conspicuous developments unfolded in the human rights arena. After the General Assembly agreed in February 1952 on including a common provision in both human rights covenants 'on the right of all peoples and nations to self-determination', Chile proposed to the General Assembly that in addition to economic and political self-determination, another paragraph stipulating the human right to permanent sovereignty over natural resources should be added.[44] These two developments sparked contentious debates which were made even more difficult by the fact that many connected legal concepts and questions remained unsettled: the concept of people's rights as opposed to sovereign rights, the implications of converging the concept of sovereign rights and human rights, the status and meaning of self-determination under international law, and finally questions of international legal protections to foreign property.

For the human rights terrain, it was the UN Commission on Human Rights at the time that was charged with drafting the two international human rights covenants. It was therefore also the venue in which Chile's proposal of including language on a people's right to self-determination over natural resources was discussed.[45] This undertaking was not uncontroversial, first, because it was not clear whether the Commission even had the authority to address which states, for example, the United States and France perceived to be a matter for relations

15 December 1959; UN, Commission on Permanent Sovereignty over Natural Resources, The Status of Permanent Sovereignty over Natural Wealth and Resources – Revised Study by the Secretariat, A/AC.97/5/Rev.1, 27 December 1960.

[40] A/RES/1803(XVII) (n 11).

[41] Common article 1, para 2.

[42] UN, General Assembly, Resolution 523 (VI) Integrated Economic Development and Commercial Agreements, 12 January 1952, preamble.

[43] ibid, para 1(b)(ii).

[44] UN, General Assembly, Resolution 545 (VI) Inclusion in the International Covenant or Covenants on Human Rights of an article relating to the right of peoples to self-determination, 5 February 1952, para 1; UN Doc E/CN.4/L24; cited after Schrijver (n 14) 49.

[45] UN, Commission on Human Rights, UN Doc E/2256/E/CN.4/669, 14 April–14 June 1952, 8.

among sovereign states rather than a human rights matter.[46] On substance, the United States also voiced its concern that linking self-determination to resource sovereignty would hinder rather than promote the progressive realisation of people's right to political self-determination and pose an obstacle to world economic development.[47] Such a view stood in stark contrast to that of many postcolonial countries which supported Chile's proposal. Their position was that people's sovereignty over natural resources was a natural and important manifestation of self-determination, and a prerequisite for the enjoyment of other human rights, and that it therefore belonged in the human rights covenants.[48] In 1955, the Commission's designated working group under Egyptian chairmanship proposed the following wording:

> The peoples may, for their own ends, freely dispose of their natural wealth and resources without prejudice to any obligations arising out of international economic co-operation, based upon the principle of mutual benefit, and international law. In no case may a people be deprived of its own means of subsistence.[49]

This proposal too was fiercely opposed by representatives of states such as the United Kingdom, the United States and Australia. The United Kingdom did not see any added benefit in using the word 'people's' as opposed to 'sovereign states', whereas Australia feared that such a provision would confer rights on national minorities vis-a-vis the central government, and the United States maintained that the new proposal did not sufficiently address the fears of foreign investors.[50] Such concerns were countered, for instance, by Saudi Arabia which observed that 'self-determination' and 'people's' were no more ambiguous than other core concepts of international law such as 'freedom', 'peace', and 'justice'.[51] Importantly, not all resource-wealthy states were in favour of framing natural wealth as a human rights issue, due to concerns about the duties that such an inclusion may impose on them.[52]

Nonetheless, the inclusion of people's rights to freely determine their natural wealth and resources is the outcome of Third World alliances, and as such a victory of the Third World project. The centrality of governing this issue in human rights terms is clear from the space given to it in both human rights covenants. Not only is it addressed in both of them in their common Article 1, but also in a separate common Article, which reiterates that nothing in the human rights covenants 'should be interpreted as impairing the inherent right of all

[46] UN, Commission on Human Rights, UN Doc E/CN.4/SR.260, 21 April 1952, 7–8.

[47] UN, General Assembly, UN Doc A/C.3/SR.646, 27 October 1955, 100.

[48] UN, General Assembly, UN Doc A/C.3/SR.643, 25 October 1955, 97.

[49] ibid, cited after Schrijver (n 14) 54.

[50] UN, General Assembly, UN Doc A/C.3/SR.669, 23 November 1955, 227; cited after Schrijver (n 14) 54.

[51] UN, General Assembly, UN Doc A/C.3/SR.672, 25 November 1955, 240; cited after Schrijver (n 14) 55.

[52] UN, General Assembly, UN Doc A/C.3/SR.671, 25 November 1955, 234; cited after Schrijver (n 14) 54.

peoples to enjoy and utilise fully and freely their natural wealth and resources'.[53] Remembering these principles as a Third World project disrupts two widely held conceptions: first, that human rights are a Western liberal project, and secondly that the 'first generation' of human rights were individual human rights.[54]

Whereas the nationalisation of petroleum reserves and infrastructure had been carried out unilaterally by Latin American countries in the first decades of the twentieth century, the high economic stakes and the diverging interests between mineral resources exporting countries in the Global South and mineral resources importing countries, meant that there was interest from many states to regulate this issue at the international level, even if the initiative came first and foremost from the states of the Global South. In October 1952, the draft resolution by Chile held that the nationalisation of natural resources was consistent with the UN Charter's commitment to self-determination.[55] It framed 'the right of each country to nationalise and freely exploit its natural wealth as an essential factor of economic independence'.[56] The resolution framed the nationalisation of mineral resources as a means for states from the Global South to generate public revenue. For Chile, the recognition of full resource sovereignty at the United Nations was a historical necessity.[57] In contrast, Mexico, which had nationalised its hydrocarbon industry in 1933, was hesitant to bring this issue before the United Nations. It considered the right to nationalise as an indisputable part of its sovereign rights. Other countries, including Australia, Canada, Iran and Saudi Arabia, supported Mexico's position.[58] Yet other countries such as the Netherlands and the United States were strongly opposed to the draft resolution as it did not mention any obligation to give adequate compensation in instances of nationalisation. They argued that the draft resolution might result in economic conditions that would deter foreign investors.[59]

Nonetheless, and despite the opposition of many resource-rich states to discussing this issue at the United Nations, Uruguay, now joined by Bolivia, submitted a revised draft resolution to the General Assembly, which was more explicit in urging states to exercise resource sovereignty in a manner conducive to economic stability, development and international economic cooperation.[60]

[53] UN, General Assembly, International Covenant on Civil and Political Rights, UNTS 999, 171, 16 December 1966, Art 47; UN, General Assembly, International Covenant on Economic, Social and Cultural Rights, UNTS 993, 3, 16 December 1966, Art 25.

[54] See generally, P Macklem, 'Human rights in international law: three generations or one?' (2015) 3 *London Review of International Law* 61; Getachew (n 15).

[55] UN, General Assembly, Economic development of under-developed countries: financing of economic development of under-developed countires: Chile: draft resolution, A/C.2/L.154, 22 October 1952.

[56] UN, General Assembly, UN Doc A/C.2/L165, 5 November 1952; cited after Schrijver (n 14) 42.

[57] UN, General Assembly, UN Doc A/C.2/SR.234, 9 December 1952; cited after Schrijver (n 14) 44.

[58] UN, General Assembly, UN Doc A/C.2/SR.231, 6 December 1652, 254; cited after Schrijver (n 14) 44.

[59] UN, General Assembly, UN Doc A/C.2/165/Corr.1, 10 December 1952, 259.

[60] ibid.

This revised resolution was adopted by the General Assembly's Second Committee on 11 December 1952 with 31 votes in favour, all of which came from Latin American, Middle Eastern, Asian and Eastern European states,with one objection from the United States and 19 abstentions.[61] Just 10 days later, the General Assembly then adopted Resolution 626, which reflected the language of compromise between states of the Global South and their demand for resource sovereignty and states which feared that the unbounded exercise of such resource sovereignty would adversely affect capital flows.[62] As a result, the resolution's recognition of resource sovereignty was a conditional one. Its exercise was contingent on the wellbeing of global markets, which demanded the uninterrupted flow of natural resources from peripheral and semi-peripheral states, to imperial and neo-imperial states.

Under the impact following the nationalisation of the Iranian petroleum industry, and the looming nationalisations in Iraq and Egypt, the General Assembly commissioned two studies to clarify the status of natural resources under international law.[63] They were conducted throughout the 1950s and were focused on the nature of the right to self-determination in conjunction with the right to permanent sovereignty over natural wealth and resources, in order to 'secure information about the actual scope and character of the right'.[64] The studies were conducted under the leadership of the UN Commission on Permanent Sovereignty over Natural Resources.[65] The Commission was composed of representatives from liberal, socialist and postcolonial states.[66] In 1959 and 1960, the Commission published one preliminary and one final study on the legal status of resource sovereignty.[67] Unsurprisingly one point of contention was that imperial states insisted that the protection of foreign investment and the safeguarding of existing property rights was part of customary international law, whereas postcolonial resource-wealthy states held the position that the principle of permanent sovereignty over natural resources also gave legality to the alteration of property regimes inherited from colonial times, including the nationalisation of petroleum, at the expense of concessionary rights, and, against the background of the nationalisations which had already taken place, were keen for the Commission to map existing praxis.[68]

[61] UN, General Assembly, UN Doc A/C.2/SR.237, 11 December 1952, 280.

[62] UN, General Assembly, Resolution 626 (VII) Right to exploit freely natural wealth and resources, A/RES/626(VII), 21 December 1952, preamble.

[63] International Court of Justice, *Anglo-Iranian Oil Co Case (United Kingdom v Iran)*, Judgment of 22 July 1952, ICJ Reports 1952, 93.

[64] UN, Commission on Human Rights, Report on the 10th Session 23 February–16 April 1954, E/2S73, April 1954, paras 322–33; UN, General Assembly, Resolution 837 (XI) Recommandations concerning International Respect for the Rights of Peoples and Nations to Self-Determination, 14 December 1954, para 1.

[65] A/RES/1314(XIII).

[66] ibid. Members of the Commision came from Afghanistan, Chile, Guatemala, the Netherlands, the Philippines, Sweden, the Soviet Union, the United Arab Republic and the United States.

[67] A/AC.97/5; A/AC.97/5/Rev.1.

[68] Schrijver (n 14) 59–68.

In its scope of study, the Commission favoured the interests of Western states. To establish the rights and duties towards foreign investors and their property, it surveyed bilateral and multilateral agreements, national policy and legislation.[69] It also did not put into question that states (ie, former imperial powers) could continue to have rights in foreign territory (ie, their former colonies), conceding only that such rights needed to be established by treaty. They could include transit rights, mining rights and the right to water resources.[70] The Commission also surveyed how international courts and international and regional organisations had viewed the validity of mineral resources contracts in the transition from colony to sovereign state with a view to the tension of safeguarding acquired rights and permitting expropriation.[71]

Perhaps most importantly, it studied the legal status of the right to permanent sovereignty over natural resources in different categories of territories, with different degrees of sovereignty from newly independent states to mandate territories, only considering African legal systems and leaving aside Latin American, Middle Eastern and Asian legal systems where the nationalisation of mineral resources was more advanced. In addition to engaging with questions of land legislation and distribution on a general level, the Commission focused on the status of mining rights in non-self-governing territories. By contrast, for territories under international trusteeship, it reviewed a broader array of sources, including national policy affecting foreign investment, trusteeship agreements, action taken by the General Assembly and the Trusteeship Council. For the Mandated Territory of South West Africa, it also reviewed mining legislation and concessions, as well as land questions.[72]

Overall, the studies were conducted primarily from an economic perspective focusing more on the regulation of the value associated with natural resources than the resources themselves. In that spirit, the Commission considered natural resources in relation to questions of economic development, such as economic diversification, balance of payments and development financing. It also examined private capital flows.

Overall, the studies did not question that international natural resources law was necessitated by the need to ensure supply from former colonies to former empires even after the end of formal imperialism.[73] This is underlined by the fact that the study of the right was informed only by its legal status in territories with no, diminished, or only recently acquired sovereignty. As the ICJ would confirm many years later though, such a right not only exists on colonial contexts, but also in fully-sovereign states.[74] Notably, self-determination is

[69] A/AC.97/5/Rev.1, ch 1.
[70] ibid, ch II, A, 2.
[71] ibid, ch III.
[72] ibid, ch IV.
[73] Anghie (n 14) 211–16.
[74] International Court of Justice, *Case Concerning Armed Activities on the Territory of the Congo (Democratic Republic of the Congo v Uganda)*, para 244.

almost completely absent from the study being referenced only in connection to General Assembly resolutions and the then still draft international human rights covenants, showing again the precarious status that self-determination enjoyed in international law at the time.[75]

Based on the studies, the next task of the Commission was to draft a resolution on permanent sovereignty over natural resources. To this end, two of the Commission's Member States, namely Chile and the Soviet Union, each developed a proposal.[76] The Soviet proposal was quickly dismissed by states from the Global North as it foresaw an unconditional right to nationalisation as well as extensive regulatory rights over the activities of foreign investors.[77] It was therefore the Chilean draft that served as the basis for what was to become Resolution 1803. With the support of eight of the Commission's nine Member States, a revised version of this proposed draft resolution was adopted and submitted to the UN Economic and Social Council (ECOSOC).[78] Unlike the two studies that had informed the Commission, the proposal by Chile linked the principle of permanent sovereignty over natural resources to the principle of self-determination. This was met with some resistance when the proposal was discussed at the ECOSOC, with for instance Japan wondering what the purpose and necessity of a right framed in this manner might be. In contrast, with reference to the Calvo Doctrine and the Drago–Porter Convention, Afghanistan applauded the linkage between self-determination and resource sovereignty, arguing that such a conceptualisation merely built on a rich Latin American legal tradition.[79] Ultimately, state representatives in the ECOSOC could not reach a consensus, so the Chilean draft proposal came to the UN General Assembly without an ECOSOC resolution to support it. At the General Assembly, it was equally met with opposition by states, such as the United States, Britain and the Netherlands.[80] The United States representative, for example, cautioned about the possible effects of such a principle on transnational trade with natural resources, and expressed their concern that the linkage to self-determination in particular could mean that the right could be interpreted as a sovereign right to expropriation without compensation.[81] Finally, in a world of economic interdependence, some US representatives saw resource sovereignty as a practical impossibility.[82]

[75] A/AC.97/5/Rev.1, 2, 200, 623.

[76] UN, General Assembly, UN Doc A/AC.97/L2, 5 May 1961; UN, Commission on Permanent Sovereignty over Natural Resources, Draft resolution submitted by Chile, UN Doc A/AC.97/L.3, 1, 10 May 1961; cited after Schrijver (n 14) 65.

[77] UN, General Assembly, UN Doc A/AC.97/L4, 16 May 1951; cited after Schrijver (n 14) 68.

[78] UN, General Assembly, UN Doc A/AC.97/L.3/Rev.2, 18 May 1961.

[79] UN, Economic and Social Council, UN Doc E/SR.1178, 2 August 1961, 172–73.

[80] UN, Economic and Social Council, ECOSOC Resolution 847 (XXXII), 3 August 1961.

[81] JN Hyde, 'Permanent sovereignty over natural wealth and resources' (1956) 50 *American Journal of International Law* 854, 857–58.

[82] Cited after C Dietrich, *Oil Revolution* (New York, Cambridge University Press, 2017) 64.

This position stayed true to the imperial premise of decolonisation that it was strictly a political matter and had no bearing on economic ones.[83] It was echoed by some parts of the scholarly community, with American jurist Hyde for instance arguing that only political relations should be characterised as colonial, while economic relations were merely those between capital-exporting (empires) and capital-importing countries (colonies).[84]

Postcolonial resource wealthy states however insisted on the necessity of this principle, and after a contentious process, which involved 26 votes in the General Assembly's Second Committee alone, the text of Resolution 1803 was finally put to a vote before the General Assembly, where it was adopted by 87 to two votes and 12 abstentions. The resolution guarantees resource sovereignty to the people (not the state) who should exercise it for the purposes of national and human development. It prohibits any interference with the exercise of resource sovereignty and encourages international cooperation and trade, private and public investment and technical assistance. It accepts that both domestic and international law governs the economic activities of foreign investors and that such activity requires permissions from recipient states. It permits expropriation of foreign investment under certain conditions, namely if national interests demand it, it is undertaken in accordance with national and international law, and if appropriate compensation is paid.[85]

The reception of Resolution 1803, among contemporary commentators, was mixed. Brownlie found it to be rather conservative noting that Western delegates had been successful in achieving last minute changes to the draft resolution in favour of foreign investment protection. He also worried that the refence to international law in key passages of the resolution would constrain rather than strengthen the scope of the principle.[86] Schachter, who was a legal counsel to the United Nations at the time, offered a more positive appraisal, finding Resolution 1803 to be well balanced. To him, it squared the colonial baggage of foreign concessions and property, and the unequal bargaining conditions under which they were obtained, with the fact that non-renewable resources acquired value largely through international markets and required cost-intensive infrastructure for their exploitation.[87]

Ultimately, in subsequent decolonisation processes, the principle of permanent sovereignty as laid down in Resolution 1803 would play only a marginal role, as the next chapter will show. Rather, it has been in the context of the present-day annexation of Palestinian territories by Israel that the principle was given meaning by the ICJ in its advisory opinion on Occupied Palestinian

[83] Boysen (n 1) 113–19.
[84] Hyde (n 81) 855.
[85] A/RES/1803(XVII) (n 11) paras 3, 4.
[86] I Brownlie, 'The Legal Status of Natural Resources in International Law (Some Aspects)' in Hague Academy of International Law (eds), *Collected Courses of the Hague Academy of International Law* (Leiden, Brill, 1979) 361; for a different perspective, see Pahuja (n 12) 95–171.
[87] Schachter (n 38) 126.

Territories.[88] In the context of examining the exploration and use of natural resources, particularly water resources located in Palestinian territories by Israel, the Court found Israel to be in breach of its obligations under the principle of permanent sovereignty over natural resources, making it the first time that this principle was applied outside a colonial context in the narrow sense.

IV. DEVELOPMENT THEORIES OF RESOURCE SOVEREIGNTY

While there was never any doubt about the importance of mineral resources supplies from the Global South to the Global North for their economic wellbeing, if resources exports actually benefited the countries that were exporting them was an open question. At the time of formal imperial rule, very little of the value that goods produced with the raw materials from the colonies had been retained as wealth there, and the revenues that were retained were often captured by a very small local elite.

This is why in addition to the question of how pre-existing property rights over mineral resources ought to be governed, and whether or not mineral resources should be considered as a public good subject to sovereign stewardship on behalf of the peoples, a contentious debate considering whether such resources should be exported to begin with, was ongoing at the time. Today, liberal development theories are of course based on the premise that this should be the case, as the previous chapter has shown, but given the impoverishment and misery of the resources-driven colonial entrerprise, if and how the export of mineral resources could benefit newly independent states was subject to fierce debate.

Yet, the 1952 General Assembly Resolution 626 already contained the premise that the exploitation of mineral resources would be beneficial to the economic development of postcolonial states, as this would permit them to acquire the capital necessary to diversify their economies.[89] Subsequent resolutions do not question the advantages of resource-exports per se, but rather acknowledge that some of the problems associated with such an economic model, such as the vulnerability to market fluctuations, needed to be managed.[90] Resolution 1515, for instance, recommends that:

> Member States and the international organs concerned should continue as a matter of urgency to seek and apply ways of eliminating both excessive fluctuations in primary commodity trade and restrictive practices or measures which have unfavorable repercussions on the trade in basic products of the less developed countries and

[88] International Court of Justice, *Legal Consequences arising from the Policies and Practises of Israel in the Occupied Palestinian Territories, Including East Jerusalem*, Advisory Opinion of 19 July 2024.

[89] A/RES/626(VII) (n 62).

[90] UN, Resolution 1514 (XV) Declaration on the Granting of Independence to Colonial Countries and Peoples, 14 December 1960, Chapeau.

> those dependent on the export of a small range of primary products, and to expand trade in these products.[91]

And, Resolution 1803 asserts that exercising resource sovereignty would be beneficial for the economic development and economic independence of post-colonial countries.[92] While the foundations for such thinking, which finds its expressions in General Assembly resolutions before 1960, it was the theory of Rostow, as laid down in his famous 1960 work *The Stages of Economic Growth: A Non-Communist Manifesto*, that laid the foundation for what was to become conventional wisdom, namely that mineral resources exports were beneficial to the economy of resource-wealthy states, which informed global economic policy by way of the foreign policies of the US Kennedy and Johnson administrations.

Rostow argued that all societies were on an upward path of economic growth that took them through five stages: namely (1) traditional society; (2) preparation for take-off; (3) take-off; (4) drive to maturity; and (5) high mass consumption. The traditional society's main characteristic was its low economic output, which Rostow attributed to the lack of modern technology. By contrast, the characteristic of a society meeting the preconditions for take-off were that it was receptive to 'modern science and technology'. Rostow found most post-colonial states to be in this stage of economic growth, attesting that they had not reached this stage endogenously, but through the colonial experience and by interactions with more 'advanced societies', characterised, among other things, by the institution of private ownership, national unity and general welfare.[93]

Rostow even asserted that the progress towards meeting the preconditions for take-off was only reached by postcolonial societies through the economic activities of the coloniser, attesting these societies to be split between the imperial and the traditional ones, and therefore suggesting that the withdrawal of all imperial activities from the colonies would bear the risk of retarding their growth unless effective institutions of a centralised nation-state were built.[94] This in turn, he alleged, required 'the emergence of the political power of a group prepared to regard the modernization of the economy as a serious, high-order political business'.[95] To then reach the next stage of economic progress – take-off – the legal integration of the national economy into the global economic system was required:

> The society makes such terms as it will with the requirements of modern efficient production, balancing off the new against the older values and institutions, or revising the latter in such ways as to support rather than to retard the growth process.[96]

[91] UN, Resolution 1515 (XV) Concerted Action for Economic Development of Economically Less Developed Countries, 15 December 1960, paras 3, 4; refered to in UN, Resolution 3167 (XXVIII) United Nations Revolving Fund for Natural Resources Exploration, 17 December 1973, Chapeau.

[92] A/RES/1803(XVII) (n 11) Chapeau.

[93] WW Rostow, *The Stages of Economic Growth: A Non-Communist Manifesto* (Cambridge, Cambridge University Press, 1960) 6.

[94] ibid, 7.

[95] ibid.

[96] ibid, 8.

Only when the political form, technical progress and global economic integration are backed by a legal order can the final stage of economic growth – high mass consumption – be achieved. This stage is distinguished by urbanisation, a high proportion of skilled labour in the overall labour force, and the ability of the majority of the population to practise consumerism.

Of course, this view did not go unchallenged. Marxists in particular developed alternative visions in the form of structuralism and dependency theories and was taken up by development economists within the United Nations, most notably Hans Singer and Raúl Prebisch.[97] Prebisch was a very influential Latin American development economist. He served as President of the Argentinian Central Bank, Executive Director of the UN Economic Commission for Latin America (ECLAC) and first Secretary-General of the UN Trade and Development Organisation; Singer was the Director of the Economic Division of the UN Industrial Development Organisation and Director of the UN Research Institute for Social Development. They are best known for the Prebisch–Singer hypothesis: the foundational work of dependency theory.

The Prebisch–Singer hypothesis describes the price relation in the world market between primary commodities and manufactured goods. It suggests that, over time, the price of primary commodities will fall relative to the price of manufactured goods, due to the terms of trade as well as the unequal distribution of the gains from technological progress favouring manufacturing over primary production. The foundations for this hypothesis were Singer's famous 1949 and 1950 articles, which cautioned that the gains of the world economy would disfavour economies that primarily relied on the export of natural resources and agricultural products.[98] Not dissimilar to Rostow, Singer observed that the economies of underdeveloped countries had a dualist structure. Export-oriented and capital-intensive sectors were often foreign owned, more technologically advanced and profitable than domestically owned sectors. Yet, unlike Rostow, Singer wondered,

> [c]ould it be possible that we economists have become slaves to the geographers? Could it not be that in many cases the productive facilities for export from underdeveloped countries, which were so largely a result of foreign investment never became part of the internal economic structure of those underdeveloped countries themselves, except in the purely geographical and physical sense? Economically speaking, they were really an outpost of the more developed investing countries. The main secondary multiplier effects, which the textbooks tell us to expect from investment, took place not where the investment was physically or geographically located but (to the extent that the results of these investments returned directly home) they took

[97] For more on Rostow's development model and its neo-marxist critiques, see E Tourme-Jouannet, *What is a Fair International Society? International Law Between Development and Recognition* (Oxford, Hart Publishing, 2013) 14–15.

[98] HW Singer, 'Economic Progress in Underdeveloped Countries' (1949) 16 *Social Research* 1; HW Singer, 'The Distribution of Gains between Investing and Borrowing Countries' (1950) 40(2) *American Economic Review* 473.

> place where the investment came from. I would suggest that if the proper economic test of investment is the multiplier effect in the form of cumulative additions to income, employment, capital, technical knowledge, and growth of external economics, then a good deal of the investment in underdeveloped countries which we used to consider as 'foreign' should in fact be considered as domestic investment on the part of industrialized countries.[99]

Singer thus located the benefits of foreign-owned industrialisation in underdeveloped countries in the home states of the investors rather than hoping for economic stimulus in host countries. He refutes the claim that foreign-driven economic growth in underdeveloped countries would have spillover effects on the local economy by referring to the dualist structure of underdeveloped economies. Singer continues:

> If we apply the principle of opportunity costs to the development of nations, the import of capital to underdeveloped countries for the purpose of making them into providers of food and raw materials for the industrialized countries may have been not only rather ineffective in giving them the normal benefits of investment and trade but may have been positively harmful. The tea plantations of Ceylon, the oil wells of Iran, the copper mines of Chile, and the cocoa industry of the Gold Coast may all be more productive than domestic agriculture in these countries; but they might have developed if those countries had not become specialized to the degree in which they now are to the export of food and raw materials, thus providing the means of producing manufactured goods elsewhere with superior efficiency.[100]

Accordingly, he finds that exporting natural resources would harm, rather than benefit, exporting economies, making them more dependent on world markets. This view contradicted global economic policy at the time, which held that through the export of a small set of primary commodities, 'underdeveloped' countries could generate the capital necessary to stimulate their economic development, recognising instead that most of the value generated in this manner would effectively contribute towards the economies of states in which the resources were utilised and processed.[101] Neither Singer nor Prebisch completely rejected the advantages of foreign investment for economic development in postcolonial states. Indeed, both argued that foreign investment and technological progress could stimulate economic growth. They merely questioned the prospect of progress under the existing terms of trade and investment of aiding capital accumulation for domestic investment or stimulating economic diversification.[102]

[99] ibid, 'The Distribution of Gains between Investing and Borrowing Countries' 475.
[100] ibid, 476.
[101] A/RES/626(VII) (n 62) Chapeau, para 1.
[102] R Prebisch, 'The Economic Development of Latin America and Its Principal Problems' (UNDEA, 1950) 2; The Prebisch–Singer hypothesis was later further developed by Frank. See AG Frank, *Latin America: Underdevelopment or Revolution* (New York, Monthly Review Press, 1971) 3–17.

However, neither Singer nor Prebisch were the only ones who were suspicious of the resource-fuelled growth narrative that was based on imitating imperial economies. American economist Paul Baran, pointed out that compared with economic activities that were labour-intensive, value generated through natural resources would be limited to a very small section of society. To that end, he pointed out that it was more useful to think in terms of transnational wealth distribution – rather than international – arguing that resource-driven wealth was primarily retained by transnational elites.[103] Baran, like Singer, did not believe that foreign investment would steer Third World economies toward industrialisation. In the absence of a significant middle class, foreign investors would capture vast gains of profits from developmental operations.[104]

We now know that these Marxist leaning development theorists were right, and that the development model popularised in Resolution 1803 which, while conceding that natural resources were both subject to the self-determination of peoples and the sovereign discretion of states, still took the export of natural resources for granted. As the previous chapter has shown, this development model has been foundational to some of the characteristics of the pathology of plenty. By focusing economic activities on the export of a limited number of natural resources, postcolonial economies were made vulnerable to the fluctuations of global markets, while experiencing variations of the Dutch disease domestically. Instead of aiding other economic sectors to flourish, the reliance of resources exports has affected them detrimentally. Instead of generating wealth for all, it has generated only wealth for some, and deepened social divisions and divides. In sum, instead of extending decolonisation to the economic sphere, the way that permanent sovereignty over natural resources was conceptualised and applied, has only aided in replacing formal colonialism with a formal market empire.[105]

V. CONCLUSION

Self-determination and permanent sovereignty over natural resources are often regarded as legal victories of Third World leaders, and in some sense, they certainly were.[106] Yet, as this chapter has shown, their adoption and interpretation

[103] PA Baran, 'On the Political Economy of Backwardness' (1952) 20 *The Manchester School* 66, 67. Similarly: G Myrdal, *Economic Theory and Under-Developed Regions* (New York, Harper & Row, 1957) 52.

[104] Baran, ibid, 69.

[105] Rajagopal for instance suggests that empire is not a geographical concept but a hegemonic concept that includes globalisation. See B Rajagopal, 'Counter-hegemonic International Law: Rethinking Human Rights and Development as a Third World Strategy' in R Falk, B Rajagopal and J Stevens (eds), *International Law and the Third World: Reshaping Justice* (London, Routledge, 2008) 67.

[106] Getachew (n 15).

were influenced by ideological and social struggles that were at least as concerned with the interests of old and new empires, and their corporations as they were with the interests of postcolonial peoples and nature. This is not to suggest that only these two principles were foundational to the pathology of plenty. As shown here, earlier legal principles such as the principle of *uti possidetis* also played an important role in translating the colonial map into a sovereign one, thus transposing economic structures into political ones. Still, the explicit entry of natural resources in the regulatory realm of international law was also a constitutive moment for the pathology of plenty.

The next chapters will show how the conception of resource sovereignty, exercised through a central government of a territorially bounded nation-state, centralised enormous power in the hands of those who represented the state, thus acting both as an incentive to grab power and a means to sustain it, both in times of peace and armed conflict. This centralisation of power as subsequent chapters will also show, has allowed wealth capture by transnational corporations and elites. Another point that this chapter has sought to make is that the way in which economic self-determination and resource sovereignty were codified, was not without alternatives. Rather, there was significant contestation, even at the highest levels of various UN organs.

4

The Hope of Plenty

I. INTRODUCTION

THIS CHAPTER EXPLORES the role of petro-states in Third World internationalism and its legal outcomes. It retraces how Iran and Algeria through two different processes reclaimed control over their mineral resources from foreign hands and, in doing so, developed and recalibrated transnational and international legal rules and altered the dynamics of Third World internationalism as it culminated in the 1974 New International Economic Order (NIEO). It sheds light on how the exceptional position that petro-states occupied among Global South states has affected their bargaining position in global affairs, permitting them to lead the push for the NIEO agenda as a model for economic development.[1] Petro-states' unique bargaining power, or, as Chaterjee has put it, their power to unleash 'economic warfare', stemmed from the global economy's dependence on petroleum products.[2] The 1973–74 oil crisis had shown how easily they could pull the threads of the interconnected global economy. By then, petroleum had come to occupy such a crucial role in global affairs that it had given rise to the formation of 'international petroleum law'.[3]

This chapter proceeds as follows: section II paints a picture of the role of natural resources in early post-Second World War Third World internationalism as it emerged through informal alliances and multilateral regionalism in the Global South. Section III dives into the history of petroleum production in Iran drawing out the evolution of the petroleum regime there from concession agreements to production-sharing agreements as well as the permanent mark that Iran has left on the conception of the international legal principle of sovereignty over natural resources as a right of the people, rather than a right of the sovereign. Section IV then shifts attention to Algeria and its struggle for true

[1] B Bollecker-Stern, 'The Legal Character of Emerging Norms Relating to the New International Economic Order: Some Comments' in K Hossain (ed), *Legal Aspects of the New International Economic Order* (London, Frances Pinter (Publishers) Ltd, 1980) 69.

[2] SK Chatterjee, 'The Charter of Economic Rights and Duties of States: an Evaluation after 15 Years' (1991) 40 *International & Comparative Law Quarterly* 669.

[3] This term can be credited to Higgins who was among the first to think of petroleum as having given rise to a delineated field in international law. R Higgins, *Themes and Theories: Selected Essays, Speeches, and Writings in International Law* (Oxford, Oxford University Press, 2009).

sovereignty over its natural resources as part of its pursuit of independence. The conclusion subsequently looks to weave the Iranian and Algerian experience back into the evolution of Third World internationalism, focusing on international producers' alliances and the processes at the United Nations (UN) in the context of the NIEO.

II. NATURAL RESOURCES IN EARLY THIRD-WORLD INTERNATIONALISM

The early years following the Second World War did not only see the institutionalisation of globalism in the form of the San Francisco, Bretton Woods, and General Agreement on Tariffs and Trade (GATT) systems but also of multilateral regionalism.[4] The earliest such regional Global South alliance was the League of Arab States, which was founded a few months before the end of the Second World War by the sovereigns of Syria, Transjordan, Iraq, Saudi Arabia, Lebanon, Egypt and Yemen.[5] The League's objectives were ambitious in scope aiming to foster cooperation and collaboration between Arab states on several civil, socio-economic and cultural issues including health and social welfare infrastructure, industry, agriculture and judicial affairs.[6] Another early milestone of regional cooperation in the Global South was the 1947 Asian Relations Conference in New Delhi. The objective of this conference, which was held several months after India's formal independence, was 'to bring together the leading men and women of Asia on a common platform to study the problems of common concern to the people of the continent'.[7] The conference laid the foundations for bilateral arrangements, such as the 1954 five principles agreed upon between India's Jawaharlal Nehru and China's Zhou En-lai guiding their countries' mutual relations, which first and foremost affirmed their intention for peaceful coexistence.[8] Whereas these earlier alliances were, at least on the surface, primarily about advancing regional cooperation, by the mid-1950s, south–south alliances had geared their objectives explicitly towards decolonisation, which is why the 1955 Bandung conference is given such importance

[4] A Singh, 'Report by Dr Anup Singh (India)' in Afro-Asian Peoples Solidarity Conference (eds), *Afro-Asian Peoples Solidarity Conference, Cairo, 1957–1958* (Moscow, Moscow Foreign Languages Publishing House, 1958) 64; cited after K McGregor and V Hearman, 'Challenging the Lifeline of Imperialism' in L Eslava, M Fakhri and V Nesiah (eds), *Bandung, Global History, and International Law: Critical Pasts and Pending Futures* (Cambridge, Cambridge University Press, 2017) 165–66.

[5] Pact of the League of Arab States, 22 March 1945; processed by Alexandria Protocol, 7 October 1944.

[6] Art 2 Pact of the League of Arab States.

[7] Jawaharlal Nehru, 'Speech', Asian Relations Conference (New Delhi, 1947).

[8] 'Joint Communiqué of Jawaharial Nehru and Zhou En-li' (28 June 1954). The principles are: (1) Respect for each other's territorial integrity and sovereignty; (2) Mutual non-aggression; (3) Mutual non-interference in each other's internal affairs; (4) Equality and mutual benefit; and (5) Peaceful co-existence.

in postcolonial histories of international law.[9] Another reason was of course that Bandung was the first transcontinental south–south conference. Of the 29 participating countries, most were from South Asian, Southeast Asian and Arab countries. The conference's objectives were to forge postcolonial alliances on key issues of international concern, as well as to develop strategies to overcome colonial legacies.

The conference also reflected the Arab League's commitment to regional cooperation on socio-economic and cultural matters. In addition, it echoed a strong commitment to the UN system, to human rights and the principle of self-determination. Participants thus called on the United Nations to recognise an independent Palestine and to admit Cambodia, Laos and Japan as members and also identified it as the suitable global institution to promote economic development, calling for the institution of a Special UN Fund to that end.[10] They shared the understanding that the end of formal colonialism had not changed the profoundly asymmetrical power structures that were embedded in the post-war global order. As Sukarno, the Indonesian Prime Minister and host of the conference cautioned, 'Colonialism has also its modern dress, in the form of economic control, intellectual control, and actual physical control by a small but alien community within a nation'.[11] The conference's First Communiqué speaks to the concern of participating countries to achieve fairer conditions for the international trade in natural resources and primary commodities. It recommends taking collective action to stabilise international commodity prices and to foster the domestic processing of primary commodities to diversify participating countries' export portfolios, in terms of products and export destinations. It also proposes to unify participating countries' positions on these issues in the UN Permanent Advisory Commission on International Commodity Trade.[12] On petroleum, the Communiqué reads that: 'The Asian-African Conference felt that exchange of information on matters relating to oil, such as remittance of profits and taxation, might eventually lead to the formulation of common policies'.[13]

The attention given to natural resources trade policy by the Bandung participants was not a coincidence. By 1952, the UN General Assembly had already passed its first resolution with the votes of states from the Global South, which had not only called for the right of all countries to freely determine the use of their natural resources, but also for the strengthening of domestic processing capacities of 'under-developed countries' of such resources.[14] The context of

[9] Eslava, Fakhri and Nesiah (n 4).

[10] This fund had been called for by the UN General Assembly two years earlier. UN, General Assembly, Resolution 724 (VIII) Economic Development of Under-Developed Countries, 7 December 1953.

[11] Sukarno, 'Opening address' Asian-African Conference (Bandung, 1955).

[12] Asian-African Conference, Final Communiqué, 24 April 1955, paras 5, 6.

[13] ibid, para 8; see also C Dietrich, *Oil Revolution* (New York, Cambridge University Press, 2017) 81.

[14] UN, General Assembly, Resolution 523 (VI), Integrated Economic Development and Commercial Agreements, 12 January 1952.

this resolution was the Iranian nationalisation of the country's oil reserves and installations, which the Iranian Parliament under Prime Minister Dr Mohammad Mosaddegh affected by a law unanimously passed in March 1951. This act was not a sudden event, but the result of prior developments.[15]

III. THE IRANIAN CONTRACT MODEL

Commonly, the history of petroleum and its production in Iran is traced to the D'Arcy concession, which had been concluded between the British millionaire William Knox D'Arcy and the Shah of Persia in 1901. It gave the concessionaire the exclusive right to search for, exploit, process, export and sell natural gas, petroleum, asphalt and ozokerite throughout vast portions of the Persian territory.[16] It also gave them the exclusive right to plan, build and own the country's petroleum infrastructure and take possession of uncultivated land for this purpose. It also granted the right to acquire cultivated land if necessary.[17] While five provinces were effectively excluded from the scope of these two exclusive rights, the agreement still foresaw that the Persian government was not to give anyone else the right to plan or build petroleum infrastructure in these territories.[18] The agreement was concluded for 60 years and provided for a fixed amount of royalties and entitled the Persian government to 16 per cent of annual profits generated by activities carried out under the concession.[19] By the time that industrial oil production and processing under this concession agreement commenced in 1913, the majority of its shares had changed hands and were owned by Burmah Oil, the predecessor of British Petroleum (BP), and its activities were carried out by its subsidiary, the Anglo-Persian Oil Company (APOC). Dissatisfaction with the terms of the concession agreement, as well as the significant drop in the profits that it generated, due to the Great Depression, led to cancellation of the D'Arcy concession in November 1932 and the conclusion of a new concession in April 1933.[20]

For Iran, the terms of the new agreement were only a marginal improvement on the D'Arcy concession. It still granted the concessionaire, APOC, the exclusive right to explore, exploit, process, transport and export petroleum and the non-exclusive right to build petroleum infrastructure.[21] APOC also still had the right to acquire privately owned lands without having to disclose the acquisition's purpose. Only for publicly owned land did the government reserve the

[15] Clifton Daniel, 'Iran stirs up acute crisis over oil' *New York Times* (25 March 1951).
[16] Art I of the D'Arcy Concession Agreement (Tehran, 28 May 1901).
[17] ibid, Arts II, III.
[18] ibid, Art VI.
[19] ibid, Arts I, IV.
[20] Agreement between the Imperial Government of Persia and the Anglo-Persian Oil Company Ltd (Teharan, 29 April 1933).
[21] ibid, Arts 1, 3.

right to refuse APOC's acquisition requests in instances in which such lands had public utility.[22] The concession also foresaw far-reaching tax exemptions for APOC, which included not only the exemption from income tax but also exemptions from almost all import taxes.[23] This left the public revenues generated by APOC entirely dependent on the government's share of its profits, which was determined by the following formula. The government was owed a fixed royalty of £0.04 for each ton of petroleum sold as well as 20 per cent of shareholder profits exceeding the threshold of approximately £670,000.[24] Notably, it was not owed any petroleum or petroleum products. Rather, the company had to sell certain petroleum products purposed for domestic consumption with a discount of 10–25 per cent from the lowest average global market price.[25] Disputes about the interpretation of the concession were to be settled by international arbitration and the rights under the concession were to be granted until 1993 with only the concessionaire having the right to terminate it prematurely.[26]

Despite its more favourable terms, the 1933 concession was in some regards more problematic than the earlier D'Arcy concession, which had been concluded before commercially sizable petroleum resources were discovered. The profit-sharing formula was not uncommon for concession agreements at the time, but as the price for petroleum increased, due to the war machinery of the Second World War as well as of post-war recovery, it soon became apparent that the terms of the 1933 concession were untenable for Iran. In this climate, Dr Mohammad Mossadegh, a foreign-trained lawyer and economist who had held public offices since the age of 14, emerged as a vocal advocate for the expansion of the concept of sovereignty to the country's petroleum operations. He is credited with spearheading the law of 1944, which prohibited the conclusion of new concession agreements without parliamentary consent as well as the law of 1947, which prohibited the conclusion of such agreements with foreign parties.[27] These laws were early precursors of the international principle of *popular* resource sovereignty, meaning the sovereignty over natural resources vested in the peoples of a country, rather than its monarch. Dr Mossadegh closely followed the developments in the legal architecture of petroleum production and was thus aware that Venezuela had passed a law that year, which provided that newly concluded concession agreements had to share the profits between petroleum corporations and the state equally.[28] In response to Iranian demands to adjust the financial provisions of the 1933 concession to a 50:50 profit share between the government and the concessionaire Anglo-Iranian Oil Company (AIOC), as APOC had been

[22] ibid, Art 4.
[23] ibid, Art 6.
[24] ibid, Art 11.
[25] ibid, Art 19.
[26] ibid, Arts 22, 26.
[27] J Bamberg, *The History of the British Petroleum Company Volume II: The Anglo-Iranian Years 1928–1954* (Cambridge, Cambridge University Press, 1994) 250–57.
[28] Dietrich, *Oil Revolution* (n 13) 31.

renamed in 1935, negotiated a supplemental agreement with Shah Mohammad Reza Pahlavi. Among other things, this agreement proposed to increase the royalty per ton of petroleum sold from £0.04 to £0.06, provided for a one-time payment of a little over £3.36 million, lifted AIOC'S unconditional income tax exemption and guaranteed that the government would receive a minimum of £4 million in revenues per year.[29] These terms did not satisfy the Iranian Parliament which, thanks to the laws it had passed just two years earlier, needed to approve this agreement. It consequentially withheld its consent, thereby paving the way for the annulment of the 1933 concession and the nationalisation of AIPC in 1951. Even more so than nationalisation itself, the parliamentary refusal of the supplemental agreement can be understood as an act of people's sovereignty over natural resources in so far as it was exercised against the monarchy, which had previously claimed the right to exercise control of the country's resource wealth for itself when it concluded the 1901 and 1933 concession agreements. This tangible internal dimension in the history of popular natural resource sovereignty is often overlooked in subsequent commentary on the formation of this legal principle.[30]

The Iranian nationalisation of the country's petroleum reserves and infrastructure came into effect on 1 May 1951 when the Iranian Oil Nationalisation Act entered into force which sent shock waves around the world. As the *New York Times* reported in its special on this subject, more than half of the petroleum consumed by Great Britain and Western Europe came from the Middle East which, at the time, was thought to be the location for over 42 per cent of the world's petroleum reserves. In the post-war tenuous climate between the West and the Soviet Union, Iran's petroleum nationalism was seen not only as threatening the world's economic recovery, but also as a threat to Western security interests. In response to Iran's refusal to enter into arbitration as provided for under the terms of the 1933 concession agreement, the United Kingdom commenced proceedings before the International Court of Justice (ICJ) asking the Court to compel Iran to accept AIOC Ltd's request for arbitration and alleging that Iran's refusal to do so deprived AIOC Ltd of any legal remedy. It further claimed that with AIOC Ltd being a British company, Iran's actions constituted an internationally wrongful act.[31] The ICJ found that it did not have jurisdiction to hear this case. This decision on jurisdiction has been seen by some as a victory for Iran under international law, which in jurisdictional terms it certainly was.[32]

[29] Arts 3, 4 of Supplemental Agreement between the Imperial Iranian Government and the Anglo-Iranian Oil Company Limited (Tehran, 17 July 1949).

[30] O Schachter, *Sharing the World's Resources* (New York, Columbia University Press, 1972); N Schrijver, *Sovereignty over Natural Resources: Balancing Rights and Duties* (Cambridge, Cambridge University Press, 1997).

[31] International Court of Justice, *Anglo-Iranian Oil Co Case (United Kingdom v Iran)*, Application instituting proceedings of 26 May 1951, ICJ Reports 1952, 93.

[32] International Court of Justice, *Anglo-Iranian Oil Co Case (United Kingdom v Iran)*, Judgment of 22 July 1952, ICJ Reports 1952, 93; D Lustig, *Veiled Power: International Law and the Private*

Yet, the decision did not resolve the merits of the dispute, namely whether Iran had violated a general principle of international law by refusing to honour the terms of the 1933 concession agreement and enter into arbitration, and whether the expropriation of AIOC Ltd by the 1951 Iranian Oil Nationalisation Act was lawful under international law. These questions would occupy the UN General Assembly, foreign ministries and international lawyers for decades to come and were thus unsurprisingly reflected in the Bandung agenda as well.[33] As for the 'Mossadegh crisis', when it could not be resolved by legal means, the British and American governments famously backed a coup d'état that removed Dr Mossadegh from office in August 1953 and installed the Shah in power who had proven to be more amenable to foreign demands. It only took little more than a year for a new agreement to be signed, which gave the rights to exploit Iran's oil wealth to a consortium of French, American, Dutch and British oil companies in which BP, the newly founded successor of AIOC held the largest share.[34]

Though this outcome was evidently far from the petroleum sovereignty that Dr Mossadegh had envisioned for his country, the terms of the 1954 agreement were a significant improvement on the 1933 concession that his government had annulled, and also from the terms of the proposed 1949 supplemental agreement that it had blocked. The 1954 agreement was not a concession in nature, but an early form of a production-sharing agreement. Today, this type of agreement is widely used in the petroleum sector. The 1954 agreement was limited to a period of 25 years and met the demands of the Iranian Parliament of sharing the profits equally between the operators and the government. Unlike in the earlier agreements, the government also preserved its sovereign prerogatives of providing public services on the lands leased by the consortium. Compared with the earlier concession agreements, this agreement did not transfer the ownership of the petroleum exploited to the consortium. As such, it decoupled the rights to exploiting the oil from processing and trading it, permitting the forming of trading companies and guaranteeing that rather than buying oil at a discounted market price, the state-owned National Iranian Oil Company (NIOC) responsible for managing the country's petroleum reserves, could buy petroleum for a price a little over the consortium's production cost. Finally, the agreement foresaw the processing of petroleum by refineries operated by the consortium and by one solely operated by NIOC.

The change in contractual form from concession agreement to production-sharing agreement is significant to international lawyers. At the time, judicial

Corporation 1886-1981 (New York, Oxford University Press, 2020) 44–78; A Leiter, 'Protecting concessionary rights: General principles and the making of international investment law' (2022) 35 *Leiden Journal of International Law* 55.

[33] For a detailed analysis of the emergence of natural resources law from a distributive-moralist perspective, see generally: O Schachter, 'Invisible College of International Lawyers' (1977) 72 *Northwestern University Law Review* 217.

[34] The Iran–Consortium Agreement of 19–20 September 1954 (Teharan, 29 October 1954).

practice suggested that while other types of concessions were subject to domestic administrative law, petroleum and mining concessions were also governed by public international law, the reasoning for this being that they governed the exploitation of sovereign exhaustible resources.[35] As such, they were distinct from other concessions, such as those on the building or operation of public infrastructure. Such concessions merely transfered vested ownership from the state to the concessionaire, which is returned back to the state when the concession elapses.[36] Other types of concessions could be subject to international law when this was provided for by an international treaty. The reasoning of the Mavrommatis concessions judgment of the Permanent Court of International Justice (PCIJ) suggests that concessions enjoying such protection could not be annulled without giving the concessionaire the right to repurchase, not even when compensation is offered.[37] By leasing the rights to exploit petroleum, rather than to transfer ownership to the territories that contain them, a breach of the rights granted under this new type of agreement would not have only been subject to international law and would not have amounted to an internationally wrongful act, unless other factors were present as well. Conceptually, the new agreement was thus in the spirit of Dr Mossadegh's campaign for petroleum sovereignty.

The evolution of the Iranian petroleum regime was a catalyst to international law developments at the time. As is well known, the decision of the ICJ not to compel Iran to participate in arbitration contributed to the emergence of the international regime of foreign investment protection.[38] Less well remembered is that the Iranian application of the concept of national sovereignty to the economic realm and its interpretation of such sovereignty being vested not only in the monarch but in Parliament was critical for shaping the international legal principle of permanent sovereignty over natural resources. Iran also quietly contributed to a paradigm shift in transnational contract law, by laying the groundwork for a new type of petroleum contract, which was a departure from the quasi-sovereign rights that earlier petroleum concessions had granted foreign companies. The 1954 agreement also contained a new formula for compensating BP for the expropriation of AIPC's assets and for a share of its prospective profits. Of the £67 million worth of local assets, which the company lost when it was expropriated in 1951, the government compensated £25 million in

[35] R Higgins, 'Natural Resources in the Case Law of the International Court' in A Boyle and D Freestone (eds), *International Law and Sustainable Development: Past Achievements and Future Challenges* (Oxford, Oxford University Press, 1998).

[36] *Saudi Arabia v Arabian American Oil Company (Aramco)*, (Arbitration) Award of 23 August 1958, ILR 1963, 117 ff.

[37] *Mavrommatis Jerusalem Concessions*, Judgment of 26 March 1925, PCIJ Ser A No 5; This interpretation is proposed by Higgins: 'Natural Resources in the Case Law of the International Court' (n 35).

[38] S Pahuja, *Decolonising International Law Development, Economic Growth and the Politics of Universality* (Cambridge, Cambridge University Press, 2011) 95–171.

addition to letting the consortium use the expropriated facilities and equipment at cost. In addition, the agreement foresaw a one-time quit claim payment of £32.4 million by its consortium partners as well as a total of US$510 million of their export profits. Unfortunately, this formula and the new contract form were sidelined in legal scholarship at the time in favour of questions surrounding the lawfulness of the expropriation and the adequate international law standard of compensation.[39]

The Iranian struggle did however influence the 'rendez-vous of elites from oil-producing countries with anti-colonial thought', which is how Dietrich has described the Bandung conference.[40] The conference's emphasis on price stabilisation, domestic processing and the diversification of exports foreshadowed what were to become economic policy objectives of Global South commodity-exporting countries for decades to come, objectives, which they chose to express not only in subsequent gatherings of global south representatives such as the Afro-Asian Peoples' Solidarity Conference in Cairo (1957), the Non-Aligned Conference in Belgrade (1961), or the Tricontinental Conference in Havana (1966) but also at the UN General Assembly, in several resolutions as well as the two studies surveying the legal architecture of natural resource governance across the world.[41]

In the context of the NIEO, the Iranian experience informed the position of its international law proponents on the legal effect on the validity of concession agreements that the principle of permanent sovereignty over natural resources had. This is exemplified by Hossain, who argued that the validity of concession agreements depended on the extent to which they fostered the interests of national development and wellbeing of the peoples of the state concerned, were lawful under their domestic law, and had been freely entered into.[42] The first condition was meant to void concessions concluded without host states' knowledge of the size and quality of their petroleum reserves; the second

[39] See, eg: KS Carlston, 'Concession Agreements and Nationalization' (1958) 52 *American Journal of International Law* 260; DP O'Connell, *The Law of State Succession* (Cambridge, Cambridge University Press, 1956); FA Mann, 'Outlines of a History of Expropriation' (1959) 75 *Law Quarterly Review* 188.

[40] Expression borrowed from CRW Dietrich, 'Mossadegh Madness: Oil and Sovereignty in the Anticolonial Community' (2015) 6 *Humanity* 63; on the impact of the early struggle over Iranian oil, see generally: S Pahuja and C Storr, 'Rethinking Iran and International Law: The Anglo-Iranian Oil Company Case Revisited' in J Crawford et al (eds), *The International Legal Order: Current Needs and Possible Responses* (Leiden, Brill | Nijhoff, 2017); Lustig (n 32) 144–78.

[41] P Chatterjee, 'The Legacy of Bandung' in Eslava, Fakhri and Nesiah (eds), *Bandung* (n 4); UN, General Assembly, Resolution 1219 (XII), Financing Economic Development (14 December 1957); UN, General Assembly, Resolution 1515 (XV), Concerted Action for Economic Development of Economically Less Developed Countries (15 December 1960); UN, Commission on Permanent Sovereignty over Natural Resources, 'The Status of Permanent Sovereignty over Natural Wealth and Resources – Preliminary Study by the Secretariat' (1959); UN, Commission on Permanent Sovereignty over Natural Resources, 'The Status of Permanent Sovereignty over Natural Wealth and Resources – Revised Study by the Secretariat' (1960).

[42] K Hossain, 'Introduction' in K Hossain (ed) (n 1) 39.

condition had the intention of shielding against stabilisation clauses; and the last condition was supposed to void colonial concessions, as well as concessions entered due to coercion.[43] From the viewpoint of public international law, whether or not resource sovereignty could affect the validity of concessions also depended on the relationship between the doctrine of acquired rights and the principle of *pacta sunt servanda* to the principle of *rebus sic stantibus*.[44] In line with the Iranian model, the NIEO provided for the prevalence of the *rebus sic stantibus* principle as it had found its way into the 1969 Vienna Convention, had been affirmed by the 1973 ICJ Fisheries decision, and had been advocated for by the Organization of Petroleum Exporting Countries (OPEC).[45] While the principle has a long lineage in international law about petroleum concessions in the context of state succession, the Aramco award had described the conflicting doctrine of acquired rights as 'the fundamental principle both of Public International Law and the municipal law of most civilized States'.[46] In contrast, the NIEO Programme of Action indirectly contradicted this decision by holding that 'states should have the right to review and revise existing arrangements in light of their national development plans and objectives'.[47] This right was by the principle of permanent sovereignty over natural resources, which the NIEO Declaration regarded as an 'inalienable right', which entitled states to, inter alia, control the exploitation of their natural resources and have the discretion of transferring their ownership or nationalise them.[48]

Bedjaoui, who had been the UN Special Rapporteur on State Succession had, just one year earlier, discussed the balance between acquired rights and *rebus sic sanctibus* for the postcolonial context and found that the inheritance of a legal order by a postcolonial successor state should not automatically imply that the concessionary regime is thereby renewed.[49] This position was reflective of, and thus informed by, the experience of his home country, as the following section will now illustrate.

[43] ibid, 39–41.

[44] This controversy was settled with the adoption of UN, 'Vienna Convention on Succession of States in respect of Treaties' UN Treaty Series, vol 1946, 3. Please note that this Convention never entered into force.

[45] OPEC Resolution XVI, 90, 'Declaratory Statement of Petroleum Policy in Member Countries' 1; International Court of Justice, *Fisheries Jurisdiction Case (United Kingdom of Great Britain and Northern Ireland v Iceland)*, Decision on Jurisdiction of 26 February 1973, ICJ Reports 1973, 3; Art 62 of the Vienna Convention on the Law of Treaties, UN Treaty Series, vol 1155, 331 (23 May 1969).

[46] *Saudi Arabia v Arabian American Oil Company (Aramco)* (n 36) 205.

[47] UN, General Assembly, Resolution 3202 (S-VI), Programme of Action on the Establishment of a New International Economic Order (1 May 1974) s V, para b.

[48] UN, General Assembly, Resolution 3201 (S-VI), Declaration on the Establishment of a New International Economic Order (1 May 1974) para 4(e).

[49] M Bedjaoui, 'Sixth Report on Succession of States in Respect of Matters other than Treaties, by Mr Mohammed Bedjaoui, Special Rapporteur – Draft Articles with Commentaries on Succession to Public Property' *Yearbook of the International Law Commission, vol II* (A/CN.4/267, 1973) 27.

IV. THE ALGERIAN MODEL OF INTERNATIONAL DIPLOMACY

Another country, which shaped Third World Internationalism on natural resources was Algeria. In contrast to the Iranian nationalisation of petroleum, which was first and foremost shaped through the reinvention of contractual relations, the Algerian path to sovereignty over its petroleum reserves was through formal decolonisation. The 'Algerian problem' has been captured in the words of the Algerian representative to the Cairo conference, Aiah Hasan:

> The colonial system was to give European settlers in Algeria the possibility to monopolise trade, natural resources and grasp hard labour for their own benefit and for the benefit of the French imperialistic capitalism. Its primary aim was the occupation of Algeria. Theft of the land was systematically organized in order to distribute it to the French settlers. The French took advantage of this opportunity. As a second step, since the Algerian's social organization was essentially tribal, hence property is in common, it was decided to apply the French Civil Code where property was codified and individual. The result was the following: In 1850, the settlers' land amounted to 100.000 hectares. In 1900, it rose to 600.000. In 1952, it was 2 million 700.000 hectares. Moreover, 11 million hectares were simply confiscated by the French state to form the 'Dominium lands'. Only 7 million hectares remained to the Algerians, ¾ of which are unfit for cultivation.[50]

The colonisation of Algerian lands and resources was achieved by both imperial law and the transplantation of French private law and its individualised conception of property. As such the French claim to Algerian petroleum reserves was not contractual, but an imperial claim, placing the question of access to mineral resources squarely at the heart of the Algerian decolonisation process. As such, the 1942 Évian Accords concluded between France and Algeria foresaw that in exchange for technical, cultural and development assistance as well as the assurance of preferential credit terms, Algeria would respect all existing rights and property titles of French natural and legal persons. They contained a freezing clause according to which all concessions held by France at the time were to remain protected from any legislative change. They further provided for the sharing of all subsoil resources located in the Algerian regions of Oasis and Saoura. Finally, the accords secured France's continued influence over Algerian mineral resources through its equal vote in a technical organisation that was to be set up to oversee the development of Algerian mineral resources extraction facilities and infrastructure and for advising on any legislative proposals affecting oil or gas production and assisting with the granting of new exploitation titles.[51] This was the context in which Houari Boumédiène entered into office in 1965 as President of Algeria and he made it a priority to change these conditions by renegotiating existing petroleum concessions to increase Algeria's

[50] A Hasan, 'The Algerian Problem' in Afro-Asian Peoples' Solidarity Conference (eds), *The Algerian Problem* (Cairo, Foreign Languages Publishing House, 1957) 112.

[51] Les accords d'Évian (18 mars 1962) s II(B).

profit shares and to ensure that SONATRACH, Algeria's state-owned oil and gas company, had the right to operate all newly assigned exploitation sites as well as the exclusive right to the transport and sale of natural gas. These efforts were, however, not sufficient to rid the Algerian mineral resource sector of the firm French grip, which the Évian Accords had secured.[52] For support and to improve Algeria's bargaining position, Boumédiène and his government thus turned to three different international venues, namely to multilateral solidarity conferences of postcolonial states, OPEC and the UN General Assembly. In doing so, he followed in the footsteps of his predecessor Ahmed Ben Bella's foreign policy, which had been equally committed to translating the ideals of Third World internationalism into concrete decolonisation outcomes.[53]

Boumédiène looked to galvanise support among postcolonial states for undoing imperial property claims to postcolonial natural resources. As the host of the first Group of 77 meeting in 1967, he advocated for the domestic processing of commodities and natural resources, and openly second-guessed OPEC's campaign for higher petroleum prices, wondering whether it was not better to instead focus on challenging the effective foreign control over subsoil resources located in the Third World. This position had been jointly articulated one year earlier at the Havana conference in 1966, where ongoing control over postcolonial economic assets by foreign powers was identified as the continuation of an empire draped in capitalism. As the conference's General Declaration put it:

> The monopolies from imperial power draw out for their benefit enormous riches from the peoples of Asia, Africa and Latin America. This spoilation has been secularly carried out under different forms. They seize the natural resources of the soil, subsoil and maritime platform, control through investments the most important sectors of industry and services as well as foreign trade, and impose their harmful conditions on the relations of international exchange, fully controlling banks and national finances.[54]

Following the earlier Bandung conference, the Secretary-General of the Arab League, Abdel Khalek Hassouna, had already commissioned the Arab League's petroleum bureau to conduct a study on oil concessions in Saudi Arabia, Iran, Kuwait, Libya and the Trucial States (today the United Arab Emirates). The study concluded that existing regimes were predatory.[55] The study's findings have been used to underline the need to renegotiate the terms of these agreements and even nullify them when appropriate. The first Arab-Petroleum Oil

[52] G Garavini, 'From Boumedienomics to Reaganomics: Algeria, OPEC, and the International Struggle for Economic Equality'(2015) 6 *Humanity* 79, 83.

[53] See generally: JJ Byrne, *Mecca of Revolution: Algeria, Decolonization, and the Third World Order* (Oxford, Oxford University Press, 2016) 172–226.

[54] 'General Declaration of the First Solidarity Conference of the Peoples of Africa, Asia and Latin America' in General Secretariat of the OS.PAAAL (ed), *First Solidarity Conference of the Peoples of Africa, Asia and Latin America* (Havana, Cuba, 1966) 153.

[55] Dietrich, *Oil Revolution* (n 13) 62.

conference had been convened in 1959, and only one year later, OPEC had been established as a forum for oil-exporting states to develop common positions towards transnational oil companies.[56] Its establishment had led the way to the forming of various other natural resources alliances among postcolonial countries, a development which had given rise to concern among early neoliberals, such as Gottfried Haberler, who believed that free trade could only flourish when it was encased in a rules-based global order.[57] Neoliberals' concern had not been international coordination on commodities trade as such, which they had seen as a preferable solution to leaving this matter to domestic policy. Rather, they had perceived the alliance formation among commodities producers as a potential threat to free trade. In the words of a 1958 GATT expert panel:

> A great advantage of international over national arrangements is that they can take into account the interests of all importing and exporting countries and can thus avoid the possibility that one country or group of countries will increase its own stability at the cost of greater instability for others. Indeed since the second world war the principle has been generally accepted that international commodity agreements should be concluded only in the case in which they are agreed upon and operated by importing and exporting countries jointly. This also avoids the possibility that they become a producer's monopoly used to exploit the consumers of the product by maintaining a price well above the price which would otherwise have ruled.[58]

The expert panel provided economic reasoning for liberalising commodities trade. It had been aware of the vulnerability of natural resource export-dependent economies to global price fluctuations. While maintaining that variations in supply and demand of commodities and raw materials could adversely affect both exporting and importing countries, it had contested that such variations were directly linked to moderate price fluctuations, concluding that the fixing of prices would not be a proportionate measure and may ultimately be detrimental rather than beneficial. The panel similarly had advised against national import or export restrictions cautioning that such measures may have incalculable consequences for the price and availability of other products. Even though it had acknowledged that, at times, political reasons may compel governments to take measures to protect their domestic economies, it had cautioned against import or export restrictions and instead advised governments to create a buffer stock of non-spoilable commodities, which should ideally be globally managed to avoid the manipulation of the price of any commodity by one country and to ensure that the supply would adjust to the demand and maintain prices at a stable level.[59]

[56] ibid, 93.

[57] The expression of encasement in the context of Geneva school neoliberals has been coined by Q Slobodian, *Globalists: The End of Empire and the Birth of Neoliberalism* (Cambridge, MA, Harvard University Press, 2018).

[58] G Haberler et al, 'Trends in International Trade: A Report by A Panel of Experts' (Geneva, General Agreement on Tariffs and Trade, 1958) 73.

[59] ibid, 65–72.

OPEC had initially not been intended as a cartel but as a forum for the exchange of economic and technical information and the development of common policies. It was only one of many Global South commodities alliances. Some merely looked to facilitate research and development, while others indeed operated like cartels engaging in price coordination. Some were global alliances that operated under the umbrella of an international organisation. For instance, a 1962 agreement signed between coffee-producing countries at the United Nations established the International Coffee Organization, and the Association of Iron-Ore-Exporting Countries was founded in 1975 under the auspices of the UN Conference on Trade and Development (UNCTAD).[60] Other alliances deliberately maintained a small but expansive membership and refused to associate with any existing international organisations, such as the Intergovernmental Council of Copper-Exporting Countries (CIPEC), which was founded to coordinate copper output, or the Alliance of Cocoa Producing Countries, which had the same objective for Cocoa with its Member States accounting for 75 per cent of global cocoa production.[61] Similarly, 92 per cent of the world's natural rubber is produced in countries which are members to the Association of Natural Rubber Producing Countries (ANRPC), which pursued the objective of promoting natural rubber over synthetic alternatives.[62] To varying degrees, all of these commodities alliances were the result of Third World internationalism, yet it was OPEC that found itself at the centre of the Third World struggle for a more equitable global economic order.[63]

In its early years, OPEC's policies were relatively moderate as both the Saudi Arabian and Iranian governments were reluctant to embrace the Egyptian and Algerian campaigns for more radical action towards the nationalisation of mineral resources. In effect, global petroleum prices in that decade stagnated at a low level.[64] Several developments towards the end of the 1960s politicised OPEC's agenda pushing it to pursue more than just better conditions for petroleum exports. By then petro-states had understood that they were in a position to weaponise the global dependency on their natural wealth. When Muammar Gaddafi took office in Libya in 1969, this coincided with an oil boom that drove petroleum prices up, both of which led to increased support for Boumédiène's

[60] International Coffee Agreement, UN Treaty Series, vol 469, 169, and vol 515, 322 (28 September 1962).

[61] See generally: KA Mingst, 'Cooperation or Illusion: An Examination of the Intergovernmental Council of Copper Exporting Countries' (1976) 30 *International Organization* 263. When CIPEC was founded in 1967, copper exports were one of the primary sources of public revenues for each of these countries, and together, their production accounted for a significant portion of exploitable copper reserves. In 1988, it was dissolved as it failed to meet its objective. Original Member States of CIPEC were Chile, Peru, the Democratic Republic of the Congo and Zambia; Abidjan Charter (1962). The Charter's original Member States were Ghana, Nigeria, Brazil, Ivory Coast and Cameroon.

[62] 'About ANRPC': www.anrpc.org/html/default.aspx?ID=4&PID=5.

[63] As Garavini notes, OPEC did not always occupy this prominent role voluntarily: Garavini (n 52) 80.

[64] ibid, 82.

demands within OPEC. In subsequent negotiations with France, Boumédiène successfully nationalised Algerian oil and gas production, and soon after all of the other OPEC countries followed Algeria's example.[65]

In the aftermath of the wave of petroleum nationalisation, the 1954 Iranian production-sharing agreement contract model replaced the concessions model as a conventional form of a petroleum contract. This had several reasons, one of which was that concessions were thought to conflict with resource sovereignty. As explained above, unlike production-sharing agreements, petroleum concessions not only transfer property and user rights but also ownership of all soil and subsoil resources.[66] Production-sharing agreements are concluded for shorter periods than concession agreements – usually 25–30 years – and provide for a higher share of the profits for host states than concession agreements.[67] At the same time, their financial regime is notoriously difficult to account for, and they frequently involve a state-owned company which is turned into a 'black box' of resource revenues.[68] As explained elsewhere, the extraordinary role that production-sharing agreements give to state-owned companies in the management of their public wealth, while such companies are simultaneously further removed from public scrutiny than other government agencies, has created the ideal conditions for grand theft by oil elites.[69]

As a final act of pushing the Third World internationalist agenda, Boumédiène called for a special session of the UN General Assembly in 1974 to propose, among other things, reform of international law to achieve a more equitable global economic order. In the context of the Iranian nationalisation of its mineral resources, international law has proven to be useful for this purpose. At the same time, it had 'not yet [been] purged of inequality and imperialism', as Bedjaoui, Boumédiène's contemporary and fellow countryman observed.[70] Conscribing international law to the project of economic justice thus required a substantial change in its normative content, an endeavour which had been fostered by international lawyers at the United Nations since the first UNCTAD in 1964.

Emblematic of this position towards international law is Georges Abi-Saab, who had arrived in Geneva in 1963. To him, postcolonial, or rather 'newly independent' states as he has referred to them, ought not to take issue with the

[65] ibid, 85.

[66] 'Oil Contracts – How to Read and Understand them' (*OpenOil*, 2012) 27.

[67] Schrijver for instance defines concession agreements transfer rights inherent to sovereignty: Schrijver (n 30) 174.

[68] 'Oil Contracts' (n 66).

[69] L Kulamadayil, 'Grand Theft in International Law' (2022) 13 Amsterdam Law School Research Paper No 2022-13.

[70] M Bedjaoui, *Towards a New International Economic Order* (New York, Holmes and Meier, 1979) 110. For a comment on the significance of the campaign of Bedjaoui in shaping postcolonial international law, see also: U Özsu, 'Determining New Selves: Mohammed Bedjaoui on Algeria, Western Sahara, and Post-Classical International Law' in J von Bernstorff and P Dann (eds), *The Battle for International Law in the Decolonization Era* (Oxford, Oxford University Press, 2019).

concept and existence of international law, but be critical of its content, as it did not reflect a decolonised world society. He understood international law to be a shield against excesses of power by former imperial states and saw it as a useful instrument for enhancing postcolonial states' political and economic objectives, but also acknowledged that the content of international law rules was connoted and did not respond to the new needs and fundamental changes of the world community.[71] Bedjaoui shared Abi-Saab's views on the potential of international law to serve in the processes of decolonisation,[72] but differed insofar as he thought that its form needed evolving. He noted that international law was not 'some sort of untouchable, sacrosanct monument' and that 'no norm is eternal and proof against the erosion of time'.[73] Bedjaoui had been a member of the Algerian delegation at the Évian and Lugrin consultations, where he took part in the negotiations of the conditions of Algeria's independence from France. He had also been Algeria's Ambassador to France in 1970 and contributed to paving Algeria's path to independence, for example by leading the renegotiations that eventually resulted in the nationalisation of Algerian mineral resources.

In the Iranian tradition of associating the control over mineral resources with popular sovereignty and in the spirit of General Assembly Resolution 1803 affirming the right to permanent sovereignty over natural resources, the people's right to self-determination was taken as the starting point for the strive towards economic justice. This right was subjected to the condition of advancing the objectives of economic development. A 1972 resolution adopted by UNCTAD is emblematic of this view. It provides that every country ought to exercise resource sovereignty in 'the interest of the economic development and well-being of its own people' and frames unwanted foreign intervention of either an economic or political nature as a 'flagrant violation' of the principles of self-determination and non-intervention that 'could constitute a threat to international peace and security'.[74] Recognising that foreign interventions in the mineral resources sector were not always a matter of choice but necessitated by the lack of access to capital to engage in capital-intensive industrial resource extraction, the UN General Assembly adopted a resolution that foresaw the establishment of a fund for natural resource exploitation managed by the United Nations. This resolution was premised on the assumption that natural resource exploitation was necessary for economic development, which is why it extended an invitation to

[71] G Abi-Saab, 'The Newly Independent States and the Rules of International Law: An Outline' (1962) 8 *Howard Law Journal* 118. For appraisal of Abi-Saab's contributions to the development of international law at the United Nations, see especially U Özsu, 'Organizing Internationally: Georges Abi-Saab, the Congo Crisis and the Decolonization of the United Nations' (2020) 31 *European Journal of International Law* 601.

[72] See also: Bedjaoui, 'Sixth Report' (n 49).

[73] Bedjaoui, *Towards a New International Economic Order* (n 70) 101.

[74] UNCTAD, Resolution 46 (III), 'Steps to achieve a greater measure of agreement on principles governing international trade relations and trade policies conducive to development', Principle II (1972).

other development institutions to collaborate.[75] Ultimately, however, this fund could not attract the necessary financial means to be operational.

Algeria's NIEO campaign was met with scepticism by countries dependent on the import of mineral resources, while the United States (US) held conflicting positions towards it. Even though Kissinger, who was the US foreign secretary at the time, voiced concerns that the draft Charter of Economic Rights and Duties of States (CERDS) did not sufficiently consider the needs of industrialised nations, the United States embraced the initiative overall, viewing it as an opportunity to improve its relations with Muslim Middle Eastern countries, which had been strained due to the US support of Israel during the 1973 Yom Kippur War.[76] To this end, nominally supporting the NIEO campaign as an act of symbolic politics was a low price to pay, as the effects of a non-binding General Assembly resolution could easily be contained by other international legal institutions, such as GATT as well as foreign policy designed to fracture Third World internationalism.[77] For this purpose, the United States stirred concerns about the disastrous economic consequences for petroleum-dependent postcolonial states that high petroleum prices would produce.[78] Many of them were indeed entirely dependent on oil imports and had been made painfully aware of that fact by a 400 per cent increase in oil prices between October 1973 and January 1974.[79]

[75] UN, General Assembly, Resolution 3167 (XXVIII), United Nations Revolving Fund for Natural Resources Exploration, 17 December 1973.

[76] Cited after CN Brower and JB Tepe, 'The Charter of Economic Rights and Duties of States: A Reflection or Rejection of International Law?' (1975) 9 *International Lawyer* 295, 299.

[77] G White, 'New International Economic Order' (1976) 16 *Virginia Journal of International Law* 323, 328–30; GW Haight, 'The New International Economie Order and the Charter of Economic Rights and Duties of States'(1975) 9 *International Lawyer* 591, 595–97.

[78] V McFarland, 'The New International Economic Order, Interdependence, and Globalization' (2015) 6 *Humanity* 217, 222–28; According to McFarland, the economic theory for Kissinger's policy was based on RN Cooper, *The Economics of Interdependence: Economic Policy in the Atlantic Community* (New York, Columbia University Press, 1968). Cooper wrote: 'Growing interdependence makes the successful pursuit of national economic objectives much more difficult'.

[79] Crude oil prices have overall significantly increased since the 1960s. There are three main phases that can be distinguished. The first phase is from 1960 to 1973 where the oil price remained at a low but stable level, peaking in 1973 at a price of US$2.7. At the time, the oil industry underwent a process of nationalisation. Before that, the 'seven sisters' – the world's largest international oil companies at the time – had dominated the oil market and had maintained oil prices at a rather stable level. This changed with the founding of OPEC in 1960 and the emergence of national oil companies. This led to a power-shift to oil-producing countries and diversified the actors and factors determining the international oil price. The first time this became evident was in 1973 when, as a response to US support for Israel in the Arab-Israeli war, some OPEC Member States decreased their production outputs and later placed embargos on the export of crude oil to the US and other countries. This caused an abrupt rise in crude oil prices. Until 1978 the price remained at a steady level. Then in 1979 the Iranian Revolution caused a fear of shortage that heavily impacted the oil price. Though the global output of oil decreased only marginally, the price spiked by roughly 10%. Subsequently, this price remained rather stable until 1985/86, when the oil price crashed by 50%. Reasons for this crash were massive oil surpluses coupled with economic recession. In the late 1980s and 1990s the crude oil price fluctuated at a smaller level. Then at the turn of the century, the price rose constantly, with the exception of 2009, when the global financial crisis decreased economic activity globally. See ML Ross, *The Oil Curse: How Petroleum Wealth Shapes the Development of Nations* (Princeton,

When the UN General Assembly ultimately adopted the NIEO under Algerian leadership, it contained several lofty objectives for natural resources. For instance, it linked the exercise of natural resource sovereignty to the end of 'all forms of foreign occupation, racial discrimination, apartheid, colonial, neocolonial and alien domination, and exploitation'.[80] The NIEO also fostered 'collective self-reliance', 'accelerated development', domestic processing, producers' associations, and higher export earnings.[81] It did however also contain specific objectives on contentious legal issues that had arisen in the context of the nationalisation of mineral resources, namely the sanctity of contracts and the conditions of expropriation.

While having left its mark on contemporary international law,[82] measured by its aspirations, its achievements have remained rather modest. Developments in and beyond international law before its adoption pacified its driving forces.[83] Changes in international development policy, among other things, in the years following the NIEO ensured that it stayed this way. Until the late 1970s, all development banks had a common policy of not providing loans for establishing an infrastructure for industrial petroleum production to developing states. This changed with decisions taken by the World Bank's Board of Governors in 1977 and 1979. In June 1977, the board decided to grant limited funding to such projects on an experimental basis. Subsequently, in January 1979, it approved a loan programme for oil and gas development projects in non-OPEC developing countries with an overall budget of US$3 billion.[84]

V. CONCLUSION

The early twentieth-century petroleum regimes of Iran and Algeria represent two complementary models of foreign appropriation of mineral resources secured by law: an intersecting regime of domestic, transnational and international law in Iran's case, and imperial law and the transplantation of French law

Princeton University Press, 2012) 52 ff; William D Smith, 'Oil as a Political Weapon' *New York Times* (20 May 1973); Richard N Cooper, 'Energy prices' *The Economist* (27 October 1979).

[80] Art 1(a) of UN, General Assembly, 'Programme of Action on the Establishment of a New International Economic Order', A/RES/S-6/3202 (1974).

[81] ibid, Art 1.

[82] Vienna Convention on Succession of States in respect of Treaties, see especially, Arts 5–10; International Court of Justice, *Case Concerning Armed Activities on the Territory of the Congo (Democratic Republic of the Congo v Uganda)*, Judgment of 19 December 2005, ICJ Reports 2005, 168.

[83] The CERDS was adopted with 120 votes in favour, merely six votes against (Belgium, Denmark, Germany, Luxembourg, the United Kingdom and the United States), and 10 abstentions (Austria, Canada, France, Ireland, Israel, Italy, Japan, Netherlands, Norway and Spain).

[84] Due to concerns for climate change, the World Bank recently announced that it will end funding for oil and gas extraction: Larry Elliott, 'World Bank to end financial support for oil & gas extraction' *Guardian* (12 December 2017), available at: www.theguardian.com/business/2017/dec/12/uk-banks-join-multinationals-pledge-come-clean-climate-change-risks-mark-carney.

in the case of Algeria. Despite these differences, the countries' path to reclaiming ownership and control over their petroleum reserves has left imprints on public international law and the transnational regime of petroleum law. Revisiting these different models permits us to consider alternatives to today's well-established international legal principles. The Iranian internal exercise of natural resource sovereignty invites us to imagine the possibility of considering natural resource sovereignty not only as public international law, but also as internationalised public law.[85] This would permit us to emphasise that it should be first and foremost the people, not their rulers, who decide what is to be done with such resources. And, Algeria's harnessing of Third World Internationalism permits a glimpse of hope that counter-hegemonic moves are possible.[86] Whereas scholars have rightfully pointed to the overemphasising of the significance of certain moments in Third World Internationalism for the development of international law, this chapter has looked to show that while the progress achieved at Bandung or in the course of the NIEO may have been modest, this should not lead one to overlook the accomplishments achieved by petro-states through bilateral, transnational and domestic law.[87] However, in light of the 'paradox of plenty' and 'resource curse' dynamics of petro-states, the optimism about these accomplishments is dampened. Not for their lack of achieving a lasting change to the international legal order, but for the cost of locking petro-states into an extractivist logic, which their wielding of influence at a global stage came at.[88]

[85] The concept of 'internationalised public law' leans on the concept of 'international public law' developed in A von Bogdandy, M Goldmann, and I Venzke, 'From Public International to International Public Law: Translating World Public Opinion into International Public Authority' (2017) 28 *European Journal of International Law* 115.

[86] Invitation for such reasoning extended by Venzke in a series of publications. See, eg: I Venzke, 'Possibilities of the Past: Histories of the NIEO and the Travails of Critique' (2018) 20 *Journal of the History of International Law* 263; I Venzke, 'What if? Counterfactual (Hi)Stories of International Law' (2018) 8 *Asian Journal of International Law* 403.

[87] R Vitalis, 'The midnight ride of Kwame Nkrumah and other fables of Bandung (Ban-doong)' (2013) 4 *Humanity* 261; K Crow, 'Bandung's Fate' in I Venzke and KJ Heller (eds), *Contingency in International Law* (Oxford, Oxford University Press, 2021).

[88] Prashad powerfully describes this trajectory from the possibilities of third-world internationalism to its demise brought about by the triumph of neoliberalism and its logic of extractivism of the Third World: V Prashad, *The Darker Nations: A People's History of the Third World* (New York, The New Press, 2008); V Prashad, *The Poorer Nations: A Possible History of the Global South* (London, Verso, 2014).

5

The Temptation of Plenty

I. INTRODUCTION

By all accounts, 2020 was a successful year for the legal regime against grand theft. That July, former Malaysian Prime Minister Najib Razak (PM Najib) was sentenced to a 12-year prison sentence for stealing billions from public coffers through the state-owned company 1MDB. Later that summer, the American investment bank Goldman Sachs admitted to its role in this theft and agreed to the costliest settlement in its corporate history. Founded in 2009 to promote the country's economic development, 1MDB was used in subsequent years to launder money for the benefit of PM Najib, his family and their associates who spent it on art, movie productions, real estate, jewellery and whatever else necessary to buy themselves access to the world's rich and famous.

Another 2020 victory involved the actions taken against the Swiss banks Julius Baer and Banca Credinvest for their roles in an affair which involved funds laundered from the Venezuelan state-owned company PDVSA. Two years earlier, the executive directors of PDVSA and Julius Baer had pleaded guilty to related criminal charges in this affair.[1]

The 1MDB and PDVSA affairs are grand theft cases as they both revolve around stolen or embezzled public wealth that was laundered through different financial institutions to enrich a selected few. Although grand theft is not a legally defined term, it is a well-known legal problem, primarily addressed through anti-corruption and anti-money-laundering (AML) law. What started with the 1977 US Foreign Corrupt Practices Act (FCPA) is now a complex, justiciable and almost universally accepted legal regime. The formation of this regime and its responses to the related crime of grand corruption is well-covered ground in international law and international relations scholarship.[2]

[1] United States District Court for the Southern District of Florida, *United States of America v Matthias Krull*, Complaint of 24 July 2018, 18-CR-20682-CMA; United States District Court Southern District of Florida, *United States v Abraham Edgardo Ortega*, Plea Agreement of 31 October 2018, 18-CR-20685-KMW.

[2] Grand corruption is defined as 'abuse of high-level power that benefits the few at the expense of the many and [that] causes serious and widespread harm to individuals and society': Unknown, 'Grand Corruption', 20 June 2022, available at: www.transparency.org/en/corruptionary/grand-corruption; KE Davis, *Between Impunity and Imperialism: The Regulation of Transnational Bribery*

Scholars commonly evaluate AML and anti-corruption law by reference to their effectiveness in achieving 'good governance' and 'the rule of law' in domestic contexts. How such laws respond to the loss of public wealth by acts of corruption is seldom scrutinised.[3] There are several reasons for this. First, grand theft, although transnational by design, is never tackled on the global terrain. On the contrary, international anti-corruption and AML law assign the responsibility to implement and oversee grand theft safeguards to domestic bureaucracies. Indeed, the body of rules referred to above as a 'legal regime against grand theft' is proliferated, and includes international, transnational and domestic rules running through private, criminal and administrative law, making a holistic appreciation of the regime rather challenging. Secondly, the most conclusive information on the regime's effectiveness is not readily available since it remains in the hands of those who provide the infrastructure for grand theft, namely financial institutions. Unfortunately, such institutions are subject to bank secrecy law which operates in a tenuous relationship with the legal regime against grand theft.[4]

Moreover, since much of this 'regime' was designed to address other crimes, such as drug trafficking or terrorism, rather than to combat the theft of public funds per se, it can be ineffective when theft occurs in the absence of these crimes. As a result, individuals found to have been involved in grand theft are frequently not prosecuted, not sentenced, or sentenced lightly. Another deficiency of the legal regime is the secrecy in which repercussions for financial institutions found to have been involved in grand theft are shrouded.

While acknowledging these difficulties, this chapter undertakes to scrutinise legal responses to grand theft, focusing particularly on the regulation of grand theft's infrastructure, ie, financial institutions. It argues that further analysis of international anti-corruption and AML law requires more serious engagement with their domestic implementation as well as their aptness to address grand theft. From a practical viewpoint, the devastating impact of grand theft on domestic economies and human livelihoods is undisputed, so, unfortunately, international law addresses it primarily through regimes designed for other regulatory objectives. From a conceptual viewpoint, reflections on the future of anti-corruption and AML law would be significantly enriched by a better understanding of the everyday operations of these regimes. This chapter can only be a first attempt at shedding light on such everyday operations.

For this purpose, the 2020 PDVSA and 1MDB affairs are used as case studies. They were selected because of their overwhelmingly positive reception: in both

(New York, Oxford University Press, 2019); KW Abbott and D Snidal, 'Values and Interests: International Legalization in the Fight against Corruption' (2002) 31 *Journal of Legal Studies* S141.

[3] Against: JC Sharman, *The Despot's Guide to Wealth Management: On the International Campaign Against Grand Corruption* (Ithaca, NY, Cornell University Press, 2017).

[4] See, eg: under Bundesgesetz über die Banken und Sparkassen (BankG), AS 1999 2405; BBl 1998 3847, 8 November 1934, Art 47.

affairs, the accountability mechanisms of the legal regime against grand theft were celebrated for having worked well, resulting in numerous criminal convictions, the recovery of stolen assets, and the imposition of sanctions against both public and corporate actors. Also, because these mechanisms were used successfully, factual accounts of the underlying schemes are available in the narrations of indictments, judgments and press releases.

The remainder of this chapter is structured as follows. Section II offers an overview of international anti-corruption and AML law and their origins. This section reaffirms other commentators' observations that the regime is quite extraordinary in its scope and design and among the most robust fields of transnational law. It also traces the regimes to their US and Swiss origins as these origins explain current divergences in legal practice. It further gives a brief overview of scholarly perspectives on international AML and anti-corruption law, to illustrate the spectrum of positions toward these two regimes.

Section III provides a factual account of the two selected case studies, the 1MDB and PDVSA money-laundering operations. The emphasis here is on information relevant to the involvement of financial institutions, rather than of executives at either PDVSA or 1MDB, to illustrate that money-laundering operations are not always, in fact, as opaque as commonly assumed. Indeed, knowledge of these operations within and among financial institutions is widespread. This supports the view that the facilitation of grand theft by such institutions is not just an exceptional occurrence, but a part of many institutions' business models.

Section IV then offers an overview of the consequences for financial institutions and individual banking employees in three jurisdictions, namely Singapore, Switzerland and the United States (US) for their involvement in the two operations. These consequences are categorised in terms of (i) individual criminal responsibility, (ii) corporate monetary consequences, and (iii) corporate structural consequences. This chapter concludes with some thoughts on the possible implications of this research for future work in this field.

II. INTERNATIONAL ANTI-CORRUPTION AND MONEY-LAUDERING LAW

What is referred to here as 'grand theft' is not itself an international law concept. Commonly, it is understood as a consequence of grand corruption and addressed through AML law.[5] As a result, international law does not regulate grand theft directly, but indirectly in pursuit of other regulatory objectives. While AML law was originally internationalised to fight organised crime, the formation of anti-corruption law can be traced back to civil society mobilisation against the distortion of democratic bargaining processes caused by the undue influence of

[5] Davis, *Between Impunity and Imperialism* (n 2).

private actors over public officials.[6] Consequentially, AML law is first and foremost concerned with the generation of funds through, or their use for, organised crime, whereas anti-corruption law is thought of as a means of restoring good governance principles and the rule of law.[7] Neither is primarily concerned with the theft of public funds by public officials: the phenomenon that this chapter has termed as grand theft.

The formation of AML law is traceable to the Financial Action Task Force (FATF), which was founded in 1989 by the G7 to address the global illicit drugs trade. For that purpose, the FATF was to 'prevent the utilization of the banking system and financial institutions for money laundering and to consider additional preventive efforts in this field, including the adaptation of the legal and regulatory systems to enhance multilateral judicial assistance'.[8] Today, FATF also links money laundering to terrorist activities and other organised crimes such as weapons trafficking. It has 37 members, among them many global financial capital hubs such as Hong Kong, Luxembourg, Singapore, Switzerland, the United Kingdom and the United States.[9] If success is measured by the degree to which formally non-binding recommendations achieved norm convergence at a global scale, then FATF's success is indeed remarkable.[10] Unlike international AML law, which has the legacy of a club governance initiative championed by the United States, anti-corruption legislation is credited to efforts by the British and German NGOs Global Witness and Transparency International.[11] Founded in 1993, both sounded alarm bells on the nexus between corruption and human rights violations.[12] Their work was supported by US corporations which felt that the 1977 FCPA had put them at a disadvantage compared with their international competitors who could still lawfully bribe foreign officials. As a result, several binding international conventions were adopted in the late 1990s and early 2000s which diffused the norm of the unlawfulness of corruption in domestic legal systems.[13]

[6] P Webb, 'The United Nations Convention Against Corruption: Global Achievement or Missed Opportunity?' (2005) 8 *Journal of International Economic Law* 191.

[7] S Rose-Ackerman, 'International actors and the promises and pitfalls of anti-corruption reform' (2012) 34 *University of Pennsylvania Journal of International Law* 447.

[8] G7, 'Economic Declaration' (Paris, 1989) para 53.

[9] Unknown, 'History of the FATF', 20 June 2022, available at: www.fatf-gafi.org/about/historyofthefatf/.

[10] KW Abbott and D Snidal, 'Hard and Soft Law in International Governance' (2000) 54 *International Organization* 421; N Krisch, 'The Decay of Consent: International Law in an Age of Global Public Goods' (2014) 108 *American Journal of International Law* 1.

[11] RO Keohane and JS Nye, 'The Club Model of Multilateral Cooperation and Problems of Democratic Legitimacy' in RO Keohane (ed), *Power and Governance in a Partially Globalized World* (London, Routledge, 2002); Abbott and Snidal, 'Hard and Soft Law in International Governance' (n 10).

[12] K Abbott et al, 'The Concept of Legalization' (2000) 54 *International Organization* 401.

[13] M Milliet-Einbinder, 'Writing off Tax Deductibility', 20 June 2022, available at: ciaotest.cc.columbia.edu/olj/oo/oo_apr00n.html; Inter-American Convention against Corruption, 35 ILM 724, 29 March 1996; African Union Convention on Preventing and Combating Corruption, 43 ILM 5, 11 July 2003; United Nations Convention against Corruption, 2349 UNTS 41, 31 October 2003;

Even though the instituting of FATF is often celebrated as the founding moment of global AML law, its development is more complicated than that. International AML law is rooted in three distinct legal fields, namely US criminal law, international anti-trafficking law, and the voluntary commitments of mostly Swiss financial institutions through instruments such as the 1988 Basel Statement on the Prevention of Criminal Use of the Banking System for Money-Laundering. American AML efforts date back to the Bank Secrecy Act of 1970, which included record-keeping duties and permitted the treasury department to impose ad hoc reporting obligations on financial institutions. This was the first brick of the American AML reporting regime which began with the duty to report foreign currency transactions that exceeded certain thresholds and later also included the duty to report transnational cash movements. Then, in the 1980s, several domestic laws were adopted to respond to tax and financial crimes. They not only established record-keeping obligations and made the reporting duties of a previously ad hoc character permanent, but also made their violation a criminal offence.[14] Accordingly, since 1986, aiding in, or concealing domestic and international money-laundering have been federal crimes that can be punished with prison sentences of up to 20 years.[15] Money laundering was first addressed in public international law in the 1988 UN Convention against Illicit Traffic in Narcotic Drugs and Psychotropic Substances (1988 Vienna Convention). This Convention required Member States to criminalise not only drug trafficking but also the transfer and concealment of its proceeds.[16] It foreshadowed subsequent international AML and anti-corruption law by, for example, establishing extraterritorial jurisdiction over nationals on foreign soil and requiring transnational collaboration and coordination among domestic authorities.[17]

The 1988 Basel Statement gives expression to the commitment of the financial sector to police itself voluntarily. It encourages banks 'to put in place effective procedures to ensure: that all persons conducting business with [them] are properly identified; those transactions that do not appear legitimate are discouraged; and that cooperation with law enforcement agencies is achieved'.[18]

Council of Europe Civil Law Convention on Corruption, ETS No 174, 4 November 1999; Council of Europe Criminal Law Convention on Corruption, Eur TS No 173, 27 January 1999.

[14] 26 US Code § 6050I Returns relating to cash received in trade or business, etc, Pub L 104-168, title XII, § 1201(a)(9), 30 July 1996, 110 Stat 1469; 18 US Code § 1956 Laundering of monetary instruments, Pub L 114-231, title V, § 502, 7 October 2016, 130 Stat 956; 18 US Code § 1957 Engaging in monetary transactions in property derived from specified unlawful activity, Pub L 111-21, § 2(f)(2), May 20, 2009, 123 Stat 1618.

[15] 18 US Code § 1956 Laundering of monetary instruments; 18 US Code § 1957 Engaging in monetary transactions in property derived from specified unlawful activity.

[16] United Nations Convention Against Illicit Traffic in Narcotic Drugs and Psychotropic Substances, 1582 UNTS 95, 20 December 1988, Art (b).

[17] ibid, Arts 4, 7, 9.

[18] BIS, Prevention of criminal use of the banking system for the purpose of money-laundering, para 6; the earliest AML commitment of Swiss banks can be found in the Swiss Bankers Association,

At the time, strict bank secrecy law in Switzerland precluded banks from reporting suspicious financial activities to law enforcement authorities. Instead, banks themselves were required to follow up on such transactions. It was only in 1990 that federal AML obligations were imposed on Swiss banks, namely the negative obligation not to impair investigations into tax crimes or the laundering of the proceeds of criminal activities.[19] The positive obligation to report suspicions of money laundering was introduced only with the adoption of the 1997 Swiss Federal Act on Combating Money Laundering and Terrorist Financing. This law codifies the Basel statement's due diligence commitments and reaffirms the individualisation of AML responsibilities grounded in the 1990 amendment to the Swiss Criminal Code.

All three fields of law share the assumptions that only 'dirty money' – ie, the proceeds of criminal activity – is laundered and that financial institutions are unwitting instruments of money laundering, not willing participants.[20] Consequentially, FATF – the poster child of international AML law – builds on the same premises.[21] FATF organisation's International Standards on Combating Money-Laundering and the Financing of Terrorism & Proliferation (FATF recommendations) encourage states to adopt domestic law requiring financial institutions to implement preventive safeguards, to cooperate with foreign agencies and to adopt effective know-your-customer protocols, which are particularly mindful of politically exposed persons.[22] Following the logic of the legal instruments from which they derive, the FATF recommendations define money laundering concerning another crime, ie, terrorism. They conceive of money laundering as an act that is first and foremost committed by individuals, or a collective of individuals, and not by a collective entity, such as a corporation or public agency.[23] This understanding of money laundering continues to inform laws and policies on this matter, including the 2020 AML action plan of the European Union.[24] So, despite its three-pronged origins and the absence of a formal international law instrument, there is now a widely shared and harmonised understanding of money laundering throughout different domestic legal systems as well as coherent legal strategies to combat it, namely by combining

'Agreement on the Swiss Banks' Code of Conduct with Regard to the Exercise of Due Diligence' (1977).

[19] Schweizerisches Strafgesetzbuch, AS 2006 3459; BBl 1999 1979; BankG, Art 2(3)(c).

[20] Compare: WC Gilmore, *Dirty Money: The Evolution of Money Laundering Counter-Measures* (Council of Europe Press, 1999).

[21] G Stessens, *Money Laundering: A New International Law Enforcement Model* (Cambridge, Cambridge University Press, 2000) 81–112.

[22] 'International Standards on Combating Money Laundering and the Financing of Terrorism & Proliferation' (FATF, Updated 2022), Rs 9–12, 24, 26.

[23] KN Schefer, 'Causation in the Corruption – Human Rights Relationship' (2010) 1 *RW Rechtswissenschaft* 397.

[24] EU Directive 2015/849 on the Prevention of the Use of the Financial System for the Purposes of Money Laundering or Terrorist Financing [2015] OJ L141, 73–117; 'Communication from the Commission on an Action Plan for a Comprehensive Union Policy on Preventing Money Laundering or Terrorist Financing' (European Commission, 2020). The action plan views AML also as a measure to strengthen good governance and investor confidence in the European economy.

a criminal law approach with a corporate due diligence approach. To this end, the FATF recommendations contain record-keeping and information-sharing requirements for financial institutions and other businesses prone to be implicated in money laundering such as law firms, real estate agencies and precious minerals traders.[25]

In contrast to AML law, international anti-corruption law is more formalised – through a plethora of international instruments – but, partly as a result, it is significantly less harmonised. The framework is nevertheless almost universally accepted, contains binding commitments, and is implemented through domestic laws and institutions. Although the congeries of international anti-corruption conventions do not share a definition of corruption or bribery, they share a minimum understanding of what these acts entail, namely quid pro quo arrangements involving public officials which distort the principle of equality in public–private bargaining processes.[26] The principal strategy of international anti-corruption law is to prevent corruption from occurring in the first place. It pursues this strategy by mandating institutional safeguards. Measures to prevent bribery entail putting in place codes of conduct alongside requirements that the income and financial interests of public officials be disclosed. It also mandates the adoption of a system of layered oversight for tax revenue collection.[27] The UN Anti-Corruption Convention encourages states to ban public officials convicted of corruption from ever holding public office or positions with state-owned companies again and, where appropriate, to suspend, reassign or remove officials who have allegedly accepted bribes.[28] Safeguards to prevent businesses from corrupting public officials include rigorous accounting standards and periodic external financial audit requirements.[29] Another important institutional safeguard mandated by international anti-corruption law is the institutionalisation of designated independent and adequately resourced domestic agencies.[30] Other components of the preventive approach to corruption include raising public awareness about its unlawfulness.

Once corruption occurs, the criminal law approach is the principal international law response to it.[31] The conventions provide for three types of

[25] 'International Standards on Combating Money Laundering and the Financing of Terrorism & Proliferation', Rs 3, 20–22.

[26] UN Anti-Corruption Convention, Arts 3, 7, 12; OECD Convention on Combating Bribery of Foreign Public Officials in International Business Transactions, S.Treaty Doc No 105-43, 17 December 1997, Art 1; European Civil Law Convention, Art 2; OAS Anti-Corruption Convention, Art VI.

[27] OAS Anti-Corruption Convention, Art III; UN Anti-Corruption Convention, Arts 8, 52; AU Anti-Corruption Convention, Art 5.

[28] UN Anti-Corruption Convention, Art 30.

[29] OECD Anti-Bribery Convention, Art 8; AU Anti-Corruption Convention, Art 5; European Civil Law Convention, Art 10.

[30] AU Anti-Corruption Convention, Art 5; UN Anti-Corruption Convention, Art 36; European Criminal Law Convention, Art 10.

[31] UN Anti-Corruption Convention, Arts 8–10, 15–19, 23, 25–27; AU Anti-Corruption Convention, Arts 5–6, 8; OECD Anti-Bribery Convention, Art 3; OAS Anti-Corruption Convention, Arts VII, IX; European Criminal Law Convention, Arts 13–15, 18.

extraterritorial jurisdiction: the active personality principle allows states to exercise jurisdiction over its nationals for acts committed abroad;[32] the passive personality principle allows domestic courts to rule on offences committed against a national abroad;[33] and the protective principle allows domestic courts to hear cases on acts committed abroad which may jeopardise sovereign rights. State parties to the African Convention can exercise this latter jurisdiction, when 'the offence, although committed outside its jurisdiction, affects, in the view of the State concerned, its vital interests or the deleterious or harmful consequences or effects of such offenses impact on the State Party'.[34] However, domestic courts seldom make use of jurisdiction under the protective principle and never to date for any case involving corruption.[35] Finally, courts can, in some instances, admit cases involving alleged corruption abroad if they potentially connect to a serious crime within their territorial jurisdiction including money laundering or concealing the proceeds of corruption.[36] So, in relation to bringing corrupt individuals to justice, international anti-corruption law is remarkably broad in scope as it is further underscored by its obligations on extradition. It requires states to extradite persons in their territory if they are investigated or prosecuted by foreign authorities for corruption or bribery. Should a state choose not to extradite such persons, it must assume jurisdiction over them itself.[37] This far-reaching *aut dedere aut judicare* principle is otherwise reserved for crimes such as acts of terrorism, hostage-taking, or torture.[38] In terms of the cooperation and information-sharing obligations among domestic agencies, international anti-corruption law is equally broad in scope, taking priority over conflicting

[32] UN Anti-Corruption Convention, Art 42; Art 15 UN Convention against Transnational Organized Crime and the Protocols thereto, 2225 UNTS 209, 15 November 2000; OECD Anti-Bribery Convention, Art 4; OAS Anti-Corruption Convention, Art VI; AU Anti-Corruption Convention, Art 10; European Criminal Law Convention, Art 17; Council of Europe, Convention on Laundering, Search, Seizure and Confiscation of the Proceeds from Crime, ETS No 141, 8 November 1990, Art 15.

[33] UN Anti-Corruption Convention, Art 42; UN Transnational Crime Convention, Art 15.

[34] UN Anti-Corruption Convention, Art 42; AU Anti-Corruption Convention, Art 10.

[35] Cases where this jurisdiction has been used in the past concerned drugs-trafficking: US District Court for the District of Puerto Rico, *United States v Paul Oliver Keller, Michael Joseph Arra, Steven Scott Aschinger and Overton Baker Pettit*, Decision and Order of 22 May 1978, Crim No 78-74; United States District Court for the Eastern District of New York, *United States v Newball et al*, Decision of 22 October 1981, 81 CR 436; Davis, *Between Impunity and Imperialism* (n 2).

[36] UN Anti-Corruption Convention, Art 42; UN Transnational Crime Convention, Art 15; European Criminal Law Convention, Art 17.

[37] OECD Anti-Bribery Convention, Arts 10(1), 10(3); UN Anti-Corruption Convention, Arts 42(3), 42(4), 44(11); UN Transnational Crime Convention, Arts 15(3), 16(1); AU Anti-Corruption Convention, Art 15; OAS Anti-Corruption Convention, Art XIII. On these different forms of jurisdiction, see generally: C Ryngaert, *Jurisdiction in International Law* (Oxford, Oxford University Press, 2015) 142.

[38] MC Bassiouni and EM Wise, *Aut Dedere Aut Judicare: The Duty to Extradite or Prosecute in International Law* (Dordrecht, Martinus Nijhoff, 1995); 'The obligation to extradite or prosecute (*aut dedere aut judicare*)' (*Yearbook of the International Law Commission*, vol II, 2014).

norms such as bank secrecy laws or diplomatic immunities. These obligations are only limited by minimum human rights guarantees.[39]

Furthermore, in the absence of corporate criminal responsibility in most domestic legal systems, international anti-corruption law, like AML law, allows for the imposition of civil and administrative penalties for violating reporting and due diligence obligations.[40] Where the two fields of law differ is in their embedded notions about the origins of the proceeds of the crimes. As mentioned, AML law assumes that laundered money and its proceeds originate from profit-oriented crimes (eg, drug trafficking). In contrast, international anti-corruption law assumes that the proceeds of corruption are not per se dirty, but that the process by which they were obtained was. Think of oil exploitation rights for example. There is per se nothing 'dirty' about a company obtaining the rights to exploit a particular oil block. Only if such rights were obtained by quid pro quo arrangements, ie, if the process of obtaining them violated anti-corruption law, do the profits made from exploiting these rights become 'dirty'. Another significant difference between the two legal fields is that AML law – by the nature of the crimes it ultimately seeks to prevent – mainly governs private actors. In contrast, anti-corruption law disciplines the interactions between public and private actors to safeguard public interests. Nowhere are these distinctive features of anti-corruption law more visible than in its tort law approach.[41] The European Civil Law Convention, for instance, asks its signatories to ensure that under their domestic tort law, persons who suffer damages as a result of corruption can access effective remedies and obtain compensation.[42] It also stipulates that legal arrangements that were concluded due to acts of corruption can be nullified.[43] To further undo the effects of corruption, asset recovery schemes offer a means of obtaining restitution. Such schemes build on tort law to repatriate laundered or embezzled foreign public funds.[44] In principle, such schemes operate as follows. The state that lost public assets due to corruption can address its claim to a civil court in the state where the proceeds of this corruption are located. If a court finds the claim to be justified, it will order law enforcement agencies to confiscate the proceeds and return the equivalent of their market value to the claimant state, after subtracting their cost and satisfying any legitimate interests of third

[39] UN Anti-Corruption Convention, Arts 38, 39, 40, 46; UN Transnational Crime Convention, Arts 12, 18; OAS Anti-Corruption Convention, Art XIV; AU Anti-Corruption Convention, Art 17; European Criminal Law Convention, Arts 19, 21, 26, 44.

[40] OECD Anti-Bribery Convention, Art 8; UN Transnational Crime Convention, Art 10; European Criminal Law Convention, Art 19.

[41] UN Anti-Corruption Convention, Art 26.

[42] European Civil Law Convention, Art 1.

[43] ibid, Arts 5, 8.

[44] UN Anti-Corruption Convention, Art 57; AU Anti-Corruption Convention, Arts 16, 18; See also: R Ivory, *Corruption, Asset Recovery, and the Protection of Property in Public International Law: The Human Rights of Bad Guys* (Cambridge, Cambridge University Press, 2016).

parties. To summarise, even though international anti-corruption and AML law are two separate legal fields pursuing distinct regulatory objectives, they complement one another in their responses to grand theft. Both heavily depend on domestic institutions to be effective and account for the transnational nature of the acts they govern, through broad extraterritorial jurisdictional provisions and international cooperation requirements on domestic agencies. Since they entered into force, many countries have introduced new AML or anti-corruption legislation leading to the formation of what I refer to here as the 'legal regime against grand theft'.

Despite its universal appeal, the emergence of this motley regime has also generated some scepticism. In 1999, the *Connecticut Journal of International Law* published a special issue on global anti-corruption efforts which gave a platform to several critical voices. At the time, anti-corruption programmes had become central to the World Bank's good governance efforts, and international as well as regional codifications of anti-corruption norms were well under way. Contributors to the special issue warned that the fight against corruption had become a pretence for pushing other donor policy preferences, such as the privatisation of public services and unrestricted foreign access to domestic economies in the Global South. They cautioned that the fight against corruption applied a double standard to the influence-taking of private actors on public officials by demonising practices elsewhere, which would be considered constitutionally protected expressions of corporate free speech in the United States. Furthermore, they pointed out that this put pressure on private–public interactions in the Third World, and created the false impression that 'Third World problems' were due to choices made on national and local levels, rather than to structural biases of the global economic system.[45] Later critics have pointed to the localised and individualised legal responses to corruption that international law proposes and that are ill-suited to fight grand corruption.[46]

In direct contrast to such views are those of scholars who perceive the embedded liberalism of international anti-corruption law not as a weakness, but as an opportunity to use the fight against corruption to promote human rights and the rule of law. In particular, international constitutional lawyers have called for the fight against corruption to be expanded to the human rights terrain. They

[45] JT Gathii, 'Corruption and Donor Reforms: Expanding the Promises and Possibilities of the Rule of Law as an Anti-Corruption Strategy in Kenya' (1999) 14 *Connecticut Journal of International Law* 407; C Thomas, 'Does the Good Governance Policy of the International Financial Institutions Privilege Markets at the Expense of Democracy?' (1999) 14 *Connecticut Journal of International Law* 551; D Kennedy, 'The International Anti-Corruption Campaign' (1999) 14 *Connecticut Journal of International Law* 455. See also: S Rose-Ackerman, 'Political Corruption and Democracy' (1999) 14 *Connecticut Journal of International Law* 363; United States Supreme Court, *Citizens United v Federal Election Commission*, Opinion of 21 January 2010, No 08-205; such a view had been put forward by, eg, BW Husted, 'Wealth, Culture, and Corruption' (1999) 30 *Journal of International Business Studies* 339.

[46] L Kulamadayil, 'When International Law Distracts: Reconsidering Anti-Corruption Law' (2018) 7 *European Society of International Law Reflections* 1.

have linked corruption with civil and political rights (eg, acts of judicial favouritism that violate the right to non-discrimination and to equal treatment before the law); socio-economic rights (eg, the embezzlement of financial resources earmarked for public services); and the erosion of democracy and the rule of law.[47] They have also argued that anti-corruption and AML laws were not sufficiently victim-focused, a shortcoming, they argue, that could easily be remedied by addressing corruption through human rights instruments. From a doctrinal viewpoint, this position is not far-fetched. Norms to prevent corruption, such as transparency requirements, depend on citizens' exercise of civil and political rights to be effective.[48] Fighting corruption and promoting human rights are normatively so intertwined that it has led Peters to suggest that corruption is a human rights violation.[49] This conception does not come without its problems. In addition to concerns that such a conception reinforces narratives that attribute corruption to the lack of resilience of local democratic institutions, some have wondered about the added value of this approach for the justiciability of claims.[50] Indeed, as this section has underlined, despite having no international enforcement mechanism of their own, international AML and anti-corruption law are sophisticated and enforceable fields in international law.

III. THE CASE STUDIES

What 1MDB and PDVSA have in common is that they are both state-owned companies. 1MDB is a Malaysian domestic development agency, financed by capital from the Malaysian public pension fund and from investments raised through bond sales. PDVSA is the extended arm of the Venezuelan government, in the sense that it manages the country's exploration and exploitation rights, and is the contracting partner for concession and production sharing agreements; it therefore, acts on behalf of the Venezuelan government in revenue collection and management. Involved in one corruption scandal after another, PDVSA has been at the centre of countless allegations of financial crimes. Unlike the relatively short-lived 1MDB affair, money-laundering schemes involving PDVSA go back decades. Not least because of its opaque and complicated history, the focus here will be limited to a series of indictments brought in 2018 in connection with one

[47] 'Final report of the Human Rights Council Advisory Committee on the issue of the negative impact of corruption on the enjoyment of human rights' (UN Human Rights Council, 5 January 2015) para 20.

[48] ibid, paras 25–33.

[49] A Peters, 'Corruption as a Violation of International Human Rights' (2018) 29 *European Journal of International Law* 1251.

[50] B Rajagopal, 'Corruption, Legitimacy and Human Rights: The Dialectic of the Relationship' (1999) 14 *Connecticut Journal of International Law* 495; KE Davis, 'Corruption as a Violation of International Human Rights: A Reply to Anne Peters' (2018) 29 *European Journal of International Law* 1289.

single money-laundering scheme. This scheme was chosen for its transnational ripple effects in terms of the AML measures triggered. In addition, its judicial aftermath complements the 1MDB affair in illustrating the possible legal consequences of grand theft. Together, the cases shed light on the legal practices in three jurisdictions, all key centres of global finance. The cases complement each other in showing how grand theft schemes operate and also in illuminating how financial institutions involved in them are then brought to justice. Also, because of the successful prosecutorial efforts in these cases, the specifics of the operations are relatively well-documented.

A. 1MDB

1MDB was founded with the assistance of Goldman Sachs shortly after Prime Minister Najib was elected into office in 2009. From its very beginnings, the company was little more than a means to misappropriate public funds for the private gain of a group of individuals tied together by Najib's young family friend Jho Low. The audacious nature of the 1MDB-related schemes and their mastermind, Jho Low, has inspired some biting book-length appraisals and political satire, depicting the affair as an illustration of the famous Bob Dylan proverb: 'Steal a little and they throw you in jail, steal a lot and they make you a king'.[51] To illustrate the tragicomedy of the spectacular failure of anti-corruption and AML safeguards in this affair over six years, its three chronological phases, as well as how it eventually came to the attention of law enforcement agencies, will now be detailed.

In its first 'Good Star' phase (2009–11), US$1 billion was reallocated from Malaysia's public services pension fund (KWAP) to 1MDB. These funds were designated to be invested in petroleum exploitation projects in Turkmenistan and Argentina in a joint venture with the privately owned Saudi Arabian oil extraction company PetroSaudi.[52] Once the funds were on the 1MDB account, Najib immediately used his influence to ensure a share of US$700 million was transferred to a Swiss RBS Coutts account, which belonged to Good Star Ltd, an offshore company founded just months earlier together with Jho Low, then 28 years old, as secretary. Despite his demonstrable involvement in 1MDB's founding as well as its business deal with PetroSaudi, Low was never formally affiliated with either PetroSaudi or 1MDB, and neither was Good Star Ltd, the company, which he not only headed but de facto also owned and controlled.[53]

[51] T Wright and B Hope, *Billion Dollar Whale: The Man Who Fooled Wall Street, Hollywood, and the World* (Paris, Hachette Books, 2018); Netflix, *Malaysia, 1MDB, and Goldman Sachs, Patriot Act with Hasan Minhaj* (2019); Bob Dylan, 'Sweetheart Like You'.

[52] United States District Court for the Central District of California, *United States of America v Real property located in Beverley Hills, California*, Complaint of, 2:16-cv-05363.

[53] United States District Court for the Eastern District of New York, *United States v The Goldman Sachs Group, Inc*, Deferred Prosecution Agreement of 22 October 2020, 20-CR-00437-MKB.

Low had purchased Good Star Ltd for the price of US$1 through another company he owned; its headquarters were at the RBS Coutts branch in Singapore and its Swiss corporate bank account had been set up with an anticipated maximum capital of US$10 million.[54]

The request to carry out a foreign currency exchange transaction of US$700 million to Good Star Ltd triggered the AML safeguards of Deutsche Bank Malaysia. This transfer did not accord with the terms of the joint venture agreement concluded between 1MDB and PetroSaudi, as it was purported by 1MDB officials. It had not been approved by Malaysia's central bank and perhaps most suspiciously of all, senior 1MDB officials did not want to disclose the beneficiary of this transaction 'to avoid any unforeseen circumstances'.[55] Telephone and email records show that Deutsche Bank employees were highly suspicious of this foreign currency exchange transaction request and that they were also aware that they could not execute this transaction without violating AML banking regulations.[56] Nonetheless, they eventually made the transfer of US$700 million to the Good Star Ltd account at RBS Coutts, where the unexpected deposit of such a large sum raised red flags (in part because the account had been set up to hold a maximum of US$10 million).[57] Indications pointing to criminal entanglements of one of its most important clients continued to accumulate over the two years during which the account was active. For instance, documents, such as a loan contract explaining the transaction from 1MDB to Good Star Ltd were only reluctantly submitted to the bank and were riddled with mistakes, such as confusing the lending and borrowing parties in a multi-million dollar loan agreement.[58] Bank employees also noted how peculiar it was that the only signatory to an account holding US$700 million in public investment capital was a young man allegedly just running a family business.[59] They also found it dubious that despite the volume of wealth he managed, Low did not use a secured corporate email account, but instead conducted all of his electronic communication from a gmail.com address.[60] By the time another series of deposits totalling US$330 million was made, that, according to the terms of the loan agreement, should have been transferred to the PetroSaudi–1MDB joint-venture account at JP Morgan, there was very little doubt left for any RBS Coutts employee involved in the management of the Good Star Ltd account, that they were hosting a money-laundering operation.[61]

[54] *United States of America v Real property located in Beverley Hills, California* (n 52) paras 44–46.
[55] ibid, para 64.
[56] ibid, paras 57–59.
[57] eidgenössisches Bundesgericht, *FINMA gegen Bank A*, 2C_422/2018.
[58] Swiss Federal Criminal Court, *Bundesanwaltschaft und eidgenössisches Finanzdepartment gegen A*, Judgment of 20 July 2020, SK.2019.55.
[59] *FINMA gegen Bank A* (n 57) para 2.3.10.1.
[60] ibid, para 2.4.1.3.
[61] *United States of America v Real property located in Beverley Hills, California* (n 52) para 94.

The financial transactions made from the Good Star Ltd account were no less dubious than those it received, as they were ill-suited to meet their purported investment objectives. For example, funds designated for investment in energy projects were instead spent on US high-end real estate or extravagant casino visits. Two transfers of US$12 million each were directly deposited into the private accounts of a Saudi prince and co-founder of PetroSaudi who, as a member of the Saudi royal family, and therefore a politically exposed person, should have been subject to additional scrutiny. Equally noteworthy is that approximately US$368 million, transferred in 11 instalments from the Good Star Ltd account to an account held by the US law firm Shearman & Sterling LLP, a firm with no apparent links to the business venture, were subsequently distributed to accounts with no investment purpose.[62] Still, RBS Coutts did not report Good Star Ltd to the Swiss Financial Market Oversight Agency (FINMA) until March 2015, four years after the account had last been used.[63] Notably, this was four years after the money-laundering scheme had been concluded and just a little over a month after news of the scheme and of RBS Coutts' involvement had become public.

The Good Star phase was followed by the 'Aabar–BVI' phase (2012). This time 1MDB employed Goldman Sachs to raise capital by underwriting two bond offerings for US$3.5 billion, allegedly to acquire energy assets.[64] The bonds were guaranteed by IPIC, a government-owned Abu Dhabi investment fund.[65] Once the capital was raised, approximately US$1.367 billion was transferred to a bank account at BSI Bank in Switzerland belonging to Aabar Investments PJS Ltd, a corporation registered in the British Virgin Islands. Like Good Star Ltd, this company had no affiliation with IPIC or 1MDB. Its name, however, is almost identical to that of a subsidiary of IPIC.[66] Once the capital was at the disposal of Aabar Investments PJS Ltd, a significant proportion was distributed to individuals associated with the scheme, including to high-ranking officials at IPIC and 1MDB.[67] This included Najib and his stepson who used it, among other things, on the movie production company Red Granite Pictures, which produced *The Wolf of Wall Street*, *Dumb and Dumber Two*, and the 2017 remake of *Papillon*.[68]

As with the Good Star Ltd scheme, the payment made under this business operation manifestly did not correspond to the stated purposes or designated beneficiaries in the corporate and contractual documents, such as bond offerings

[62] United States District Court for the Central District of California, *United States of America v the real property known as the Viceroy L'Ermitage Beverly Hills*, 20 July 2016, Case 2:16-cv-05368.

[63] *Bundesanwaltschaft und eidgenössisches Finanzdepartment gegen A* (n 58) para 2.3.20.

[64] *United States of America v Real property located in Beverley Hills, California* (n 52) paras 121–42.

[65] ibid, paras 132, 33, 41.

[66] ibid, paras 134, 43.

[67] ibid, paras 177, 81, 87, 203.

[68] ibid, paras 212–16.

or joint venture or sale agreements. Whereas some funds reached a contractual partner of 1MDB (namely Tanjong Energy and Genting Power Holdings), more than half of the net capital at 1MDB's disposal was transferred over to Aabar Investments PJS Ltd, a company with whom it had no documented business ties. From there, funds were then wired through an account at the Singaporean branch of Standard Chartered Bank and subsequently distributed to various accounts of different members of the 1MDB money-laundering scheme in the United States, the Netherlands and Luxembourg. The highly suspect nature of the scheme's financial transactions was recognised and documented by bank employees from each of the numerous financial institutions involved. Yet, as in the case of Good Star Ltd, no complaint was registered with Swiss, Singaporean, US, Dutch or Luxembourgian authorities at the time.[69]

As a result, the 1MDB money-laundering operation could continue into its third phase, the 'Tanore' phase. In March 2013, only a year after the Abar–BVI bond sales, 1MDB once again commissioned Goldman Sachs to conduct another bond sale raising US$3 billion overall.[70] This time, the bonds were guaranteed by the government of Malaysia through a letter signed by PM Najib. The alleged purpose of the bond sales was to raise funds for a joint venture with IPIC Aabar. Yet, as in the Aabar–BVI scheme, once the funds were raised, US$1.26 billion were diverted into an account at Falcon Bank in Singapore held by Tanore Finance Corporation, an offshore cooperation with one listed beneficial owner, Tan Kim Loong, who had no professional affiliations to any of the business entities involved in the joint venture but was a known associate of Jho Low.[71] As with the Swiss BSI and RBS Coutts accounts, the Falcon Bank account of Tanore Finance Corporation was merely a gateway account from which funds were distributed, either to accounts personally held by IPIC or 1MDB officials, PM Najib, his friends and family or Jho Low and his associates, or to accounts owned by shell corporations that these individuals beneficially owned. Among the banks involved were BSI branches in Singapore and Switzerland, ING Netherlands and Falton in Zurich.[72] Everything about the nature of the financial transactions, the alleged urgency with which they were made, their beneficiaries and their use to buy Van Gogh paintings and New York luxury apartments rather than investments into energy infrastructure projects caught the attention of the AML compliance departments of the various financial institutions involved. Yet again, no action was taken by any of them.[73]

Given the financial flows of the 1MDB affair, it seems abundantly clear that none of the three schemes described here was so subtle, opaque or complex

[69] *United States of America v the real property known as the Viceroy L'Ermitage Beverly Hills* (n 62) paras 112–226.

[70] *United States of America v Real property located in Beverley Hills, California* (n 52) paras 231–42.

[71] ibid, para 243.

[72] ibid, paras 243–58.

[73] ibid, paras 266–90.

that they could escape all AML safeguard measures. Instead, these measures simply proved to be inconsequential in practice. Grand theft in the 1MDB affair took place at the core of global financial markets, not in the obscurities of offshore jurisdictions. Funds stolen were raised with the help of, laundered through, and unlawfully misappropriated by established financial institutions. Yet, despite all of this, investigations into 1MDB's schemes only took concrete form in January 2015 when Xavier Justo, the then former director of PetroSaudi, blew the whistle by providing evidence on the Good Star Ltd scheme to the well-connected British journalist Clare Rewcastle Brown. Brown had reported on 1MDB for years and had published corruption and embezzlement allegations on her platform, the Sarawak Report.[74] As sister-in-law of former British Prime Minister Gordon Brown, she had been able to do so since her ties to the British Prime Minister shielded her from repercussions for her investigatory work into 1MDB. Justo was not so lucky. Shortly after he came forward to Brown, he was arrested in Thailand on charges of corporate blackmail, convicted and subsequently jailed for 18 months until Swiss authorities were able to negotiate his release. One has to wonder, had it not been for Justo who was disgruntled enough to come forward, and for Brown who was not only courageous enough to publicise his evidence of money laundering but also in a priviledged enough situation to initiate an investigation into an affair involving a sitting prime minister and members of the Saudi and Abu Dhabi royal family and their friends, would we have ever known about the 1MDB grand theft operations? By the time the investigations triggered by Justo's data leak commenced, more than two years had elapsed since the last of the three phases of the 1MDB operation had concluded. In this time, the 1MDB conspirators had been anything but discrete about their theft, with Low and his associates flaunting it in plain sight by splurging on week-long gambling extravaganzas with Hollywood movie producers, birthday parties with media darlings such as Paris Hilton, and New Year's Eve celebrations with famous actors such as Leonardo DiCaprio, who even thanked his generous friends by name in his Golden Globe acceptance speech. Yet, despite all of these conspicuous indications of ongoing financial crime, no decisive measures against any of the individuals, companies or financial institutions involved were ever taken until the 2015 data leak.

B. PDVSA

In 2018, Floridian authorities indicted several individuals belonging to an international money-laundering conspiracy tied to the Venezuelan state-owned company PDVSA. This was not the first criminal enterprise involving PDVSA that American law enforcement agencies uncovered. This time, however, they had

[74] C Rewcastle Brown, 'Sarawak Report', 20 June 2022, available at: www.sarawakreport.org/.

placed an informant within the operation who had worn a concealed recording device, which provided them with ample evidence of the criminal operations. As a result, the 2018 indictments were by far the most successful ones indicting senior officials at PDVSA, including one of its directors. Concretely, charges were brought against eight individuals for their involvement in a money-laundering network that had embezzled funds from PDVSA for four years. Authorities also uncovered evidence exposing the Swiss financial marketplace yet again for its lax AML efforts as it was revealed that one of the executive directors of Julius Baer – a medium-sized Swiss private bank based in Zurich – had been assigned to attract members of the so-called Bolibourgeoisie, ie, rich Venezuelan clients who are suspected to have come to their wealth through favouritism or corruption. A subsequent Swiss investigation into the bank's business practices from 2009 to 2018 found that the bank's business model was premised on appealing to lucrative high-risk clients by prioritising their requests for anonymity and secrecy over enforcing legally mandated AML safeguards. As a result, the bank's client records were more often than not incomplete. Moreover, despite demonstrably knowing of corruption allegations against some of their clients, Julius Baer employees continued to carry out transactions for them of sums as high as 70 million CHF.[75] In the context of this particular PDVSA money-laundering scheme, it came to light that the Julius Baer executive, Matthias Krull, advised his co-conspirators on how to structure financial flows in a manner that would not trigger AML safeguards when they moved embezzled PDVSA funds out of Venezuela and onto the international financial marketplace. Even though Krull was the only Julius Baer employee criminally charged before the District Court for the Southern District of Florida, the findings by the Swiss authorities leave no doubt that Julius Baer as a whole was actively and willingly involved in this and other money-laundering schemes. In this regard, Julius Baer's involvement is comparable to that of Goldman Sachs in the 1MDB operations. As part of the scheme, US$1.2 billion were embezzled between 2014 and 2015 alone. The network used the corporate structures to conceal their crimes in a fairly simple yet effective manner, as their first operation in December 2014 illustrates well. The operation was conducted as follows: the shell company Rantor Capital CA concluded a loan contract for over 7.2 million Bolivars which, at the time, was worth the equivalent of €35 million with PDVSA. A few days later, it concluded an assignment contract with the Hong Kong shell company Eaton Global, assigning this company its rights as a creditor to the PDVSA loan. Eaton Global then sent a notice of assignment letter to PDVSA in which it gave the company the option of cancelling its debt of €35 million by paying Eaton Global US$600 million within 180 days. As implausible as this may sound in economic terms, the loan and assignment contracts together with the notice letter proved

[75] V Mathys and L Tobias, 'Serious AML failings at Julius Baer' (FINMA, 20 February 2020), available at: finma.ch/en/news/2020/02/20200220-mm-jb/.

to be sufficient to satisfy legal AML safeguards.[76] Another option chosen to launder funds from PDVSA was to designate them as investments. To this end – and just as in the 1MDB affair – the PDVSA conspirators simply founded several fake joint ventures to purportedly invest in. Indeed, the transfer of funds for investment purposes is perhaps most prone to being misused for money laundering. As long as the contractual agreements providing the basis for the transfer exist, few financial institutions will investigate the plausibility or reasonableness of an investment.

These factual accounts in the PDVSA and 1MDB affair illustrate that grand theft not only requires the services of financial institutions, but also their cooperation and assistance. The affairs also show that the assumption that money-laundering operations are difficult to detect is not always accurate. They highlight that due to the sanctity of the autonomy of parties under contract law, even the most nonsensical contractual arrangements can serve as a fig leaf for grand theft.[77] Though the two cases cannot be conclusive, the fact that it took whistle-blowers in both instances to bring these schemes to the attention of law enforcement agencies at the very least invites further reflection and study of the policing function that the legal regime on grand theft attributes to financial institutions. Under the current regime, such institutions have more to gain from concealing grand theft than they have from reporting it as the following section shows.

IV. LEGAL RESPONSES TO GRAND THEFT

This section recounts the legal consequences of grand theft for involved institutions and individuals. The purpose is to show how the remaining features of the legal regime against grand theft operate in practice. It will distinguish between individual criminal accountability mechanisms, measures imposed to reform corporate conduct, and monetary penalties and other fees imposed on individuals and financial institutions found to have participated in grand theft. These categories do not mirror conventional legal typologies, as monetary fees and penalties can be the result of a decision taken under civil, criminal or administrative law. The categories were chosen to reflect the practical impact of legal measures as they are felt by financial institutions. This overview can only be partial since the primary sources are either available only selectively or not at all. For a regime hailed for its potential to promote transparency, as well as liberal democracy and the rule of law, this secrecy is highly problematic as it prevents domestic constituencies which have been victims of grand theft from holding their governments accountable for the funds returned to them in cases in which

[76] *United States of America v Matthias Krull* (n 1) paras 46–47.

[77] For a constructivist view of global finance, see generally: K Pistor, *The Code of Capital: How the Law Creates Wealth and Inequality* (Princeton, NJ, Princeton University Press, 2019).

grand theft is detected. Such funds not only include the return of misappropriated assets but, in the best case scenario, also significant amounts in civil, administrative and penal fines.

A. Individual Criminal Responsibility

The most headline-grabbing criminal sentence in the 1MDB affair was the 2020 conviction of PM Najib for his involvement in the Good Star Ltd scheme. The Kuala Lumpur High Court convicted him of undue influence, abuse of power and unlawful enrichment as a public servant.[78] A previous investigation into his role in the 1MDB operations, initiated in 2015 as a result of the data leak by Justo, had ended abruptly when he replaced Malaysia's Attorney-General. The 2020 decision against him would have been highly unlikely had he not lost the Malaysian general elections in 2018. Najib appealed unsuccessfully, and, with a Federal Court denying his final appeal in 2022, he is now serving his prison sentence.[79]

Only one day after the 2020 High Court judgment against him, the Swiss Federal Criminal Court rendered another judgment in the 1MDB affair finding the compliance officer responsible for overseeing the Good Star Ltd account at RBS Coutts guilty of having violated his reporting obligations under the Federal Act on Combating Money Laundering and Terrorist Financing. The Swiss judgment highlights the paradox between corporate culpability and individual accountability in this domain. It establishes that many RBS Coutts employees including senior-level officials were repeatedly made aware of the corruption and money-laundering allegations against their customer Jho Low, and of the highly suspect nature of the financial transactions on the Good Star Ltd account.[80] Still, Swiss prosecutorial authorities were not in a position to bring further charges. Under Swiss law, banks can create internal competence and responsibility structures that allow them to limit criminal liability for their involvement in money laundering, however grave and widespread it may be, to a few individuals, typically their compliance officers. Further, the judgment highlights that in strictly economic terms the severity of sentencing for those convicted of having violated their reporting obligation under the Federal Act on Combating Money Laundering and Terrorist Financing – the only obligation for which non-compliance may result in a criminal conviction – does not necessarily

[78] Kuala Lumpur High Court, *Prosecuter against Najib Nazak*, 27 July 2020; the Court found a violation of s 23 Malaysian Anti-Corruption Commission Act; Anti-Money Laundering, Anti-Terrorism Financing and Proceeds of Unlawful Activities Act; Penal Code.

[79] Court of Appeal, Putrajaya, *Dato' Sri Mohd Najib Hj Abd Razak v PP*, Decision of 8 December 2021, W-05(SH)-(231-233)-07-2020; Federal Court of Malaysia, *Dato' Sri Mohd Najib bin Hj Abd Razak v Pendakwa Raya*, Judgment of 23 August 2022, Nos 05(L)-289-12/2021(W); NO 05(L)-290-12/2021(W); 05(L)-291-12/2021(W).

[80] *Bundesanwaltschaft und eidgenössisches Finanzdepartment gegen A* (n 58) s 2.3.

disincentivise non-compliance with AML safeguards. The convicted compliance officer at RBS Coutts was sentenced to the payment of a fine of 50,000 CHF, which is only a little more than a third of what he earned in bonus payments, namely 140,000 CHF, for his work overseeing the Good Star Ltd account.[81] In this sense, the Swiss implementation of international AML law's criminal law approach not only exonerates financial institutions' senior management officials – who are responsible for fostering a culture of non-compliance –but it is also very limited in scope and, at least in economic terms, inapt to the purpose of deterrence.

The 'lightness' of the Swiss approach to individual responsibility stands out when comparing this sentence with the measures taken by the Singaporean authorities in 2017 concerning the 1MDB affair. There, two directors of the Singapore branch of BSI bank were respectively sentenced to two and 18 weeks imprisonment, as well as fines of S$10,000 and S$24,000, for failing to meet their AML reporting obligations under Singaporean law and for forging reference letters misrepresenting Jho Low's sources of income in the 2013 Tanore scheme. Similarly, the director of the Singapore branch of Falcon Bank was sentenced to 28 weeks imprisonment and a fine of S$128,000 for failing to comply with AML reporting obligations and purposefully misleading the Monetary Authority and Commercial Affairs Department of Singapore (MAS).[82] Furthermore, an account manager at BSI Singapore received a 30-month prison sentence for witness tampering in addition to a 24-month prison sentence on charges of money laundering and related forgery.[83] Finally, Singaporean authorities issued prohibition orders ranging from six years to indefinitely against these and other individuals that have since prevented them from working in the financial sector in Singapore.

Among the individuals who received a 10-year prohibition order was Tim Leissner, the former chairman of Goldman Sachs Southeast Asia and participating managing director of Goldman Sachs who, in August 2018, pleaded guilty to criminal charges brought against him before a US court. Leissner admitted to the bribery of foreign public officials and the circumvention and violation of internal accounting controls to enable Goldman Sachs' involvement in setting up 1MDB and securing the 1MDB bond sales services contracts.[84]

[81] ibid, para 3.3.

[82] Monetary Authority of Singapore (MAS), '1MDB-Related Regulatory Actions and Criminal Proceedings', 22 July 2022, available at: www.mas.gov.sg/-/media/MAS/News-and-Publications/Press-Releases/Summary-of-1MDB-Related-Court-and-Regulatory-Actions_as-at-30May17.pdf.

[83] ibid, 2.

[84] United States District Court for the Eastern District of New York, *United States v Tim Leissner*, Complaint of 7 July 2018, 18-CR-439; 15 US Code § 78d–1. Delegation of functions by Commission, Pub L 100-181, title III, § 308(a), 4 December 1987, 101 Stat 1254; 15 US Code § 78d–2. Transfer of functions with respect to assignment of personnel to chairman, Pub L 100-181, title III, § 308(a), 4 December 1987, 101 Stat 1255; 15 US Code § 78d–3 – Appearance and practice before the Commission, Pub L 107-204, title VI, § 602, 30 July 2002, 116 Stat 794; 15 US Code § 78m – Periodical and other reports, Pub L 114-94, div G, title LXXXVI, § 86001(c), 4 December 2015, 129 Stat 1798.

According to a US law – which requires any person convicted of corruption or money laundering to forfeit any property and its proceeds derived from such acts – he was ordered to forfeit US$43.7 million.[85] A joint indictment of Jho Low and the former head of investment of Goldman Sachs Malaysia, Roger Ng has only been partially tried so far.[86] Whereas law enforcement authorities have not yet succeeded in locating Jho Low, Roger Ng was tried before a federal jury in New York and found guilty of participating in bribery and money laundering.[87] He was sentenced to 10-years' imprisonment. This decision is under appeal.[88]

Comparable to the involvement of Goldman Sachs' Tim Leissner and Roger Ng in the 1MDB operation is that of Julius Baer banker Matthias Krull in the PDVSA affair. Krull who pleaded guilty to conspiracy to commit money laundering before a US district court was never criminally charged in Switzerland.[89] Krull's original sentence of 10-years' imprisonment with a US$50,000 fine and US$600,000 in foreclosure was recently reduced by 65 per cent to 3.5 years, a degree of reduction which is highly unusual in the US criminal justice system, even in the case of cooperating witnesses.[90] Still, the case and judgment against him remain extraordinary. Prosecutions of bankers for financial crimes remain the exception rather than the rule. Even if such crimes are successfully prosecuted, sentences are frequently light and mostly limited to monetary fines and forfeitures. Prison sentences are exceptional, and despite a guilty plea in 2018, Leissner has, to this date, not been sentenced.

Criminal law is not, in any case, the only or even optimal response in these cases. Grand theft does not occur when a few individuals go rogue. It is the result of a corporate culture that measures the cost of compliance against the margin for profit. Considering this, the individualisation of guilt of the criminal law approach seems ill-suited by design to the extent that it permits financial institutions to externalise liability. At the same time, how the criminalisation of money laundering is currently implemented is notably lax, supporting the widely held suspicion that criminal justice systems across the

[85] 18 US Code § 981 – Civil forfeiture, Pub L 111-203, title III, § 377(3), 21 July 2010, 124 Stat 1569; 28 US Code § 2461 – Mode of recovery, Pub L 109-177, title IV, § 410, 9 March 2006, 120 Stat 246; *United States v Tim Leissner*, para 51.

[86] United States District Court for the Eastern District of New York, *United States v Low Taek Jho and Ng Chong Hwa*, Indictment of 3 October 2018, 18-CR-00538.

[87] United States District Court for the Eastern District of New York, *United States v NG Chong Hwa*, Trial Conviction of 8 April 2022, 18-CR-00538.

[88] 'Former Goldman Sachs Managing Director Sentenced to 10 Years in Prison for His Role in Massive Bribery and Money Laundering Scheme', Press Release, United States Attorney's Office, Eastern District of New York, 9 March 2023, available at: www.justice.gov/usao-edny/pr/former-goldman-sachs-managing-director-sentenced-10-years-prison-his-role-massive.

[89] *United States of America v Matthias Krull*; 18 US Code §1956 Laundering of monetary instruments.

[90] Jay Weaver, 'Feds slash Swiss banker's sentence in Venezuelan money laundering case in Miami' *Miami Herald* (24 March 2021), available at: www.miamiherald.com/news/local/article250155995.html.

world are far more lenient towards white-collar crime than towards blue-collar crime. Just imagine if the sums in question here had been stolen by (non-violent) physical theft. What would the legal consequences for the responsible individuals have been then?

B. Corporate Monetary Payments

Given the inadequacy of individual criminal responsibility to address the corporate culture in financial institutions that enable or even encourage grand theft, other legal consequences, which affect financial institutions as a whole, take on a particular significance. Two such legal mechanisms stand out, namely monetary penalties and corporate structural reform mandates. To the extent that the relevant information is available, the legal basis, volume and beneficiaries of monetary payments imposed on financial institutions will shortly be examined here. This section only engages with the 1MDB affair as conclusive information on fines and penalties in the PDVSA affair is not available, and even the overview of penalties and fines in the 1MDB affair may be incomplete as information of this sort is made available only very inconsistently. This is a surprising finding in and of itself given that the legal regime countering grand theft is premised on the values of transparency and accountability: unfortunately, its practice – at least as it pertains to monetary fines collected by public authorities from financial institutions – is neither transparent nor accountable.

In Singapore and under the 1970 Monetary Authority of Singapore Act, MAS should 'foster a sound and reputable financial centre' and 'conduct integrated supervision of the financial services sector' including directing the sector's efforts to combat money laundering and the financing of terrorist activities to this end.[91] The law limits the scope of the regulations and directions that MAS can enact to due diligence and record-keeping obligations and the fines that it can impose to S$1 million. This maximum fine can only be exceeded if a financial institution has already been fined for violating MAS's AML or terrorist financing directives. Considering this, the fines imposed on eight Singaporean branches of multinational financial institutions in connection with the 1MDB affair appear rather high. The legal basis for imposing them was MAS Notices 101.4 and 626, which spell out AML obligations for financial institutions and merchant banks.[92] Table 1 below lists details about the fines MAS ordered financial institutions to pay in connection with the 1MDB affair. They collectively amount to S$29.1 million, which is approximately US$17.4 million.

[91] Monetary Authority of Singapore Act, 1970.

[92] Notice 626 Prevention of Money Laundering and Countering the Financing of Terrorism; Notice 1014 Prevention of Money Laundering and Countering the Financing of Terrorism.

Table 1 Penalty payments imposed on merchant banks and other financial institutions in Singapore by May 2017

Breaches of Merchant Banks' AML obligations under MAS Notice 1014	
BSI (41 breaches)	S$13.3 million
Falcon (14 breaches)	S$4.3 million
Coutts & Co Ltd (24 breaches)	S$2.4 million
Breaches of Financial Institutions' AML obligations under MAS Notice 626	
DBS Bank Ltd (10 breaches)	S$1 million
UBS AG (13 breaches)	S$1.3 million
Standard Chartered Bank (28 breaches)	S$5.2 million
Credit Suisse (7 breaches)	S$0.7 million
United Overseas Bank (9 breaches)	S$0.9 million
	S$29.1 million (**approx US$17.4**)

Unfortunately, MAS has not released details on the breaches which these financial institutions are being penalised for. Based on the absence of any indication to the contrary in MAS press releases – the only primary source available in this matter – it appears that MAS did not impose any measures leading to the forfeiture of any profits generated through 1MDB's operations. The monetary cap on fines and the absence of any regulations on the proceeds of money laundering either in the 1970 MAS law or MAS Notices 1014 and 626 would appear to indicate that MAS does not have the authority to require banks to disgorge such profits. It is also not clear whether these fines are civil or criminal, since both can be imposed under the 1970 MAS Act. Unfortunately, there is also no information available as to whether or not MAS required any additional measures of a non-monetary nature, such as the implementation of additional internal accountability mechanisms.

Turning now to Switzerland, it should be noticed that the monetary fines imposed by Swiss authorities are similarly difficult to ascertain because information released by the press office of FINMA varies in its specificity from case to case. As is the case with MAS in Singapore, FINMA press releases are the only available primary sources on measures imposed against specific Swiss financial institutions for violating their AML obligations, as FINMA orders themselves are not published. FINMA however regularly publishes information updates on its reviews of banks' AML efforts, legislative developments and relevant court rulings. Under Swiss law, FINMA can confiscate corporate profits generated by financial institutions by grave violations of the supervisory responsibilities of an executive officer.[93] The purpose of this provision is to re-establish the 'natural state of affairs', which characterises such confiscation of profits as an

[93] Federal Act on the Swiss Financial Market Supervisory Authority, AS 2018 5247.

administrative rather than a punitive measure. This conception then affects how the amount of profit for seizure is calculated, namely not as the value generated by unlawful acts or omissions, but by a formula borrowed from Swiss anti-trust law and Swiss jurisprudence on 'agency without authorisation'. Under this formula, only the net value generated is considered as profit, which means that all costs of generating such profit are subtracted from the net profit.[94] The analogy of the violation of supervisory responsibilities to 'agency without authorisation' reaffirms not only the conception that the responsibility for the violation of AML safeguards in financial institutions can be individualised, but also implies that the conduct of individuals can be seen in isolation from corporate conduct and that it is in its nature contradictory to corporate interests. This reasoning justifies the protection of corporate interests from the AML transgressions of specific bank employees, which is a core principle of Swiss regulation in this field. Based on the information available, it is clear that FINMA seized RBS Coutts' profits of 6.5 million CHF and 2.52 million CHF in profits from Falcon Bank Ltd.[95] It has also announced that it will seize 70 million CHF in profits from BSI, which is 25 million CHF less than it had originally announced. This reduction is the result of the legal formula for profit calculation outlined above.[96]

While the Swiss practice of profit seizure is certainly more far-reaching than the apparent practice in Singapore, it is still problematic that under the Swiss formula for profit calculation, the costs for financial institutions involved in money laundering are effectively paid for by the victims of grand theft: the people of the country from which the laundered funds originate. Like any other capital, sovereign capital does not only carry its value, but it is also a potential source of investment. It raises significant equity questions that the financial institutions which unlawfully benefited from grand theft can recover their costs from the margin of profit they generated by facilitating its theft.

The United States has the most transparent criminal accountability process with the indictments and judgments of US courts offering detailed information about the money-laundering schemes and the individuals involved. Aside from investigative journalism, US legal documents are by far the most detailed sources of information on the details of the 1MDB and PDVSA grand thefts, and without them, the information provided by Swiss or Singaporean national agencies would have been even more difficult to unlock. The US judgment that has attracted the most attention by far is that against Goldman Sachs in connection

[94] *FINMA gegen Bank A* (n 57) paras 2.3–2.5.

[95] V Mathys, 'FINMA sanctions Coutts for 1MDB breaches' (FINMA, 2 February 2017), available at: www.finma.ch/en/~/media/finma/dokumente/dokumentencenter/8news/medienmitteilungen/2017/02/20170202-mm-coutts.pdf?sc_lang=en&hash=D75E335E4BCA9561B83537DA63F37744; 'Falcon sanctioned for 1MDB breaches' (FINMA, 11 October 2016), available at: www.finma.ch/en/news/2016/10/20161011-mm-falcon/.

[96] T Lux, 'FINMA reassesses disgorgement of profits in BSI case' (FINMA, 22 October 2020), available at: www.finma.ch/en/news/2020/10/20201022-mm-bsi-gewinneinziehung/#:~:text=FINMA%20has%20more%20precisely%20reassessed,the%20original%20CHF%2095%20million.

with the 1MDB affair, as it is the first time Goldman Sachs has admitted to corporate misconduct. For its role in raising US$6.5 billion in bond sales, Goldman Sachs pleaded guilty to conspiring to defraud the United States, to having conducted prohibited foreign trade practices, and to have acted contrary to numerous provisions of US anti-corruption law.[97] The bank agreed to pay US$2.9 billion in disgorgement and penalties.[98] The plea agreement accounts for US$1.9 billion, of which more than US$1.3 billion is owed to financial, regulatory and judicial authorities in the United States, the United Kingdom, Singapore and Hong Kong. Table 2 below lists the amount and nature of the payments as they are described in the plea agreement.

Table 2 Distribution of Goldman Sachs payments according to its plea agreement of October 2020

Goldman Sachs 1MDB Penalties under Plea Agreement	
Federal Reserve System (FED)	Civil penalty US$154 million
US Securities and Exchange Commission (SEC)	Civil penalty US$400 million
	Disgorgement US$606 million
New York State Department of Financial Services	Civil penalty US$150 million
United Kingdom Financial Conduct Authority	Civil penalty US$63 million
United Kingdom Prudential Regulation Authority	Civil penalty US$63 million
Attorney-General's Chambers of the Republic of Singapore	(Not specified) US$122 million
Hong Kong Securities and Futures Commission	(Not specified) US$350 million
	US$1.908 billion

It is not clear what proportion of these fines will be paid to Malaysian state coffers.[99] Unlike the Swiss formula on illicit profit calculation, under this plea agreement, the disgorgement, ie, Goldman Sachs' earnings from the services it provided to 1MDB, had to be returned in full and the bank could not recover the costs for its involvement in this scheme. This standard of profit calculation has been applied by US courts to all individuals and entities held accountable for their involvement in the 1MDB scheme. In addition to ordering that the value of the assets purchased with the laundered funds must be returned, consent judgments by the District Court for the Central District of California also

[97] 15 US Code § 78m – Periodical and other reports; 18 US Code § 371 – Conspiracy to commit offense or to defraud United States, Pub L 103–322, title XXXIII, § 330016(1)(L), 13 September 1994, 108 Stat 2147.

[98] US Justice (Office of Public Affairs), 'Goldman Sachs Charged in Foreign Bribery Case and Agrees to Pay Over $2.9 Billion', available at: www.justice.gov/opa/pr/goldman-sachs-charged-foreign-bribery-case-and-agrees-pay-over-29-billion.

[99] United States District Court for the Eastern District of New York, *United States v Goldman Sachs (Malaysia) Sdn Bhd*, Plea Agreement of 22 October 2020, 20-CR-00438-MKB.

ordered the confiscation of any profits made from these assets. This concerns, for instance, the proceeds and profits of the movies produced by Red Granite Pictures Inc including *The Wolf of Wall Street*.[100] So, the US approach is the most far-reaching in terms of holding corporate entities accountable. Even if the Goldman Sachs plea agreement is still exceptional, its overall emphasis on the financial institution as an accountable corporate entity appears to be a promising approach to grand theft. At the same time, it is unfortunate that a significant proportion of the payments due was returned to non-Malaysian national agencies. This hardly seems fair. Under US jurisdiction, a settlement agreement between the Malaysian government and Goldman Sachs was concluded, but this agreement is not publicly available. However, the *New York Times* reported that Goldman Sachs agreed to pay Malaysia US$2.5 billion to

[100] United States District Court for the Central District of California, *United States of America v 'The Wolf of Wall Street' Motion Picture, including any rights to profits, royalties and distribution proceeds owned to Red Granite Pictures, Inc or its affiliates and/or Assigns*, Complaint of, 2:16-cv-05362; United States District Court for the Central District of California, *United States of America v One Bombarder Global 5000 Jet Aircraft, bearing manufacturer's serial number 9265 and registration number N689WM, its tools and appurtenances, and aircraft logbooks*, Complaint of 20 July 2016, 2:16--cv-05367; United States District Court for the Central District of California, *United States of America v any rights to profits, royalties and distribution proceeds owned by or owned to JW Nile (BVI) Ltd, JCL Media (EMI Publishing Ltd), and/or Jynwel Capital Publishing Group North America Holdings, Inc, and DH Publishing LP*, Complaint of, 2:16-cv-05364; *United States of America v Real property located in Beverley Hills, California* (n 52); United States District Court for the Central District of California, *United States of America v All Business assets of the Viceroy L'Ermitage Beverly Hills, including all chatels and intangible assets, inventory, equipment, and all leases, rents and profits derived therefrom*, Complaint of, 2:16-cv-05369; *United States of America v the real property known as the Viceroy L'Ermitage Beverly Hills* (n 62); United States District Court for the Central District of California, *United States of America v All rights to and interest in Symphony CP (Park Lane) LLC, held or acquired, directly or indirectly, by Symphony CP Investments LLC and/or Symphony CP Investments Holdings LLC, including any interest held or secured by the real property and appurtenances located at 36 Central Park South, New York, New York, known as the Park Lane Hotel, any rights to collect and receive any profits and proceeds therefrom, and any interest derived from the proceeds invested in the Symphony CP (Park Lane) LLC by Symphony CP Investments LLC and Symphony CP (Park Lane) LLC*, Complaint of, 2:16-cv-05370; United States District Court for the Central District of California, *United States of America v one pen and ink drawing by Vincent Van Gogh titled 'Law Maison de Vincent à Arles'; one painting by Claude Monet titled 'Saint-Georges Majeur'; and one painting by Claude Monet titled 'Nympheas Avec Reflets De Hautes Herbes'*, Complaint of, 2:16-cv-05366; United States District Court for the Central District of California, *United States of America v Real Property located in New York, New York, 118 Greene Street (NYC) LLC*, Complaint of, 2:16-cv-05375; United States District Court for the Central District of California, *United States of America v. Real Property located in New York, New York, 80 Columbus Circle (NYC) LLC*, Complaint of, 2:16-cv-05374; United States District Court for the Central District of California, *United States of America v Real Property located in New York, New York, Park Laurel Acquisition LLC*, Complaint of, 2:16-cv-05371; United States District Court for the Central District of California, *United States of America v Real Property located in Beverly Hills, California, Laurel Beverly Holdings LLC*, Complaint of, 2:16-cv-05379; United States District Court for the Central District of California, *United States of America v Real Property in London, United Kingdom, owned by Qentas Holdings*, Complaint of, 2:16-cv-05380; United States District Court for the Central District of California, *United States of America v Real Property located in Los Angeles, California, Oriole Drive (LA) LLC*, Complaint of, 2:16-cv-05378.

settle all criminal charges, in addition to compensating Malaysia for any shortfalls from the sale of assets seized by US government authorities.[101]

C. Mandated Corporate Structural Changes

Both FINMA and MAS have required specific changes in the corporate structure of financial institutions found to have facilitated grand theft schemes. These measures could be important in preventing future grand thefts. For example, in response to their serious breaches of Singaporean AML law, MAS revoked BSI's banking licences temporarily and Falcon Bank's permanently. Also, FINMA has required banks to change their internal reward and promotion policies, adjust risk assessment protocols for politically exposed persons, and improve monitoring systems for high-risk transactions. Beyond operational adjustments, it has also required banks to take organisational measures such as strengthening a board of directors' independence or instituting a committee responsible for overseeing corporate conduct and compliance. Finally, in severe cases of corporate misconduct, FINMA has issued several temporary bans including a ban on entering into new business relationships with foreign politically exposed persons as well as bans on conducting any major transactions.[102]

V. CONCLUSION

The purpose of this chapter has been to highlight the need to understand grand theft as a legal problem in and of itself, rather than through the lens of corruption, money laundering, or human rights violations. It has been suggested that the existing legal regime, though robust on the books, evidences deficiencies in practice. Given the regime's relative 'newness', international law scholars have so far focused on its design, its legalisation and its relation to other legal fields. This chapter has drawn attention to the need for more engagement with the domestic implementation of international anti-corruption and AML law, particularly as regards the functions and responsibilities attributed by these regimes to financial institutions. It has refuted the validity of the premise that

[101] Alexandra Stevenson and Matthew Goldstein, 'Goldman Sachs and Malaysia Reach $3.9 Billion Settlement in 1MDB Scandal' *New York Times* (20 July 2020).

[102] Lux (n 96); V Mathys, 'FINMA concludes proceedings against Banca Credinvest' (FINMA, 6 October 2020), available at: www.finma.ch/en/news/2020/10/20201006-mm-verfahren-banca-credinvest/#:~:text=These%20proceedings%20have%20now%20been,regulations%20between%202013%20and%202017; 'FINMA concludes final 1MDB proceedings' (FINMA, 20 July 2018), available at: finma.ch/en/news/2018/07/20180720-mm-rothschild/; 'Update on 1MDB proceedings against JP Morgan' (FINMA, 21 December 2017), available at: www.finma.ch/en/news/2017/12/20171221-mm-jpm/#:~:text=At%20the%20end%20of%20June,J.P.%20Morgan%20(Switzerland)%20Ltd.

they are inadvertent infrastructure providers for criminal activity and demonstrated that they have also been willing participants. It has further highlighted, that responses to grand theft vary significantly across jurisdictions. While some scholarship on this is beginning to emerge, such work focuses on criminal law, and is frequently inhibited by the lack of access to relevant legal material.[103] The grand theft vernacular permits shifting efforts from disciplining corruption in the Global South by international means, to disciplining financial institutions in the Global North by primarily domestic ones. By flagging issues of accessibility of relevant primary material, this chapter has also highlighted that the everyday operation of this regime is shrouded in secrecy and removed from public and scientific scrutiny. In addition to the broader accountability issues that this raises, it is also a significant obstacle to monitoring the regime's effectiveness. In the absence of a robust evidence base, further reliance on financial institutions in the fight against global crime (as is the case of recent legislation such as the US Global Magnitsky Act and EU Council Regulation 2020/1998), are mere acts of faith. The effectiveness of these laws thus requires close monitoring.[104] Employing the techniques of investigative journalism and turning scholarly attention from easily available legal materials to other materials – not typically considered by international lawyers or readily accessible – unlocks a rich and important field of study. To this end, it is worth paying closer attention to the work of domestic financial market oversight authorities. This not only permits a better appreciation of the rule of law and distributive justice questions inherent in the problem of grand theft, but it may also open up new avenues for the convergence of legal analysis with legal activism.

[103] R Ivory and T Søreide, 'The International Endorsement of Corporate Settlements in Foreign Bribery Cases' (2020) 69 *International & Comparative Law Quarterly* 945; F Lüth, 'Corporate non-prosecution agreements as transnational human problems: transnational law and the study of domestic criminal justice reforms in a globalised world' (2021) 12 *Transnational Legal Theory* 315.

[104] Civil society organisations have for instance already called out the enabling role of European financial institutions in the bypassing of Magnitsky sanctions. 'Undermining Sanctions: Evidence suggests scandal-hit billionaire Dan Gertler is trying to dodge US sanctions using a suspected money-laundering network' (Global Witness & PPLAAF, 2020).

6

The Peril of Plenty

Oil was the most vital war material at that time, and personally, I thought we started the war for the sake of the oil.[1]

Admiral Watanabe (Japanese naval officer) 1956

I've been saying, take the oil. I've been saying it for years. Take the oil. They still haven't taken the oil. They still haven't taken it. And they hardly hit the oil. They hardly make a dent in the oil.[2]

Donald Trump (then US presidential candidate) 2016

I. INTRODUCTION

In response to the Russian invasion of Ukraine in February 2022, Western states were quick to identify the energy sector of Russia, ie, its exports of petroleum and natural gas, as the Achilles heel of the Russian war economy. Immediately stopping all Russian mineral resources imports was an obvious action to take, but the problem was that the European Union (EU), and in particular its largest economy Germany, was dependent on Russian energy imports.

Accompanied by controversial policy choices, which included reactivating coal and nuclear power plants, the European Union (EU) eventually introduced a sanctions regime severely limiting energy relations between EU Member States and Russia.[3] Measures in place at the time of writing included: a prohibition on imports from Russia of oil and coal; a price cap related to the maritime transport of Russian oil; prohibitions on exports to Russia of goods and technologies in the oil refining sector; and prohibitions on new investments in the

[1] Cited after Appeal Board, *NV de Bataafsche Petroleum Maatschappij and Others v The War Damage Commission*, Case Note of January 1956 (1956) 5 *International & Comparative Law Quarterly* 84.

[2] Maggie Haberman and David E Sanger, 'Transcript: Donald Trump Expounds on His Foreign Policy Views' *New York Times* (26 March 2016), available at: www.nytimes.com/2016/03/27/us/politics/donald-trump-transcript.html.

[3] European Council, Special meeting of the European Council (30 and 31 May 2022) – Conclusions, CO EUR 19 CONCL 4, 31 May 2022, paras 27–30; EU Regulation 2022/1904, [2022] OJ L259I/3; EU Regulation 2022/2367 [2022] OJ L311I/1, Art 1; European Council meeting (20 and 21 October 2022) – Conclusions, CO EUR 27 CONCL 6, 21 October 2022, paras 17–20.

Russian energy and mining sector.[4] With the cost of oil and gas sky-rocketing, the effects of these measures were most acutely felt by low-income households. Yet, while many could barely afford to heat their homes, oil and gas corporations were doing better than ever, reporting historic profit margins.[5] This was in part because many European energy companies continued trading Russian products. According to Global Witness, the Shell corporation traded US$430 million worth of Russian liquified natural gas in the first 10 months of the conflict alone, and Dutch and Cyprus-based traders Vitol and Gunvor traded approximately 222 million barrels of oil and oil products with an estimated worth of well over US$3 billion, in the first 12 months of the conflict.[6]

Armed conflicts have always been moments of wealth redistribution and war profiteering goes hand-in-hand with existential anxieties, tangible misery and the loss of livelihood. Natural resources, including mineral ones, have frequently played a significant part in this redistribution. While the orthodox view is that industrial resource production requires stable conditions, conflict and political turmoil present opportunities for transnational capital to acquire oil and mining assets well below their market value.[7]

Pushing back against ideas of 'newness', this chapter hopes to show how resource wars are highly regulated occurrences for which international law's moralist aspirations decisively clash with its deference to hegemony and capitalism.[8] This is of course not a novel insight. It has been discussed in the context of the laws of war, their inaptitude in making sense of economic and ecological injustices, and the effects of investment treaties on the protection of foreign property as opposed to domestically held private property as well as

[4] For updates, see 'EU restrictive measures against Russia over Ukraine (since 2014)', 13 August 2023, available at: www.consilium.europa.eu/en/policies/sanctions/restrictive-measures-against-russia-over-ukraine/#economic.

[5] See: www.reuters.com/business/energy/big-oil-doubles-profits-blockbuster-2022-2023-02-08/.

[6] 'Shell estimated to make hundreds of millions trading Russian gas since the Ukraine invasion', 12 August 2023: available at: www.globalwitness.org/en/campaigns/stop-russian-oil/shell-estimated-make-hundreds-millions-trading-russian-gas-ukraine-invasion/; 'One year on: Western companies traded 533 million barrels of Russian oil', 13 August 2023, available at: www.globalwitness.org/en/campaigns/stop-russian-oil/one-year-western-companies-traded-533-million-barrels-russian-oil/.

[7] Erika Solomon, Guy Chazan and Sam Jones, 'Isis Inc: how oil fuels the jihadi terrorists' *Financial Times* (15 October 2015), available at: www.ft.com/content/b8234932-719b-11e5-ad6d-f4ed76f0900a; N Klein, *The Shock Doctrine: The Rise of Disaster Capitalism* (London, Macmillan, 2007) 360–82.

[8] Using the typology by Le Billon, the term 'resource war' is used here to describe different types of armed conflict linked to mineral resources including conflicts that are fought over access and control over mineral resources; that are financed by resources revenues; that involve resources plunder by belligerent occupying forces; and in which extraction sites are strategically targeted: P Le Billon, *Wars of Plunder: Conflicts, Profits and the Politics of Resources* (London, Hurst, 2012); M Bavinck, L Pellegrini and E Mostert, *Conflicts over Natural Resources in the Global South: Conceptual Approaches* (London, CRC Press, 2014). For a critique of 'newness', see OC Okafor, 'Newness, Imperialism, and International Legal Reform in Our Time: A TWAIL Perspective' (2005) 43 *Osgoode Hall Law Journal* 171.

public property in times of armed conflict.[9] To add to the literature, this chapter draws attention to how normative progress has been achieved and undone, not only by mere power politics but also by how occupying powers' law and legal reasoning is absorbed into national and international law. By zooming in on four cases concerning mineral resources in armed conflict, this chapter hopes to show how capitalism intersects with victor's justice when it concerns questions of mineral resources property rights, as well as questions of legal authority over their governance. It also shows how foreign and private property structurally enjoy a higher level of protection than communal and public property. It does so by first describing the spectrum of scholarly positions with regard to the governance of mineral resources in times of armed conflict and occupation. It then turns to the specific question of the treatment of mineral resources as property focusing on four specific legal cases. With a view to tracing how international doctrinal developments interact with the exercise of military control, this chapter's approach is to contextualise doctrinal developments.

II. INTERNATIONAL LAW AND THE ENVIRONMENT IN TIMES OF ARMED CONFLICT: POWER POLITICS OR LEGAL PROGRESS?

In response to targeted attacks on the natural environment in the Second World War, and the Vietnam and Gulf wars, several environmental law frameworks emerged, complementing property-based approaches to the protection of the natural environment in the laws of armed conflict.[10] Also, in recognition of how natural resources, or rather the monetary value they represent were cause for, and means of armed conflict, several soft law instruments, as well as a tailored sanctions regime were developed, which address the economic ties between armed conflict and mineral resources.[11] In sum, one can speak of the existence of a legal regime addressing the role of the natural environment and mineral resources in times of armed conflict. This regime is made up of specific treaties and conventions prohibiting certain types of warfare, known to be harmful to the natural environment such as the Biological Weapons Convention, the Environmental Modification Convention, the Chemical Weapons Convention,

[9] T Ackermann, *The Effects of Armed Conflict on Investment Treaties* (Cambridge, Cambridge University Press, 2022).

[10] UN, General Assembly, Additional Protocol I of the Geneva Conventions Relating to the Victims of International Armed Conflict, UNTS 1125, 3, 8 June 1977, Art 55. For one example of the *ius cogens* approach to property, see Special Court for Sierra Leone, *Prosecutor against Moinina Fofana and Allieu Kondewa*, Judgment of 2 August 2007, SCSL-04-14-T-785; See generally: R Falk, 'Environmental Warfare and Ecocide: Facts, Appraisal, and Proposals' (1973) 4 *Bulletin of Peace Proposals* 80.

[11] 'UN Sanctions: Natural Resources – Research Report' (United Nations Security Council, 2015); D Dam-de Jong, 'UN natural resources sanctions regimes: incorporating market-based responses to address market-driven problems' in L Van den Herik (ed), *Research Handbook on UN Sanctions and International Law* (Cheltenham, Edward Elgar, 2017).

and the Treaty on the Prohibition of Nuclear Weapons, as well as soft law instruments (eg, the 2020 ICRC Guidelines on the Protection of the Natural Environment in Armed Conflict), and customary law as spelled out in the 2022 ILC Draft Principles on the Protection of the Environment in Armed Conflict.[12]

The scholarly community's response to the emergence of this regime has been mixed. Some view the legal protection of nature and her resources in times of armed conflict as a story of progress. They point to the responsiveness of international law to resource wars as evidence that law can 'catch up' with time and adapt to societal change viewing the fragmentation and specialisation of international law as an opportunity for, rather than a challenge to, progress.[13] Sandholtz, for instance, observes that over time international legal rules have transformed from 'to the victor belongs the spoils' to the 'prohibition of plunder'.[14] Others do not doubt the adaptability of international law but question its ability to deliver justice.[15] Yet others point out that power rather than law determines what is considered permissible, and what is not. Falk's work is emblematic of this position. Taking stock of the evolution of the protection of the natural environment in times of armed conflict, he shows that *ius in bello* norms protecting the environment were selectively applied to justify 'punitive peace' during the 1990/91 Gulf War and the Yugoslav wars, or disregarded completely by the more powerful party to the conflicts in Kosovo, Vietnam and Iraq.[16] Yet others argue that, given the potential multigenerational consequences associated with the pollution of water systems, the degradation of ecosystems, and the contamination of air and soil, contemporary legal responses simply do not correspond to the severity of the issue, and that further developments, such as the institution of the crime of ecocide, are necessary.[17] Some proponents of this view treat environmental consciousness – or rather an understanding of the potentially catastrophic effects of environmental warfare for present and future

[12] United Nations, International Law Commission, Draft principles on protection of the environment in relation to armed conflicts, *Yearbook of the International Law Commission*, vol II, Part 2, 2022.

[13] M Bothe et al, 'International Law Protecting the Environment During Armed Conflict: Gaps and Opportunities' (2010) 92 *International Review of the Red Cross* 569; KE Boon, 'UN Sanctions as Regulation' (2016) 15 *Chinese Journal of International Law* 543; Jong (n 11); JG Stewart, *Corporate War Crimes: Prosecuting the Pillage of Natural Resources* (Open Society Justice Initiative, 2010); C Droege and M Tougas, 'The Protection of the Natural Environment in Armed Conflict – Existing Rules and Need for Further Legal Protection' (2013) 82 *Nordic Journal of International Law* 21.

[14] W Sandholtz, *Prohibiting Plunder: How Norms Change* (Oxfordd, Oxford University Press, 2007) 9–11.

[15] E Cusato, *The Ecology of War and Peace: Marginalising Slow and Structural Violence in International Law* (Cambridge, Cambridge University Press, 2021).

[16] R Falk, 'The Inadequacy of the Existing Legal Approach to Environmental Protection in Wartime' in JE Austin and CE Bruch (eds), *The Environmental Consequences of War* (Cambridge, Cambridge University Press, 2000). See also: M Koskenniemi, '"The Lady Doth Protest Too Much" Kosovo, and the Turn to Ethics in International Law' (2002) 65 *Modern Law Review* 159.

[17] T Lindgren, 'Ecocide, genocide and the disregard of alternative life-systems' (2018) 22 *International Journal of Human Rights* 525.

generations and ecosystems far beyond the territorial boundaries of the conflict parties – as a new insight. Yet, as the ancient practice of 'salting the earth' in the villages and towns of surrendering parties to a conflict shows, creating environmental conditions which do not permit the sustainment of life, has always been part and parcel of warfare. In sum, in line with the increased consciousness for ecological matters and the significance and value of mineral resources, a sophisticated legal regime has emerged, yet when and how the norms of this legal regime have been applied is not quite as straightforward to diagnose. A point, which will be illustrated by zooming in on how property of, and sovereignty over natural resources has been interpreted and applied.

III. PROPERTY, SOVEREIGNTY, OR THE SPOILS OF WAR?

The value that mineral resources represent have been a cause for, and a factor in armed conflict and in situations of occupation.[18] This raises several important questions for international law and its role in resource wars. As Knop has eloquently pointed out, international law is highly vested in the representational work it requires the state to perform on behalf of its people.[19] At the same time, as Okowa has drawn attention to, its state-centricity and recognition of formal sources of governmental authority has led to its inability to make sense of, and adequately address, non-state actors' authority.[20] In the context of non-international armed conflict, this representational work favours state agents over non-state actors. This is because the principle of permanent sovereignty over natural resources vests the right to trade natural resources in a state's formal government. In the past, this has led to an inability to respond to instances in which non-state armed groups or, for that matter, occupying powers, concluded mineral contracts on behalf of the people under their effective control. To a lesser extent, the same is true for mineral contracts concluded by occupying powers on behalf of the people in occupied territory, with the 2024 International Court of Justice (ICJ) Advisory Opinion on Israeli Policies and Practices in Occupied Palestinian Territories having great significance for legal clarity on this issue.[21]

Commonly, mineral resources, their extraction sites and infrastructure are thought of as falling under the scope of Articles 53 and 55 of the Hague

[18] See generally: Le Billon (n 8).

[19] K Knop, 'Statehood: territory, people, government' in J Crawford and M Koskenniemi (eds), *The Cambridge Companion to International Law* (Cambridge, Cambridge University Press, 2012) 101. See also: A Cassese, *Self-Determination of Peoples: A Legal Reappraisal* (Cambridge, Cambridge University Press, 1995) 5.

[20] P Okowa, 'Natural Resources in Situations of Armed Conflict: Is There a Coherent Framework for Protection?' (2007) 9 *International Community Law Review* 237; P Okowa, 'Sovereignty Contests and the Protection of Natural Resources in Conflict Zones' (2013) 66 *Current Legal Problems* 33.

[21] International Court of Justice, *Legal Consequences arising from the Policies and Practices of Israel in the Occupied Palestinian Territories, Including East Jerusalem*, Advisory Opinion of 19 July 2024.

Convention on the Laws and Customs of War. Article 53 stipulates the conditions under which an occupying power can take possession of public and private property, which is when it is for military necessity. It further states that in instances of the seizure of private property, the occupying power must restore or compensate once the armed conflict has ended. Article 55 then further specifies that an occupying power must administer public property in occupied territory, and must safeguard it and its proceeds, and may only use it following the rules of *usufruct*.[22] Whether mineral resources are private or public property, under what conditions they can be seized and exploited by an occupying power, and what concrete rights and obligations result from such acts are questions that have preoccupied courts numerous times, with cases relating to Japanese and Israeli occupation having long served as authoritative case law. With the 2024 ICJ Advisory Opinion on Occupied Palestinian Territories, being both detailed and specific on the use of private and public property by occupying powers, as well as their rights to enter into mineral resources contracts on behalf of the population under their occupation, it can be expected that this Opinion will become the authoritative reference point for future disputes. These cases, and the Advisory Opinion will now be presented briefly.

A. The Oil Stocks Case

During the Second World War, Japanese armed forces occupied the Dutch East Indies – contemporary Indonesia – and took over control of petroleum production sites in occupied territory, which had been run by Dutch concessionaires. Upon taking control, the Japanese military repaired the production facilities and infrastructure which had been deliberately damaged by the concessionaires before the occupation to prevent Japanese forces from continuing oil production on their sites. Once repaired, the Japanese military continued to exploit existing production sites without expanding production to new sites. They used some of the oil for their purposes but also shipped large quantities to Singapore where it was stored until the British army, which took over control in Singapore in 1945, seized it. In response, the Dutch concessionaires of the petroleum sites the oil originated from demanded compensation before a special appeals board. This board dismissed the claim arguing that oil in the ground was *res nullius* meaning that the first to take possession of it would also be its rightful owner. Setting aside other possibly applicable laws, including domestic law, the board further reasoned that Article 53 of the Hague Convention was to be interpreted permissively, meaning that it entitled Japan, as occupying power, to some of the oil.[23] The board's decision was successfully challenged before the Court

[22] Also recognised as a principle of customary international law, see ibid, para 124.

[23] Appeal Board, *NV de Bataafsche Petroleum Maatschappij and Others v The War Damage Commission* (n 1).

of Appeal of Singapore, which accepted that the seizure of the appellants' oil installations was purposefully carried out as part of a larger plan of Japan to supply the military and civilian needs of Japan during the war. Contrary to the appeal board, it considered that the assets seized were private property, rather than *res nullius*. As a result, it treated decisions by the Nuremberg Tribunals on the seizure and destruction of private property as precedent and concluded that in the case before it, the acts of the occupying power constituted a violation of the protection of private property.[24] The Court further held that crude oil in the ground did not constitute movable property suitable for military purposes, which is why occupying powers had no lawful basis to exploit it.[25] Finally, concerning the reserves held in stock, the Court found that following Article 53, Japan had had the obligation to return these to the concessionaires once armed activities had ceased.[26] In sum, it determined that the acts of the Japanese and British armies were wartime plunder. To this day, the decision of the Singaporean Court of Appeal is regarded as authoritative case law.[27] Yet, when the occupation by Israel of Palestinian territories and that of neighbouring countries raised the question of the occupying power's right to dispose of petroleum reserves in occupied territory again years later, the legal reasoning of this decision was simply disregarded.

B. 1967 Israeli Occupation

From 1967 onwards, Israeli military forces occupied the Gaza Strip and the Sinai (Egypt), the West Bank (Jordan) and the Golan Heights (Syria). During its occupation, Israel continued existing oil production in the Sinai's Abu Rhodeis fields in occupied Egyptian territory, increased output levels, and allegedly used up to 55 per cent of the oil produced in occupied territories for its domestic energy demand. In response to contemporary critics who regarded this practice as unlawful and considered that *ius in bello* at most permitted the maintenance of oil production at the levels predating occupation, but certainly not its increase,[28]

[24] SGCA, *Singapore, Bataafsche Petroleum v The War Damage Commission (Singapore Oil Stocks)*, Judgment of 13 April 1956 (1957) 51 *American Journal of International Law* 802; United States Military Tribunal, Nuremberg, *USA v Alfried Felix Alwyn Krupp von Bohlen und Halbach, et al*, Judgment of 31 July 1948, Case No 58; United States Military Tribunal, Nuremberg, *USA v Friedrick Flick, et al*, Judgment of 22 December 1947, Case No 5; United States Military Tribunal, Nuremberg, *USA v Carl Krauch, et al*, Judgment of 30 July 1948, Case No 57.

[25] SGCA, *Singapore, Bataafsche Petroleum v The War Damage Commission (Singapore Oil Stocks)* (n 24) 809.

[26] ibid, 811.

[27] M Paparinskis, 'Singapore Oil Stocks Case', 18 August 2023, available at: opil.ouplaw.com/display/10.1093/law:epil/9780199231690/law-9780199231690-e408.

[28] BM Clagett and OT Johnson, 'May Israel as a Belligerent Occupant Lawfully Exploit Previously Unexploited Oil Resources of the Gulf of Suez?' (1978) 72 *American Journal of International Law* 558.

Israel insisted that, as an occupying power, it had the right to continue, expand and modernise existing oil production sites in occupied territories, as long as the revenues they generated were then used to meet the needs of the population living under occupation.[29] It went on to argue that, as an occupying power, it had the right to take possession of public property[30] and that the obligations of *usufruct* under international law were 'to utilise and exploit the oil fields only as a *bonus paterfamilias* would' as *ius in bello* could not be interpreted 'to cause economic paralysis of occupied territory'.[31] In sum, the Israeli position was that *usufruct* in Article 55 of the Hague Convention, as it was interpreted in British and US military manuals and existing case law, did not prohibit the exploitation of new oil fields. On the contrary, it found that the writings of eminent international lawyers suggested that the principle should be interpreted to prohibit the destruction of public resources and their exploitation beyond what is useful or necessary.[32] Even more so, it argued that a prohibition to exploit new oil fields would be contrary to the purpose and objective of the Hague Conventions as halting oil production in areas dependent on oil revenues would result in severe economic deprivation of the population in occupied territory.[33] Finally, and as a matter of policy, the Israeli position was that oil prospection and production increased the value of land and was thus in the interests of the sovereign state that the occupied territory was part of and that not exploiting existing oil wells would cause them to fall into disrepair.[34]

Of course, this position was in direct contradiction to the findings of the Court of Appeal in the *Singapore Oil Stocks* case. Furthermore, Israel's position was not shared by even its closest allies, with the United States arguing that the principle of *usufruct* indicated that Israel had no right to develop new oil fields, and that even if new oil fields could be lawfully developed, the oil produced could only be used for the needs of the peoples in occupied territory. The United States further cautioned that Israel was not entitled to grant commercial concession agreements to a third party, and that it was under an obligation to respect the existing concession agreement.[35]

So, even at the time, it was clear that the Israeli interpretation of the permissibility of *ius in bello* on mineral resources exploitation in occupied territory by the occupying power was in direct contradiction to established case law. Yet, it is the language and reasoning of this governmental position that found its way into the 2011 Israeli High Court decision concerning mining and quarrying

[29] 'Ministry of Foreign Affairs Memorandum of Law on the Right to Develop New Oil Fields in Sinai and the Gulf of Suez' (1978) 17 *International Legal Materials* 432.

[30] ibid, para 11.

[31] ibid, para 12.

[32] ibid, para 2.

[33] ibid, para 3.

[34] ibid.

[35] 'United States: Department of State Memorandum of Law on Isreal's Right to Develop New Oil Fields in Sinai and the Gulf of Suez' (1977) 16 *International Legal Materials* 733.

activities being conducted by Israel in occupied territory. The Court first dismissed the assertion that international law prohibited the mining of minerals in territories held under belligerent occupation by the occupying force or by others to whom such a force had granted concessions.[36] It then distinguished between 'occupation' and 'prolonged occupation', arguing that in instances of prolonged occupation, *ius in bello* obligations of the occupying state needed adjusting to permit it to safeguard economic wellbeing and promote economic development in occupied territory.[37] Based on this, it determined that the quarrying operations in question were in the best interests of those under occupation given the 'common economic interests of both the Israeli and Palestinian parties and the prolonged period of occupation'.[38] The decision triggered fierce opposition on doctrinal grounds, with seven Israeli academics issuing an expert opinion to contest the Court's judgment, including its interpretation that the occupying power was authorised to make 'reasonable use' of the natural resources located in occupied territory and the capital that they yielded, and that quarrying activities were allowed by quarries that were not in operation before the occupation.[39]

There are a few issues that are particularly noteworthy about this case. Some are fairly obvious, namely the doubts about the Court's neutrality and impartiality that its uptake of the highly contested 1978 Israeli government position in its legal interpretation and reasoning raises. This underlines the legitimacy concerns that come with any attempt to adjudicate conflicts between the occupier and the occupied in the courts of the occupier, but also places this decision in the imperial tradition of making and re-making *ius in bello*.[40] It relies on the Vitorian logic of justifying colonial conquest and violence with the promise of civilisation by trade.[41] This argumentative pattern is not unique to this judgment but has been employed by other courts to justify Israeli settler colonialism with the logic of improvement.[42] As Bhandar notes, despite economic interests not being the principal driving force of Israeli settler colonialism, the rationale of European colonial endeavours, such as the promise of improving the

[36] Israeli High Court of Justice, *Yesh Din – Volunteers for Human Rights, et al v Commander of the IDF Forces in the West Bank, et al*, Judgment of 26 December 2011, HCJ 2164/09.

[37] ibid, para 10.

[38] ibid, para 13.

[39] G Harpaz et al, 'Expert Legal Opinion' (Jerusalem, Yesh Din, 2012) para 94.

[40] F Megret, 'From "Savages" to "Unlawful Combatants": A Postcolonial Look at International Humanitarian Law's "Other"' in A Orford (ed), *International Law and Its 'Others'* (Cambridge, Cambridge University Press, 2006) 278–316; G Simpson, *Great Powers and Outlaw States: Unequal Sovereigns in the International Legal Order* (Cambridge, Cambridge University Press, 2004); D Kennedy, *On Law and War* (Princeton, NJ, Princeton University Press, 2006).

[41] M Koskenniemi, 'Empire and International Law: The Real Spanish Contribution' (2011) 61 *University of Toronto Law Journal* 1.

[42] B Bhandar, *Colonial Lives of Property: Law, Land, and Racial Regimes of Ownership* (Durham, NC, Duke University Press, 2018) 141–45. See also: Nathaniel Berman, 'Israel's Supreme Court Is No Human Rights Savior. Just Ask the Palestinians' *Haaretz* (14 February 2023), available at: www.haaretz.com/israel-news/2023-02-14/ty-article-opinion/.premium/israels-supreme-court-is-no-human-rights-savior-just-ask-the-palestinians/00000186-4f2d-d603-a7bf-cfbfe0360000.

productivity of land and labour, and thereby augmenting the standard of civilisation in colonised, or, in the present instance, occupied territory, have found their ways into Zionist thought.[43] This reasoning comes with an astonishing neglect of the legal principles of the postcolonial global legal order.

For example, the judgment does not consider the possible legal implications of the principles of permanent sovereignty over natural resources, or the principle of people's right to economic self-determination.[44] It does not mention either of them at all. This is despite their applicability outside the colonial context already being well established at the time that this judgment was rendered.[45] One way to look at this would be as an instance of flawed legal reasoning, as has been done by expert legal opinion. Yet, this raises all the more questions about the decision's singular ICRC law in practice status for the interpretation of *usufruct* in the laws of war. By reading promises of 'development' and 'modernity' into *usufruct*, the Court takes a restrictive norm, intended to prevent plunder and pillage, and turns it into a permissive, even noble obligation to advance economic and social interests in occupied territory for the sake of progress:

> [T]he royalties paid to the Civil Administration by the operators of the Quarries are used to finance the operations of the military administration, which promotes various kinds of projects aimed to benefit the interests of the Area. In their Reply, the Respondents (the Quarries) also emphasized that their activities have been contributing to the economic development and to the modernization of the Area in many ways, such as training of employees, payment of royalties and supplying quarrying products necessary for construction purposes. It was stated further that a significant portion of their quarrying products is being marketed both to Palestinians and to Israeli settlers (at a rate that varies from one quarry to another) and that granting the remedy as requested under the petition will inflict a fatal blow not only upon them, but also upon their employees and service providers among the local population, for which the quarries serve as a source of livelihood.[46]

The logic put forward by the Court here is reminiscent of a welfarist development discourse, as it had been used by former imperial powers in the context of decolonisation to justify their continued influence in newly independent states.[47] It is also the same language and reasoning that was deployed by US authorities in

[43] Bhandar (n 42) 119–39.

[44] UN, General Assembly, Resolution 1803 (XVII) Permanent Sovereignty over Natural Resources, A/RES/1803(XVII), 14 December 1962; UN, General Assembly, International Covenant on Civil and Political Rights, UNTS 999, 171, 16 December 1966, Art 1; UN, General Assembly, International Covenant on Economic, Social and Cultural Rights, UNTS 993, 3, 16 December 1966, Art 1.

[45] International Court of Justice, *Case Concerning Armed Activities on the Territory of the Congo (Democratic Republic of the Congo v Uganda)*, Judgment of 19 December 2005, ICJ Reports 2005, 168.

[46] *Yesh Din – Volunteers for Human Rights, et al v Commander of the IDF Forces in the West Bank, et al* (n 36) para 19.

[47] HW Arndt, *Economic Development: The History of an Idea* (Chicago, IL, University of Chicago Press, 1989), 49–87.

occupied Iraq after the invasion in 2003 to justify their interventions in economic affairs and governance of petroleum resource, as will be discussed below.

Israeli authorities have continued to give out mining permits on Occupied Palestinian Territory until this day, which effectively means that they have controlled mining activities for, example in the West Bank, for the last 60 years. It is against this backdrop that the ICJ considered the scope of an occupying power's right to govern and use natural resources in occupied territory in its 2024 Advisory Opinion. The Court affirmed that the principle of *usufruct* conveyed on the occupying power the responsibility to 'safeguard the capital' that these natural resources translated to, and that their use may not exceed what is necessary for the purposes of meeting the needs of the population under occupation. For the first time, it also found that such natural resources had to be used in a sustainable matter and without causing environmental harm.[48] Building on its earlier jurisprudence, which had recognised the principle of permanent sovereignty over natural resources as a principle of customary international law and as applicable outside the colonial context, the ICJ examined whether the situation in occupied Palestinian territory amounted to a violation of this principle.[49] In an earlier decision, it had found that the principle was not violated, due to the absence of governmental policy to plunder natural resources in occupied territory.[50] Relying among other things on the fact that of the 10–12 million tons of raw material produced in Area C of the West Bank by 11 Israeli-operated quarries in 2015, approximately 10 million tons were exported to Israel, with the Israeli state additionally capturing significant public revenue from these activities through royalties and user fees, the ICJ found there to be a government policy in place that was inconsistent with the right of Palestinians to permanent sovereignty over natural resources:

> On the basis of the evidence before it, the Court considers that Israel's use of the natural resources in the Occupied Palestinian Territory is inconsistent with its obligations under international law. By diverting a large share of the natural resources to its own population, including settlers, Israel is in breach of its obligation to act as administrator and usufructuary. In this connection, the Court recalls that the transfer by Israel of its own population to the Occupied Palestinian Territory is contrary to international law … Therefore, in the Court's view, the use of natural resources in the occupied territory cannot be justified with reference to the needs of that population … In light of the above, the Court also concludes that Israel's policy of exploitation of natural resources in the Occupied Palestinian Territory is inconsistent with its

[48] United Nations, Conference on Environment and Development, Rio Declaration on Environment and Development, 1992, Art 23; ILC Conflict and Environment Draft Principles, Principle 20.

[49] *Legal Consequences arising from the Policies and Practises of Israel in the Occupied Palestinian Territories, Including East Jerusalem* (n 21) para 125; *Case Concerning Armed Activities on the Territory of the Congo (Democratic Republic of the Congo v Uganda)* (n 45) para 244.

[50] *Case Concerning Armed Activities on the Territory of the Congo (Democratic Republic of the Congo v Uganda)* (n 45) para 242.

> obligation to respect the Palestinian people's right to permanent sovereignty over natural resources.[51]

In sum, the Advisory Opinion of the ICJ, even if not binding, is still highly authoritative in character for the case of the Occupied Palestinian Territories. In that sense the Court can only be commended for expressing its interpretation of international law in such stark terms. At the same time, the situation that the Court examined was also an extreme instance of foreign rule, which, as the ICJ recognised in the same Opinion, amounted to annexation of the territories concerned, leaving one to wonder about the threshold this decision may set.[52] It is also worth noting that the transfer of natural resources – or of the value they generate from those living under occupation to the occupying power – is exceptionally straightforward in this case, and that in most wartime contexts, the ways in which natural resources and their wealth are disappropriated frequently involve foreign corporations as well as some collaborators representing the people under occupation.

Instances in which violations of resource sovereignty do not result from direct resources transfer, but from efforts of the occupying power to liberate the domestic natural resources sector to facillitate the entry of foreign corporations, continue to elude international law. Arguably, however, such efforts can and do in practice amount to instances of enrichment at the expense of the population under occupation, as will now be illustrated.

C. Iraq

In the wake of the 2003 invasion of Iraq, it did not take long for the US administration to turn its attention towards the governance of Iraqi petroleum production and reserves. In the context of the push for a new international economic order, Iraq had nationalised its petroleum reserves and infrastructure, which had previously been owned by the concessionaire consortium Iraq Petroleum Company (IPC), formed by foreign companies. From the mid-1970s to the 1990s, petroleum production was conducted entirely by the then nationalised IPC, but following the Iraqi invasion of Kuwait, the government of Saddam Hussein entered into several development and production contracts with Chinese, Russian and French companies. This was in part in an attempt to circumvent economic sanctions which had been imposed against Iraq in response to their invasion of Kuwait, and in part to obtain foreign capital investments in the country's petroleum installations and infrastructure, which heavy bombings during the Gulf War had left in a desolate state. Still, in 2003, the country's petroleum was primarily

[51] *Legal Consequences arising from the Policies and Practises of Israel in the Occupied Palestinian Territories, Including East Jerusalem* (n 21) para 133.

[52] ibid, para 179.

managed and run by the state-owned company IPC, a fact that the US government sought to change as quickly as possible.

In March 2006, the US Congress appointed the Baker–Hamilton Commission, composed of current and former US politicians, bureaucrats and members of the judiciary, to develop strategic recommendations for the peacebuilding and reconstruction process in Iraq.[53] Within 10 months, the Commission put forward its recommendations addressed to the US government. Among other things, their report included recommendations on the future of the Iraqi oil sector. Recognising its critical importance for the Iraqi economy, the Commission recommended that the US government should help the Iraqi government to prepare a new fiscal and legal framework conducive to foreign investment; to have the US military work with Iraqi security forces and private security companies to protect the petroleum infrastructure; and to press the Iraqi government to reduce subsidies in the energy sector by working with the International Monetary Fund so that Iraqis would pay market value for oil products, in the hope that this would address fuel shortages in the country.[54] In addition, the US government should encourage international public and private investment in the Iraqi petroleum sector, and assist Iraqi leaders 'to reorganize the national oil industry as a commercial enterprise'.[55] In short, the Commission proposed a full reversal of the country's petroleum nationalisation that had taken place in the 1970s, by inviting foreign companies into the country, and by engaging in a fully-fledged market liberalisation of the sector, down to the price for domestic consumption, in what was a war-torn economy.

The Commission's recommendations were met with open ears by the US government, which had already mandated BearingPoint, an international business consultancy, to advise the Iraqi Ministry of Oil on the development of a new foreign investor-friendly oil code.[56] From the perspective of the US government, BearingPoint had been an obvious choice for this task. As early as December 2003, the consultancy published a USAID-funded study on the ways forward for a 'sustainable Iraqi oil industry'. The study strongly positioned itself against state-owned petroleum production and in favour of a liberalised corporate oil sector arguing that this would, among other things, enhance the rule of law.[57] By February 2007, the Iraqi transitional cabinet had approved a new hydrocarbon law designed to liberalise the petroleum sector and attract foreign investment, but when the code was put before the Iraqi Council of Representatives, it could not get the necessary support to pass as it was unpopular

[53] 'Iraq Study Group Fact Sheet', 18 August 2023, available at: www.usip.org/publications/2006/12/iraq-study-group-fact-sheet.

[54] JA Baker III et al, *The Iraq Study Group Report* (New York, Vintage Books, 2003) recommendation 62.

[55] ibid, recommendation 63.

[56] Antonia Juhasz, 'It's still about oil in Iraq' *Los Angeles Times* (8 December 2006).

[57] 'Options for Developing a Long Term Sustainable Iraqi Oil Industry' (Washington DC, BearingPoint, 2003) 32–46.

among the Iraqi people.[58] A poll found that 63 per cent preferred national, and state-owned, rather than foreign and corporate petroleum production, and less than 9 per cent felt that they had been sufficiently informed about the proposed new oil code.[59]

In light of this resistance, the Iraqi Ministry of Oil in consultation with the US administration drafted terms for petroleum service contracts which, in a non-competitive process, were given to Western oil companies, including ExxonMobil, Shell, BP and Total. These contracts were met with lots of criticism, not only for the US involvement in drafting them but also because the need for bringing in foreign companies for the tasks specified under the terms of the service contracts was not clear. Under the terms of a hydrocarbon service contract, a company is paid a fixed fee by the state to conduct specific activities, such as repairs and maintenance services. The service contracts given out in the wake of the failed attempt to pass the draft Iraqi oil bill concerned repairs for which IPC certainly had the necessary expertise, and for which it had already undertaken a significant bulk of the works required, raising serious questions why these services were then contracted out to foreign companies. This was even more acutely felt because service contracts do not incentivise foreign investment to the same degree as production-sharing agreements, the commonly used instrument in the petroleum sector, which in effect meant that transnational corporations ended up with lucrative deals paid out of Iraq's state coffers, at a comparatively low risk for investment.

More importantly, these contracts positioned them again in the Iraqi oil sector, reversing their ousting by the 1970s nationalisation, and also securing access of Western companies to this sector. When the service contracts were given out in 2008/09, they were only awarded to Western companies, while contracts that the Iraqi government had concluded with Russian and Chinese corporations before the 2003 invasion were nullified.[60] The failure of the 2007 draft petroleum bill was a successful exercise of the Iraqi peoples' right to freely determine over their natural wealth and resources. Nonetheless, important parallels between the policy and rhetoric of the Israeli government in the 1960s/1970s and the US government in the 2000s can be identified. One is the logic of improvement through the use of mineral resources which, even if not used to justify occupations as such, legitimised interventions or even takeovers in the law and governance of mineral resources in occupied territory. The other is the insistence that resource extraction even in conditions in which armed activities were still ongoing, would be beneficial to peace and reconstruction processes. At the same

[58] Edward Wong and Sheryl Gay Stolberg, 'Iraqi Blocs Opposed to Draft Oil Bill' *New York Times* (3 May 2007).

[59] D Dougherty, 'Oil Change International: Iraq Survey Results' (Washington DC, Custom Strategic Research, 2007).

[60] Waleed Ibrahim and Ahmed Rasheed, 'Iraq oil ministry to push ahead with deal tender' *Reuters* (16 June 2009); Peter S Goodman, 'For Iraq's Oil Contracts, a Question of Motive' *New York Times* (29 June 2008).

time, the prioritisation of mineral resources exports over their availability and affordability in occupied territory leaves very little doubt that the insistence on mineral resources operations even in times of armed conflict does not principally serve the wellbeing of the people in occupied territory but the interests of the occupying force and global energy security.

D. Gaza Offshore Reserves

The same can be said about US energy policy in the context of the international armed conflict between Israel and Palestine in Gaza. In summer 2023, the Israeli government approved plans to move forward with natural gas production in the Mediterranean Sea in Palestinian territorial waters off the coast of Gaza.[61] Such plans had been pursued for a long time by the Palestinian Authority in order to ensure energy security in Palestinian territories but had been repeatedly vetoed by the Israeli government as occupying power over its concerns that the revenues generated from the export and sale of gas might be used by Hamas to fund attacks against Israel.[62] Now, in response to the attacks of 7 October 2023 by Hamas which killed more than 1,200 Israeli civilians and which were conducted out of Gaza, the Israeli government has retaliated with extreme force and blatant disregard for civilian life. In the four months since the attacks by Hamas, Israeli military operations by land and air in Gaza have caused more than 26,000 civilian casualties, and left only 14 of the 36 hospitals there operational.[63] The situation for civilians in Gaza is so dire that the ICJ in its order of 26 January 2024 found the Gaza Strip to be in a 'catastrophic humanitarian situation' and ordered Israel to take 'immediate and effective measures to enable the provision of urgently needed basic services and humanitarian assistance'.[64]

Despite this, so far the US position has been to support the Israeli government even against allegations of crimes against humanity, war crimes and genocide voting, for example, against a UN General Assembly Resolution calling for a humanitarian ceasefire, suspending its funding to the UN Relief and Works Agency for Palestine Refugees in the Near East (UNRWA).[65] This is why

[61] Reuters, 'Israel gives nod to Gaza Marine gas development, wants security assurances' *Reuters* (18 June 2023), available at: www.reuters.com/business/energy/israel-gives-nod-gaza-marine-gas-development-wants-security-assurances-2023-06-18/.

[62] Reuters, 'Palestinians, seeking new developer, offer 45 pct stake in Gaza gas field' *Reuters* (4 April 2018), available at: www.reuters.com/article/israel-palestinians-gas-idUSL5N1RH2D5/.

[63] UNOCHA, 'Hostilities in the Gaza Strip and Israel | Flash Update #104' (28 January 2024), available at: www.unocha.org/publications/report/occupied-palestinian-territory/hostilities-gaza-strip-and-israel-flash-update-104-enarhe.

[64] International Court of Justice, *Application of the Convention on the Prevention and Punishment of the Crime of Genocide in the Gaza Strip (South Africa v Israel)*, Order of 26 January 2024.

[65] UN, General Assembly, Resolution E-10/21 Protection of civilians and upholding legal and humanitarian obligations, A/RES/ES-10/21, 30 October 2023; M Miller: www.state.gov/statement-on-unrwa-allegations/'*US Department of Justice* (26 January 2024); US policy towards Gaza has

it is of particular note that in late November 2023, Amos Hochstein, the US President's energy security adviser, during his visit to Israel made it a priority to advocate for the development of Palestinian offshore gas reserves 'on behalf of the Palestinians'.[66] While to some observers it may appear cynical that the very same state which has so far taken very little action to safeguard civilian life in Gaza is showing such concern for its post-war economic development; being met with such behaviours is, unfortunately, far from uncommon.[67]

IV. CONCLUSION

The value that natural resources represent gives rise to the peril of plenty. Despite considerable international law-making momentum, on nature and natural resources in armed conflict, international law remains astonishingly permissive with regard to the appropriation of natural resources in times of armed conflict and occupation, particularly when it concerns natural resources that are still subject to sovereign, rather than private property rights. In light of the added incentive that natural resources represent to prolong belligerent occupation, or to effectively annex land, as has been the case with Area C in the West Bank, this permissiveness is reminiscent of the 'to the victor belongs the spoil' era in the laws of war. To return to the initial question of this chapter, whether international law governance of natural resources in armed conflict represents a story of progress, this chapter has shown that this is not the case, at least not if progress is measured not by the mere presence of international law, but also by its ability to safeguard against the peril of plenty.

While this chapter has focused on state conduct, the dissonance between progress made through the adoption of treaties and through jurisprudence, on the one hand, and the tangible real-world outcomes of these legal developments, on the other, is also evident in the realm of international criminal responsibility.[68] This issue has been extensively discussed by others, particularly with respect to natural resources.[69] International criminal law prohibits the pillaging of public, private, movable and immovable property in both international

led to a case being brought against the Biden Administration alleging that the Administration lends support to the commitment of genocide. See United States District Court for the Northern District of California, *Defense for Children International-Palestine v Biden*, Complaint of 13 November 2023, 4:23-cv-05829-JSW.

[66] Mina Al-Oraibi, 'US envoy Hochstein says offshore gas belongs to the Palestinian people' *The National News* (19 November 2023), available at: www.thenationalnews.com/mena/palestine-israel/2023/11/19/us-envoy-hochstein-tells-the-national-offshore-gas-belongs-to-the-palestinian-people/.

[67] Klein (n 7).

[68] Art 8(2)(a)(iv); (b)(xiii) ICC Statute; International Criminal Court, Trial Chamber II, *The Prosecutor v Jean-Pierre Bemba Gombo*, Judgment of 21 March 2016, ICC-01/05-01/08, 115.

[69] Stewart (n 13); MB Taylor, *War Economies and International Law* (Cambridge, Cambridge University Press, 2021).

and non-international armed conflicts.[70] This prohibition is understood to apply equally to natural resources. In the case of publicly owned natural resources, such a prohibition applies when property is seized for reasons not specified under the Geneva or Hague Conventions, namely military necessity or the fulfilment of the needs of the civilian population. For the seizure of private property, an additional condition applies. When it is seized, fair compensation must be offered. Furthermore, knowingly receiving pillaged property, whether as a gift or through purchase, can also constitute a violation of the prohibition against pillage in international criminal law.[71]

Notably, the Special Court for Sierra Leone found former Liberian President Charles Taylor responsible for aiding and abetting the looting of various resources, including diamonds, by members of the non-state armed group, the Revolutionary United Front (RUF). This case highlighted that, for the purposes of international criminal responsibility, mineral resources in the ground are considered to be 'lootable property', and that attacks on such property were not only intended to exploit resources and extract value but also to inflict psychological and material harm on the population at large.[72]

The dualism of liberal and humanitarian values reflected in the prohibition of pillage, viewing property both as an individual and collective right, as well as a means of human survival, has been distorted within the international criminal responsibility framework in the sense that the prohibition acknowledges that individual, public and corporate property may be pillaged, while limiting the scope of criminal responsibility to natural persons. All the while, it is inconceivable that the threshold for criminal responsibility for the pillaging of natural resources could be met without the involvement of state or corporate entities. In the case of the war in Angola, for instance, this pillaging of diamonds has specifically been associated with the company De Beers.[73] While this gave rise to the Kimberley Process Certification Scheme, as a soft law instrument to create transparency and accountability in the supply chain of diamonds, the relevations of De Beers involvement with blood diamonds never gave rise to any criminal responsibility. In sum, as was the case for the temptation of plenty and in relation to AML, and anti-corruption law, for the peril of plenty too, international law gives corporations the benefit of being possible victims, and possible problem solvers, but does not make sense of corporate conduct as a cause for the peril of plenty.

[70] Art 8(2)(a)(iv); (b)(xiii) ICC Statute; International Criminal Court, Trial Chamber II, *The Prosecutor v Jean-Pierre Bemba Gombo* (n 68) 115.

[71] Stewart (n 13) 68, 63–66.

[72] Special Court of Sierra Leone, *Prosecutor v Charles Ghankay Taylor*, Judgment of 26 April 2012, SCSL-03-01-T-1283, para 2020.

[73] 'A Rough Trade: The Role of Companies and Governments in the Angolan Conflict' (Global Witness, 1998).

7

The Pain of Plenty

I. INTRODUCTION

In December 2022, the United Nations (UN) Office for the Coordination of Humanitarian Affairs (UN-OCHA) announced that it anticipated humanitarian crisis responses in Afghanistan, the Democratic Republic of the Congo (DRC), Ethiopia, Nigeria, Somalia, South Sudan, Sudan, Syria, Ukraine and Yemen to each require more than US$1 billion in funding. The UN agency further announced that a total of US$51.5 billion would be required to meet the world's overall humanitarian needs, which is to deliver life-saving assistance to every person affected by an armed conflict or natural disaster. This appeal was the biggest in the history of UN-OCHA, yet it represents not even a quarter of the profits that five oil corporations reported for 2022.[1] Shell, Chevron, ExxonMobil, Equinor, TotalEnergies and BP combined profits for that year were US$219 billion. ExxonMobil alone reported profits of US$55.7 billion.[2] All five corporations roughly doubled their earnings in 2021 and also surpassed their previous profit records by a wide margin.[3] Why is it of interest to read global humanitarian appeals and reported profits of global energy companies in conjunction? Measured by per capita earnings from crude oil production, South Sudanese and Venezuelans should be among the economically most secure people in the world, as should be the inhabitants of the oil-wealthy Niger Delta.[4] Yet, the opposite is true: they are among those who live most precariously. For these communities, their resource wealth has not translated into prosperity, but destitution.

[1] Unknown, 'Global Humanitarian Overview 2023' (Geneva, Office for the Coordination of Humanitarian Affairs). It should be noted that this number does not reflect the humanitarian needs resulting from the devastating earthquakes in Turkey and Syria on 6 February 2023.

[2] Ron Bousso, 'Big Oil doubles profits in blockbuster 2022' *Reuters* (8 February 2023).

[3] In the case of Shell by US$10 billion. See, eg: Isabeau van Halm, 'Big Oil profits soared to nearly $200bn in 2022' *Energy Monitor* (8 February 2023); Evan Halper, 'Shell adds to oil industry's record profits, with $41.6 billion' *Washington Post* (2 February 2023).

[4] In 2021, South Sudan had a population of 10.75 million and Venezuela 28.2 million people. Nigeria is a populous state with more than 213 million people, oil production however takes place first and foremost in the Niger Delta, which has somewhere between 30–40 million inhabitants. See: www.data.worldbank.org/indicator/SP.POP.TOTL?locations. 'Leading oil-producing countries worldwide in 2021' (27 February 2023), available at: www.statista.com/statistics/237115/oil-production-in-the-top-fifteen-countries-in-barrels-per-day/.

The relationship between unimaginable wealth and unspeakable misery is not unique to petro-states. The DRC is one of the resource-richest countries in the world, yet 69.7 per cent of its population lives on less than US$1.50 per day.[5] The country has significant crude oil and natural gas reserves, but its most important economic sector is mining. Diamonds and other gemstones, gold, copper, cobalt, tin, tantalum and tungsten are all found in abundance in the DRC and some are almost exclusively found there. In 2020, 69 per cent of global cobalt supplies, an essential ingredient of rechargeable batteries and indispensable to the production of portable electronic devices and green technologies, were sourced in the DRC.[6] This has, however, not only not translated to prosperity, but instead caused a great deal of grief. An estimated two million persons work in the Congolese artisanal mining sector and another 400,000 in the industrial sector.[7] *Creuseurs*, ie, artisanal miners, are the first link in global supply chains of electronic vehicles, smartphones, laptops, tablets, jewellery and other common consumer products. Many weapon system supply chains start with them as well. It is illustrative to remember that the nuclear bombs dropped on Hiroshima and Nagasaki claimed their first victims in Shinkolobwe. Just like the devastation of their explosion unfolded over generations, so did the effects of their making, with the mining communities in and around Shinkolobwe exhibiting all the symptoms associated with exposure to radioactive radiation. Once the mines in Shinkolobwe were depleted of uranium with about 3,000 tons having been shipped to the United States as part of the Manhattan Project, the still radioactive site became populated with *creuseurs* digging for cobalt and copper; 15,000 of them were counted at the site at the turn of the century.[8] Depending on the minerals and ores sourced, 10–50 per cent of all *creuseurs* are women, and child labour is rampant with roughly 50 per cent of the global supply of copper having been tainted by some form of child labour.[9]

Most *creuseurs* work without personal protective equipment. As a result, injuries are common, as is constant back and neck pain as well as headaches. Mining communities have higher rates of respiratory illnesses and cancer. Cruelly, artisanal mining without adequate protection also detrimentally affects miners' reproductive health as cobalt is not only in and of itself toxic but also commonly found in sediments that include other toxins including uranium. Exposure to these substances, not only by the *creuseurs* themselves but also through contaminations of freshwater resources and soil, causes higher rates

[5] 'Democratic Republic of Congo' (30 March 2023), available at: www.data.worldbank.org/country/congo-dem-rep.

[6] AL Gulley, 'One hundred years of cobalt production in the Democratic Republic of the Congo' (2022) 79 *Resources Policy* 1.

[7] See, eg: 'Democratic Republic of Congo: Artisanal and Small-Scale Mining Sector' (28 February 2023), available at: www.delvedatabase.org/resources/delve-country-profile-democratic-republic-of-congo.

[8] Frank Swain, 'The forgotten mine that built the atomic bomb' *BBC Future* (4 August 2020).

[9] 'DRC Country Profile' (n 7).

of miscarriage, children born with disabling differences, prematurely and/or with low birth rates. Also, gender-based discrimination characterises the mining sector with female *creuseurs* commonly being paid less for the same output. In sum, where there is precarity, there is violence. In the mining sites of the Congo, this violence is perpetuated over generations, with both the land and its people left violated and scarred once the soil is stripped of all that holds value rendering it barren, poisoned and uninhabitable. As a result, immediate or eventual displacement and erasure of local communities are inherent to the mining frenzy.[10]

Devastating human misery in the presence of immeasurable fortunes – that is the pain of plenty. Its manifestations are multi-fold. They include high rates of absolute poverty, higher likelihood of exposure to cancerous substances, higher rates of children born with physical or mental disabilities, higher rates of hunger and malnutrition, higher rates of children out of school, higher exposure to bodily harm, higher rates of forced displacement and dispossession, and finally, higher likelihood of loss of identity and eventual erasure. The pain of plenty is therefore both an immediate result of mineral resource extraction as well as of its implications for the governance and political economy at a local, regional and national scale.

Even though not termed as such, the pain of plenty has been a significant issue for international law. Earlier chapters have already engaged with some concrete legal responses to the pain of plenty including the adoption of good governance regimes such as the 'Extractive Industries Transparency Initiative', the 2016 'OECD Due Diligence Guidance for Responsible Supply Chains of Minerals from Conflict-Affected and High-Risk Areas', and the 'Kimberley Process Certification Scheme'. This chapter engages with the possibilities and pitfalls of human rights responses to the pain of plenty.[11] Such responses are varied. In terms of judicial responses, human rights courts have been used to seek redress for violations caused by state action and failures leading to human rights violations in the context of resource extraction.[12] Similarly, domestic courts have been seized with civil claims for violations of corporate due diligence and duty of care standards resulting in domestic and extraterritorial human rights violations, or, in instances of claims brought under the US 'Alien Tort Statute', for aiding and abetting grave violations of international law.[13] Efforts towards facilitating the

[10] On conditions in Congolese artisanal mining communities, see S Kara, *Cobalt Red: How the Blood of the Congo Powers our Lives* (New York, St Martin's Press, 2023).

[11] See generally: J Gilbert, *Natural Resources and Human Rights: An Appraisal* (Oxford, Oxford University Press, 2018); M-C Petersmann, *When Environmental Protection and Human Rights Collide: The Politics of Conflict Management by Regional Courts* (Cambridge, Cambridge University Press, 2022).

[12] Committee on the Rights of the Child, *Sacchi et al v Argentina et al*, Decision of 22 September 2021, Communication Nos 104/2019; 105/2019; 106/2019; 107/2019; 108/2019; European Court of Human Rights, *Greenpeace Nordic and Others v Norway*, Application of 15 June 2021, App No 34068/21.

[13] United States Court of Appeals for the Ninth Circuit, *John Doe v Unocal Corporation et al*, Settlement of 18 September 2002, 395 F.3d 932; United States Supreme Court, *Kiobel, individually*

piercing of the corporate veil to hold corporations accountable for the actions of their subsidiaries as well as for human rights violations occurring down their supply chains have resulted in the adoption of laws requiring corporations to adhere to due diligence standards in their supply chains.[14] They have also given rise to the nascent trend towards the inclusion of references to human rights in bilateral and multilateral trade and investment treaties, of either a general nature or by reference to a specific framework such as the 'OECD Guidelines for Multinational Enterprises'.[15] The frustration with the lack of accountability for corporate human rights violations motivated considerable efforts in defining the human rights obligations of business enterprises, which ultimately pursue the adoption of a binding treaty.[16] Finally, within the UN human rights mandate system the pain of plenty has received significant attention. First, UN mandate holders – including the special rapporteurs on extreme poverty, food, indigenous peoples, racial discrimination, foreign debt and a healthy environment – have sounded alarm bells.[17] Secondly, mandates pertaining directly or indirectly to the adverse effects of mineral resource extraction have been institutionalised,

and on behalf of her late husband Kiobel et al v Royal Dutch Petroleum co et al, Judgment of 17 April 2013, 569 US 108 (2013); United States Court of Appeals, District of Columbia Circuit, *DOE VIII v Exxon Mobil Corporation*, Decision of 13 September 2010, Nos 09-7125, 09-7127, 09-7134, 09-7135; Court of Appeal, The Hague, *Fidelis Ayoro Oguru et al v Shell Petroleum NV et al*, Judgment of 29 January 2021, 200.126.804 (case a); 200.126.834 (case b); The Hague District Court, *Vereniging Milieudefensie and others v Royal Dutch Shell*, Judgment of 26 May 2021, C/09/571932/HA ZA 19-379.

[14] Proposal for a Directive of the European Parliament and of the Council on Corporate Sustainability Due Diligence and amending Directive (EU) 2019/1937, 2022/0051 (COD), 23 February 2022; Gesetz über die unternehmerischen Sorgfaltspflichten in Lieferketten, BGBl. I 2021 S. 2959, 3 March 2021; Loi relative au devoir de vigilance des sociétés mères et des entreprises donneuses d'ordre, loi n° 2017-399, 27 March 2017; Modern Slavery Act, 2015 c 30, 26 March 2015.

[15] eg: see Reciprocal Investment Promotion and Protection Agreement between the Government of the Kingdom of Morocco and the Government of the Federal Republic of Nigeria, 3 December 2016, art 18; Agreement on Encouragement and Reciprocal Protection of Investments between the Kingdom of the Netherlands and the United Arab Emirates, 23 November 2013, art 2(3); Investment Cooperation and Facilitation Treaty between the Federative Republic of Brazil and the Republic of India, 25 January 2020, art 12. See also: General Assembly, Report of the Working Group on the issue of human rights and transnational corporations and other business enterprises: Human rights-compatible international investment agreements, A/76/238, 27 July 2021.

[16] JG Ruggie, *Just Business: Multinational Corporations and Human Rights* (New York, WW Norton & Company, 2013).

[17] United Nations, Human Rights Council, Global extractivism and racial equity: Report of the Special Rapporteur on contemporary forms of racism, racial discrimination, xenophobia and related intolerance, 14 May 2019; United Nations, Human Rights Council, Report of the Special Rapporteur on the rights of indigenous peoples, James Anaya: Extractive industries operating within or near indigenous territories, A/HRC/18/35, 11 July 2011; United Nations, Human Rights Council, Report on the 'just transition' in the economic recovery: eradicating poverty within planetary boundaries, A/75/181/REV.1, 9 October 2020; United Nations, General Assembly, Report of the Independent Expert on the effects of foreign debt and other related international financial obligations of States on the full enjoyment of all human rights, particularly economic, social and cultural rights, Attiya Waris, A/77/169, 15 July 2022; United Nations, General Assembly, Report of the Special Rapporteur on the situation of human rights defenders, A/71/281, 3 August 2016.

most notably those on climate change.[18] Diagonally opposed to this law-making and development dynamic is a frustration with human rights, which manifests most evidently in the cynical turn of some scholars who purport that human rights have run their course.[19] Such totalising critiques are problematic. Human rights, despite all of their shortcomings, remain a powerful discourse with counter-hegemonic potential as has been illustrated, for instance, in the context of development and climate change, but also to give meaning to war crimes, crimes against humanity and violence at a genocidal scale.[20] As such, disregarding human rights completely is a position of privilege unaffordable to those who experience the pain of plenty.[21] At the same time, the critique of human rights law and its intricate link to legitimising legally structured inequalities cannot be discounted. Such critiques have first and foremost focused on the relationship of human rights law with power and hegemony and its role in the global spread of neoliberalism.[22] It notes that human rights were, among other things, sanctifying planned misery,[23] that they were 'powerless companions' and 'not enough'[24] or 'fellow travellers'[25] to neoliberalism, or that they simply came in too late.[26] Indeed, as Baxi has pointedly noted, human rights have emerged as the only 'universal ideology' that enhances 'both the legitimisation of power and the praxis of emancipatory politics'.[27]

[18] General Assembly, Mandate of the Special Rapporteur on the promotion and protection of human rights in the context of climate change, A/HRC/RES/48/14, 13 October 2021; Also of note is the renewal of the mandate on the effects of foreign debt. See Human Rights Council, Mandate of the Independent Expert on the effects of foreign debt and other related international financial obligations of States on the full enjoyment of all human rights, particularly economic, social and cultural rights, A/HRC/RES/43/10, 29 June 2020.

[19] See, eg: S Hopgood, *The Endtimes of Human Rights* (Ithaca, NY, Cornell University Press, 2013); PB Harris, 'The Humanitarian God in the Political Marketplace' (2016) 7 *Humanity* 325.

[20] JT Gathii, 'Africa and the Radical Origins of the Right to Development' (2020) 1 *TWAIL Review* 28; P Paiement, 'Urgent agenda: how climate litigation builds transnational narratives' (2020) 11 (1–2) *Transnational Legal Theory* 121; 'Gaza: Halt the war now to save children from dying of imminent famine', available at: www.ohchr.org/en/press-releases/2024/03/gaza-halt-war-now-save-children-dying-imminent-famine-un-committee-warns; PA Agudo et al, 'Gaza: UN experts decry bombing of hospitals and schools as crimes against humanity, call for prevention of genocide' (19 October 2023), available at: www.ohchr.org/en/press-releases/2023/10/gaza-un-experts-decry-bombing-hospitals-and-schools-crimes-against-humanity.

[21] PJ Williams, 'Alchemical notes: Reconstructing ideals from deconstructed rights (1987) 22 *Harvard Civil Rights-Civil Liberties Law Review* 401.

[22] JT Gathii, 'Promise of International Law: A Third World View' (2020) 114 *Proceedings of the ASIL Annual Meeting* 165.

[23] S Marks, 'Human Rights and Root Causes' (2011) 74 *Modern Law Review* 57.

[24] S Moyn, *The Last Utopia, Human Rights in History* (Cambridge, MA, Harvard University Press, 2010); S Moyn, *Not Enough: Human Rights in an Unequal World* (Cambridge, MA, Harvard University Press, 2018).

[25] J Whyte, *The Morals of the Market: Human Rights and the Rise of Neoliberalism* (London, Verso, 2019).

[26] K McNeilly, 'Are Rights Out of Time? International Human Rights Law, Temporality, and Radical Social Change' (2018) 28 *Social & Legal Studies* 817.

[27] U Baxi, 'Voices of Suffering and the Future of Human Rights' (1998) 8 *Transnational Law & Contemporary Problems* 125, 126.

This chapter takes neo-extractivism as a point of departure to review human rights responses to the pain of plenty. Doing so permits it to complicate the power relationships, which neoliberal human rights critiques often frame as a binary relationship between global capital and subalterns, namely by reintroducing the state to the power equation. In particular, human rights critiques foregrounding the state-centrism of human rights law to explain their inaptitude to respond – let alone reverse structural inequalities – tend to neglect the central role of some governments in creating the conditions for structural inequality to fester.[28] By zooming in on the neo-extractivist state, this chapter attempts to break with the – at times caricaturist – imaginary of postcolonial and Third World states as empty vessels to neoliberalism by shifting attention to a type of statehood. This permits complicating the neoliberal connotation of structural inequality and reinvigorates the conversation on the possibilities and pitfalls of human rights.

II. NEO-EXTRACTIVISM

As described in the introductory chapters of this book, the 'resource curse' refers to problematic patterns of mineral economies, such as their vulnerability to global commodity market price fluctuations and their tendency to crowd out other sectors, such as the manufacturing and services sectors.[29] In contrast, the 'paradox of plenty' scholarship describes the corrosive effect that the presence and extraction of mineral resources may have on liberal public institutions.[30]

Drawing on both strands of scholarship, neo-extractivism has emerged as a concept that focuses on the problematic dynamic between global commodities capitalism and the mineral resources-enabled concentration of political power in the domestic sphere. Neo-extractivism seeks to explain the stagnant or even regressive development trajectories of mineral economies. Having its origins in development studies, it has been conceptualised primarily with a view to Latin American states. It purports that international trade is, among other things, premised on the exchange of natural resources for processed goods, a dynamic that it identifies as being the result of deliberate policy choices rather

[28] To this end, another helpful category has been that of the 'cunning state'. See S Randeria, 'The State of Globalization: Legal Plurality, Overlapping Sovereignties and Ambiguous Alliances between Civil Society and the Cunning State in India' (2007) 24 *Theory, Culture and Society* 1.

[29] R Auty, *Sustaining Development in Mineral Economies: The Resource Curse Thesis* (London, Routledge, 1993); JD Sachs and A Warner, 'The Big Push, Natural Resource Booms and Growth, (1999) 59 *Journal of Development Economics* 43; P Collier, *The Plundered Planet: Why We Must – and How We Can – Manage Nature for Global Prosperity* (Oxford, Oxford University Press, 2010).

[30] ML Ross, *The Oil Curse: How Petroleum Wealth Shapes the Development of Nations* (Princeton, NJ, Princeton University Press, 2012); TL Karl, *The Paradox of the Plenty: Oil Booms and Pedro States* (Berkeley, CA, University of California Press, 1997); T Mitchell, *Carbon Democracy: Political Power in the Age of Oil* (New York, Verso, 2011); P Le Billon, *Wars of Plunder: Conflicts, Profits and the Politics of Resources* (London, Hurst, 2012).

than a natural phenomenon.[31] In 1945, two-thirds of the world's petroleum was produced in the United States, but by 2020, with the United States still being the largest oil producer, this share had dropped to 20 per cent with 28 per cent then being produced by Gulf states.[32] This shift in production to the Gulf region and the Global South is the legacy of imperial and foreign mercantilist conquest, which, in the context of decolonisation and Third World Internationalism in the late 1940s to the 1970s had given rise to today's unique regime of petroleum extraction based primarily on production-sharing agreements.[33] Under these agreements, petroleum operations in Global South and Gulf states are typically operated by a consortium of state-owned and transnational enterprises, a pairing that symbolises the symbiotic relationship between transnational capital and domestic political power. The dynamic of this relationship defines neo-extractivism.

In the Latin American context, neo-extractivism is perceived to be the latest stage in the exploitation of the continent's people and resources.[34] It is thought to have taken place in two phases, namely the 'neoliberal phase' (the 1970s–2000s) and the 'reprimitisation phase', which began in the 2000s and is still ongoing. The neoliberal phase was characterised by global capitalist developmentalism that has become synonymous with the World Bank's structural adjustment programmes. In this phase, economies in Latin America and elsewhere in the Global South were disciplined by the promise of development, which would materialise through the creation of market-friendly institutions and the attraction of foreign investment. The neoliberal phase, as Slobodian points out, was, among other things, characterised by the creation of institutional conditions, including legal ones, that would permit a free market to flourish, or, as he puts it, with the 'encasement' necessary to sustain a global marketplace.[35] To give one example, while the foundations for it had been set years earlier, the development and proliferation of today's regime of foreign investment protection were accelerated in the neoliberal phase.[36] It also prepared the conditions for the reprimitisation phase which was induced by the increase in demand for mineral resources due to the spread and intensification of resource-intensive consumption patterns associated with economic development and 'the Western

[31] H Veltmeyer and JF Petras (eds), 'Introduction' in *The New Extractivism: A Post-Neoliberal Development Model or Imperialism of the Twenty-First Century?* (London, Zed Books, 2014).

[32] US EIA, 'What countries are the top producers and consumers of oil?', 11 August 2024, available at: www.eia.gov/tools/faqs/faq.php?id=709&t=6.

[33] D Lustig, *Veiled Power: International Law and the Private Corporation 1886–1981* (New York, Oxford University Press, 2020).

[34] The other stages being colonial extractivism, liberal capitalist extractivism and peripheral-Fordist extractivism. See, eg: U Brand, K Dietz and M Lang, 'Neo-Extractivism in Latin America. One Side of a New Phase of Global Capitalist Dynamics' (2016) 11 *Ciencia Política* 125, 136–41.

[35] Q Slobodian, *Globalists: The End of Empire and the Birth of Neoliberalism* (Cambridge, MA, Harvard University Press, 2018).

[36] T St John, *The Rise of Investor–State Arbitration; Politics, Law, and Unintended Consequences* (Oxford, Oxford University Press, 2018).

way of living'. Throughout the reprimitisation phase, the United States has still accounted for 20 per cent of the world's petroleum consumption but only for approximately 4 per cent of the global population. In comparison, China and India combined, which are home to 35 per cent of the global population and have rapidly growing and export-driven manufacturing sectors, have accounted for 18.8 per cent of global petroleum consumption. As a result of these developments, as well as of the financialisation of petroleum and commodities markets, the global petroleum price sky-rocketed in the early 2000s, right up into the global economic crisis of 2007/08 from which it recovered and remained relatively stable and on a high level, right up until the beginning of the COVID-19 pandemic in early 2020, when the price suddenly dropped significantly. Now, in the post-pandemic global economy, petroleum prices have again risen so significantly that they have contributed to record levels of global inflation, leading to a rise in extreme poverty.

Overall, the price development of petroleum has led to a further shift towards petroleum production in mineral economies. In 2019, 96.7 per cent of Venezuelan oil exports were petroleum products, which is a significant increase compared with 1998, when the share had been 68 per cent.[37] A similar pattern, even if a less extreme one, has been reported for Ecuador. The reprimitisation phase has brought lots of issues with it, many of which are well known by resource-curse theorists. States in which the economy has measurably shifted towards the export of mineral resources have also suffered from a loss of livelihood for those working in other sectors, as well as comparatively higher levels of inflation, which particularly affect the poor and vulnerable. So, while the GDP of a country going through the reprimitisation phase may suggest that it has enjoyed economic growth through the higher valorisation of its mineral resources, a closer look often reveals that only a very limited part of the population benefits from this growth, whereas the majority loses out. Importantly, the economic growth achieved through reprimitisation comes at the cost of ecological destruction, which is rarely considered when the success of this development model is measured. This is because environmental costs often only become visible after some time and affect people on the margins, permitting such costs to be spatially externalised and temporarily postponed.[38]

III. ILLUSTRATIONS OF THE RESPONSIVENESS TO INTERNATIONAL HUMAN RIGHTS LAW

In particular, early international human rights law had bought into the hypothesis that human development in post-colonial countries could be promoted with

[37] 'Annual Statistical Bulletin 2022: Venezuela facts and figures', 6 November 2022, available at: www.opec.org/opec_web/en/about_us/171.htm.

[38] Brand, Dietz and Lang (n 34) 136.

public revenues generated by the extraction of mineral resources. This argument was received wisdom at the United Nations from the 1950s onwards, even though it was certainly not uncontested even then.[39] Yet, despite the effectiveness of mineral resource extraction as a development model having been called into question, early cases by UN human rights treaty bodies were construed as balancing acts between the right to economic development and the protection of the cultural rights of minorities and indigenous peoples.

The Human Rights Committee decided its first communications on mineral resource extraction in indigenous territories by heavily relying on Article 27 of the International Covenant on Civil and Political Rights (ICCPR). The Article protects the rights of minorities and is therefore a collective right, but is only justiciable for individuals. In contrast, the Human Rights Committee determined that Article 1 ICCPR, which provides for the people's right to self-determination and sovereignty over their natural resources is therefore also a collective right that can be held not only by the peoples of a nation state but also by indigenous peoples, was not justiciable for individuals.[40]

The Human Rights Committee interpreted the protection of minorities as also protecting indigenous people's ways of living closely associated with their lands and resources.[41] It found the scope of this right to include that the presence of indigenous communities did not preclude extractive operations in and of themselves, as long as such operations did not interfere with the traditional lifestyle of communities to such a degree that a continuation of this lifestyle was no longer possible.[42] At the time, the Human Rights Committee considered mineral resource extraction as a means of economic development and therefore to be a matter of majoritarian collective interests, against which the interests of indigenous communities needed to be weighed. Reflecting on this point, former Human Rights Committee member Nisuko Ando noted, 'the outright refusal by a group in a given society to change its traditional way of life may hamper the economic development of the society as a whole'.[43]

The balancing act that early decisions of the Human Rights Committee thus proposed was not one between contractual or concessionary rights of extractive companies and human rights, but between the right to development exercised by the state and the cultural rights of minorities and indigenous peoples.[44] This

[39] United Nations, General Assembly, Resolution 523 (VI) Integrated Economic Development and Commercial Agreements, 12 January 1952; HW Singer, 'Economic Progress in Underdeveloped Countries' (1949) 16 *Social Research* 1; R Prebisch, 'The Economic Development of Latin America and Its Principal Problems (UNDEA, 1950).

[40] Human Rights Committee, *Lubicon Lake Band v Canada*, Decision of 26 March 1990, Communication No 167/1984.

[41] United Nations, Human Rights Committee, General Comment No 23, The Rights of Minorities (Art 27), CCPR/C/21/Rev.1/Add.5, 8 April 1994, paras 3.1., 6.1.

[42] *Lubicon Lake Band v Canada* (n 40) para 13.3.

[43] ibid, Appendix I.

[44] Human Rights Committee, *Länsman et al v Finland*, Decision of 8 November 1994, Communication No 511/1992.

balancing act has woven the extractivist development model into the fabric of international human rights jurisprudence, permitting the pain of plenty to be construed as a minority rights issue and as the natural cost of the promise of overall better human rights outcomes for the nation state as a whole.[45] This is a legacy that human rights law responses to the pain of plenty still struggle to overcome. Overcoming it requires reversing the assumption that, under a fictional normal state, resource extraction is beneficial to the overall state of human rights, and that only under irregular conditions is this not the case. In turn, achieving this requires unbinding human rights from the promise of capitalist modernity, a linkage which is commonly seen as being inherent to human rights law rather than a result of its appropriation.

The argument here is not that indigenous, peasant, tribal and other minorities do not particularly suffer from the pain of plenty, nor to suggest that they do not require special protection. Rather, it is to argue that in the context of extractivism, the interests of minorities are not in a conflicting relationship with majoritarian interests, but a harmonious one. When a state permits the violation of indigenous rights through resource extraction, it does not serve its population, but rather corporate, consumer and shareholder interests, oftentimes spacially far removed from its territory and with the social and ecological costs that it bears over time far outweighing the profit that resource extraction generates in the present.[46]

The tenuous relationship between indigenous rights, and those construed as majoritarian, is woven into the indigenous rights regime itself. The ILO Indigenous and Tribal Peoples Convention and the UN Declaration on Indigenous Peoples protect the special relationship of such communities with their lands. Under the UN Declaration, indigenous people have the right to their archaeological and historical sites and it envisions redress mechanisms in case of violations of that right.[47] It also recognises the significance of including indigenous people in decision-making processes and of their consent to any activity conducted on these territories. In contrast, the 1987 ILO Convention stipulates that if the state retained ownership of mineral and sub-surface resources, extractive operations could be carried out, as long as the state consulted concerned communities, compensated damages resulting from such operations, and offered an equitable share of the profits to affected communities.[48]

[45] Pillars of liberal development theory include, eg: WW Rostow, *The Stages of Economic Growth: A Non-Communist Manifesto* (Cambridge, Cambridge University Press, 1960); W Brandt et al, 'North – South: A Programme for Survival' (1980) Independent Commission on International Development Issues.

[46] J Dehm, 'The Temporalities of Environmental Human Rights' in K McNeilly and B Warwick (eds), *The Times and Temporalities of International Human Rights Law* (Oxford, Hart Publishing, 2022).

[47] United Nations, OHCHR, Declaration on the Rights of Indigenous Peoples, A/RES/61/295, 3 September 2007, Art 11.

[48] International Labour Organization, Indigenous and Tribal Populations Convention, C107, 26 June 1957, Art 15(2).

Set against this backdrop, the development of the Inter-American human rights bodies' 'right to communal property' and '*vida digma*' doctrines, have certainly helped to strengthen the indigenous rights regime in innovative ways, namely by reinterpreting a human right intricately linked to capitalism through a communal lens, and by reading a civil right – the right to life – through a socio-economic one.[49] Building on the right to private property,[50] the doctrine of the right to communal property acknowledges the special relationship of indigenous and tribal communities with their lands and natural resources.[51] The first decision to develop it was the 2001 *Case of the Mayagna (Sumo) Awas Tingni Community v Nicaragua*, where the Court found that property should be interpreted with due regard to the cultural context and that therefore the indigenous understanding of communal property rather than the conception of property as an entitlement of individuals should be applied.[52] The right to communal property not only entails the right to land but also to all subsoil resources.[53] Since then, the Court has gone on to acknowledge that 'human rights treaties are living instruments' that must evolve to reflect 'current living conditions'. Thus, under the rules of interpretation laid down in Article 29(d) of the Inter-American Court of Human Rights and Article 31 of the Vienna Convention on the Law of Treaties, the Court interpreted the right of property in light of the indigenous rights regime.[54] It defined the scope of indigenous the right to communal property to give peoples who had traditionally possessed the land, legal ownership over it, which entails the official recognition and registration of their ownership as a collective title by the state.[55] At the same time, even this remarkably progressive judicial doctrine has its limits. Even under this

[49] On the significance of the progressive Inter-American human rights jurisprudence, see G Pentassuglia, 'Towards a Jurisprudential Articulation of Indigenous Land Rights' (2011) 22 *European Journal of International Law* 165; J Auz, 'Human rights-based climate litigation: A Latin American cartography' (2022) 13 *Journal of Human Rights and the Environment* 114.

[50] Art XXIII, American Declaration of the Rights and Duties of Men. See also: 'Indigenous and Tribal Peoples' Rights over their Ancestral Lands and Natural Resources, Norms and Jurisprudence of the Inter-American Human Rights System' (Inter-American Commission on Human Rights, 2009).

[51] For a concise definition of the right to communal property, see EA Daes, 'Prevention of Discrimination and Protection of Indigenous Peoples, Indigenous Peoples' Permanent Sovereignty over Natural Resources' (Commission on Human Rights, 2004) para 40.

[52] Inter-American Court of Human Rights, *Case of the Mayagna (Sumo) Awas Tingni Community v Nicaragua*, Judgment on Merits, Reparations and Costs of 31 August 2001. See also: Inter-American Court of Human Rights, *Case of the Yakye Axa Indigenous Community v Paraguay*, Judgment on Merits, Reparations and Costs of 17 June 2005.

[53] Inter-American Court of Human Rights, *Case of the Saramaka People v Suriname*, Judgment on Merits, Reparations and Costs of 28 November 2007, Series C No 172.

[54] Inter-American Court of Human Rights, *Case of the Kichwa Indigenous people of Sarayaku v Equador*, Judgment on Merits and Reparations of 27 June 2012, Series C No 245.

[55] *Case of the Mayagna (Sumo) Awas Tingni Community v Nicaragua* (n 52) paras 101, 51, 64; Inter-American Court of Human Rights, *Sawhoyamaxa Indigenous Community v Paraguay*, Judgment on Merits, Reparations and Costs of 29 May 2006; *Case of the Saramaka People v Suriname* (n 53) para 194.

doctrine, the involuntary loss of indigenous territories by the legitimate transferral to 'innocent third parties' can be compensated not only by the recovery of such lands but also by the provision of other lands of the same size and quality.[56] In its decision on the Saramaka People, the Court specified the criteria for legitimately restricting the right to property for resource extraction purposes. It elaborated that the granting of resource exploitation concessions in indigenous territories required the effective participation of the concerned community in a development, investment, exploration and extraction plan. Furthermore, 'independent and technically capable entities' were to conduct environmental and social impact assessments. Finally, indigenous communities were to benefit equitably from the profit generated by resource extraction.[57]

Under African human rights law, human rights violations resulting from resource extraction are similarly construed as an issue isolated to local communities and indigenous peoples, rather than a structural human rights problem. For instance, in a case concerning the eviction of the Ogiek people from their lands in the Mau Forest, the African Court of Human Rights found clearly and decisively in favour of indigenous land rights, acknowledging however that such rights could be restricted for public purposes, if such restrictions were necessary and proportional, once consultations with affected communities had been undertaken.[58] Of particular interest here, is the Court's rationale concerning the people's right of free disposal over natural wealth and resources. The Court noted that while this right – like the rights to economic self-determination and sovereignty over natural resources – was primarily intended to protect against foreign occupation and dispossession, it found that it could nonetheless also be invoked internally against any deprivation from free access to food crops and other resources.[59]

Some have argued that human rights law, despite its liberal undercurrent and the resulting emphasis on the rights of the individual, its limited enforceability, and limited applicability to businesses, particularly transnational corporations, is amenable enough to address systemic human rights violations, resulting from government failures to enact and enforce policy, which would prevent such violations from occurring at a massive scale.[60] A milestone decision in this debate has been the famous 2001 Ogoni decision by the African Commission on Human

[56] *Sawhoyamaxa Indigenous Community v Paraguay* (n 55) paras 128–30; *Case of the Saramaka People v Suriname* (n 53).

[57] *Case of the Saramaka People v Suriname* (n 53) para 129.

[58] African Court of Human Rights, *African Commission on Human and Peoples' Rights v Kenya*, Judgment of 26 May 2017, App No 006/2012.

[59] ibid, paras 195–201.

[60] Heri has made this argument for the European human rights law regime, by arguing that the Court's doctrine of affording special protection to the vulnerable should be extended to those who suffer the most from climate change: C Heri, 'Climate Change before the European Court of Human Rights: Capturing Risk, Ill-Treatment and Vulnerability' (2022) 33 *European Journal of International Law* 925.

and Peoples' Rights.[61] The communication alleged, among other things, that the exploitation of petroleum by a consortium formed by a Nigerian state-owned company and Shell Petroleum resulted in many avoidable oil spills, causing severe ecological damage. The Commission sided with the applicants and in so doing decisively moved the adverse impacts of resource extraction beyond the scope of cultural rights in finding that Nigeria had violated the right to freedom from discrimination to life to property, to health, to family life, to the free disposal of wealth and natural resources and to a satisfactory environment.[62] With the decision's findings on the involvement of public security forces in the commission of grave human rights violations under the direction of a transnational corporation setting the stage for milestone cases against the Shell corporation, the decision's remarkable findings on state obligations have been somewhat overlooked.[63] The Commission affirmed the state obligation to respect the collective right of a people to the free use of their natural resources as an exercise of their right to permanent sovereignty over their natural resources.[64] Whereas this reasoning has so far been interpreted as a strengthening of the right to free and prior informed consent, in light of the pain of plenty and the well-documented likelihood of sights of resource extraction becoming 'sacrifice zones', one could also read the Commission's reasoning as a default assumption of the right to non-use. To this end, the Commission noted that state obligations include protecting from political, economic and social interferences as part of the enjoyment of human rights.[65]

One effect of the argumentative structure, which frames the pain of plenty as an issue that can be remedied by appropriate safeguard measures to prevent it from affecting distinguishable groups of vulnerable people, is that this has triggered significant legalisation and law-making developments.[66] To illustrate this point, two of such processes, namely the greening of human rights, as well as

[61] African Commission on Human and Peoples' Rights, *The Social and Economic Rights Action Center and the Center for Economic and Social Rights v Nigeria*, Decision of 27 May 2002, Communication No 155/96.

[62] ibid, paras 10, 68.

[63] See, eg: *Fidelis Ayoro Oguru et al v Shell Petroleum NV et al* (n 13); UK Supreme Court, *Okpabi and others v Royal Dutch Shell PIC and another*, Judgment of 12 February 2021, [2021] UKSC 3; *Kiobel, individually and on behalf of her late husband Kiobel et al v Royal Dutch Petroleum co et al* (n 13).

[64] *The Social and Economic Rights Action Center and the Center for Economic and Social Rights v Nigeria* (n 61) para 46.

[65] ibid, para 47.

[66] On corruption, see generally: 'Extractive Industries Transparency Initiative (EITI)', 19 April 2023, available at: www.eiti.org; On conflict prevention, see generally: International Conference on the Great Lakes Region, Protocol Against the Illegal Exploitation of Natural Resources; Nagoya Protocol on Access to Genetic Resources and the Fair and Equitable Sharing of Benefits Arising from their Utilization to the Convention on Biodiversity; 'Toolkit and Guidance for Preventing and Managing Land and Natural Resources Conflict' (United Nations and European Union, 2012); Kimberley Process Certification Scheme; R177 – Chemicals Recommendation.

the introduction of human rights norms in transnational law, will be presented in the following two sections.

A. The Right to a Healthy Environment

As mentioned in chapter two, section VI of this book, both the artisanal and industrial extraction of mineral resources are harmful to nature. To give one example, the practice of introducing hydrochloric acid to increase the soil's porosity as well as the injection of steam and onsite burning to increase the oil's viscosity damage soil and subsoil formations while the toxic waste water produced through such practices contaminates freshwater systems. The environmental degradation that results from such practices affects the enjoyment of numerous human rights in various ways. To give just one example, the use of hazardous substances and unsound waste management has been found to violate, among other things, the human rights to property, culture, health, life, food and water.[67] The varied nature of human rights violations that result from environmental degradation, and destruction by mineral resource extraction, has significantly contributed to the development of the human right to a 'clean, healthy and sustainable' environment. This right was explicitly recognised by the Human Rights Council in 2021.[68] Yet, it existed long before in regional human rights law, international environmental law and international development law, as well as in domestic constitutional law.[69] The first recognition of this right in international development law dates back to the 1972 Stockholm Declaration (principle 2) and the 1992 Rio Declaration (principle 1).[70] It is recognised in Inter-American, African and Arab human rights instruments, as well as by members of the Association of Southeast Asian Nations (ASEAN).[71] In the European context, the absence of the right to a healthy environment from the original canon of human rights law has in part been rectified through

[67] United Nations, Human Rights Council, Report of the Special Rapporteur on the human rights obligations related to environmentally sound management and disposal of hazardous substances and waste, C Georgescu, A/HRC/21/48, 2 July 2012; United Nations, General Assembly, Report of the Special Rapporteur on the implications for human rights of the environmentally sound management and disposal of hazardous substances and wastes: The impact of toxic substances on the human rights of indigenous peoples, A/77/183, 28 July 2022.

[68] United Nations, Human Rights Council, Resolution 48/13, The human right to a clean, healthy and sustainable environment, A/HRC/RES/48/13, 18 October 2021.

[69] According to a path-breaking study, 155 states recognise some form of the right to a healthy environment in their constitutions. See: DR Boyd, *The Environmental Rights Revolution: A Global Study of Constitutions, Human Rights, and the Environment* (Vancouver, UBC Press, 2011).

[70] For a detailed chronology of the development of this right, see: Gilbert (n 11) 179–58.

[71] Additional Protocol to the American Convention on Human Rights in the Area of Economic, Social and Cultural Rights, Art 11; African Charter on Human and Peoples' Rights, Art 24; Arab Charter on Human Rights; ASEAN Human Rights Declaration, Art 28(f).

jurisprudential norm development, primarily under the Convention's right to private and family life.[72]

Inter-American jurisprudence has been particularly illuminating concerning the normative content of this right.[73] To that end, it identifies several state obligations that result from this right. One obligation is to guarantee a healthy environment suitable for human life on a non-discriminatory basis, including by providing basic public services. Another is to promote environmental protection and conservation. Framing it in analogy to, but not as an economic and cultural right, inter-American human rights jurisprudence identifies availability, accessibility, sustainability, acceptability and adaptability as necessary conditions for the enjoyment of this right, while at the same time accepting that evaluating whether or not this right is violated requires applying criteria for environmental soundness including: atmospheric conditions, quality and sufficiency of water sources, air and soil quality; adequate waste management; energy resources; and the protection of biodiversity and forestry resources.[74] In 2024, the Inter-American Court of Human Rights decided a landmark case on human rights violations resulting from heavy metal contamination through copper mining where, among other things, it found that the right to a healthy environment had been violated.[75]

With its internationalisation and growing use by human rights bodies, the right to a healthy environment as a clear example of an anthropocentric approach to the protection of nature, has been subjected to a lot of critical scrutiny. Critics have rightfully pointed out that this approach values and protects nature only to

[72] European Court of Human Rights, *López Ostra v Spain*, Judgment of 9 December 1994, App No 16798/90; European Court of Human Rights, *Case of Guerra and Others v Italy*, 19 Febuary 1998; European Court of Human Rights, *Case of Ledyayeva, Dobrokhotova, Zolotareva and Romashina v Russia*, Judgment of 26 October 2006, App Nos 53157/99, 53247/99, 53695/00 and 56850/00; European Court of Human Rights, *Taskin and Others v Turkey*, Judgment of 4 March 2004, App No 46117/99; European Court of Human Rights, *Tatar v Romania*, Judgment of 27 January 2009, App No 3675/04; European Court of Human Rights, *Di Sarno and Others v Italy*, Judgment of 10 January 2012, App No 30765/08. The 2000 EU Charter on Fundamental Rights contains a reference to the protection of the natural environment, albeit under the premise of the objective of sustainable development. See Art 37 Charter of Fundamental Rights of the European Union.

[73] Inter-American Court of Human Rights, *Advisory Opinion on the Interpretation of Article 1(1), 4(1) and 5(1) of the American Convention on Human Rights*, Advisory Opinion of 15 November 2017, OC-23/17.

[74] Inter-American Court of Human Rights, *The Environment and Human Rights (State Obligations in relation to the environment in the context of the protection and guarantee of the rights to life and to personal integrity: Interpretation and scope of Articles 4(1) and 5(1) in relation to Articles 1(1) and 2 of the American Convention on Human Rights)*, Advisory Opinion of 17 November 2017, OC-23/17.

[75] Inter-American Court of Human Rights, *Case of the Inhabitants of La Oroya v Peru*, Judgment of 23 November 2023, Petition 1473-06; For a comment, see Thalia Viveros-Uehara, 'La Oroya and Inter-American Innovations on the Right to a Healthy Environment' (*Verfassungsblog*, 16 May 2024), available at: verfassungsblog.de/la-oroya-and-inter-american-innovations-on-the-right-to-a-healthy-environment/.

the extent that it serves humankind.[76] On this matter, the Inter-American Court of Human Rights, referencing cases by Columbian,[77] Ecuadorian[78] and Indian[79] courts, has observed that:

> [A]s an autonomous right, the right to a healthy environment, unlike other rights, protects the components of the environment, such as forests, rivers and seas, as legal interests in themselves, even in the absence of the certainty or evidence of a risk to individuals. This means that it protects nature and the environment, not only because of the benefits they provide to humanity or the effects that their degradation may have on other human rights, such as health, life or personal integrity, but because of their importance to the other living organisms with which we share the planet that also merit protection in their own right.[80]

While this reconciliation of the rights of nature doctrines emerging from the Global South with the human right to a healthy environment is promising, the uptake of this particular interpretation of this right by other legal systems, including those in the Global North, remains to be seen. Overall, the 'greening of human rights', ie, the use of human rights to protect the natural environment, is one of the most dynamic fields of international law, and as such an important means to make up for the limited justiciability of most environmental law regimes. This is also evidenced by the surge in climate litigation.[81]

At the same time, the multiple forms of violence that mineral resource extraction produces, and the resulting difficulties of framing them in traditional human rights terms, have led to the jurisprudential creation of what one may refer to as composite rights, such as the *vida digma* doctrine, or the right to communal property. The Inter-American *vida digma* doctrine interprets the right to life as encompassing more than the protection from being arbitrarily killed, to also include the protection from any interference by the

[76] See, eg: U Natarajan, 'Who Do We Think We Are? Human Rights in a Time of Ecological Change' in J Dehm and U Natarajan (eds), *Locating Nature: Making and Unmaking International Law* (Cambridge, Cambridge University Press, 2022); A Grear, 'Deconstructing Anthropos: A Critical Legal Reflection on "Anthropocentric, Law and Anthropocene, Humanity"' (2015) 26 *Law and Critique* 225.

[77] Constitutional Court of Columbia, *Atrato River*, Decision of 16 November 2016, T-622/16.

[78] Constitutional Court of Ecuador, *Judgment No 218-15-SEP-CC*, Judgment of 9 July 2015, Case No 1281-12-EP.

[79] High Court of Uttarakhand, *Lalit Miglani v State of Uttarakhand & others*, Order of 30 March 2017, App. No. CLMA 3003/17.

[80] *Advisory Opinion on the Interpretation of Article 1(1), 4(1) and 5(1) of the American Convention on Human Rights*, para 62; see also: Inter-American Court of Human Rights, *Case of Indigenous Communities Members of the Lhaka Association Habitat v Argentina*, Judgment of 6 February 2020.

[81] P Dupuy and JE Viñuales, *International Environmental Law* (Cambridge, Cambridge University Press, 2018), 297 ff; Dutch Supreme Court, *Netherlands v Stichtig Urgenda*, Judgment of 20 December 2019, ECLI:NL:HR:2019:2006; Bundesverfassungsgericht, *BVerfG, Beschluss des Ersten Senats vom 24. März 2021*, 1 BvR 2656/18 -, Rn. 1-270; European Court of Human Rights, *Duarte Agostinho and Others v Portugal and 32 Other Member States*, Complaint of 9 February 2020, App No 39371/20.

state, or non-state actors, with the socio-economic conditions that sustain a life in dignity.[82]

The right to communal property acknowledges the special relationship of indigenous and tribal communities with their lands and natural resources as being distinct from the conceptions of property.[83] Using the right to private property[84] as a starting point, the Inter-American Court of Human Rights acknowledged that the conception of property was contingent on cultural context and that an indigenous conception of communal property should therefore also be protected under human rights law.[85] The Court further specified that the right to communal property also entailed the right to sovereignty over natural resources, including subsoil resources.[86] Despite this progressive norm development, the Court – not unlike the Human Rights Committee in its early decision on indigenous rights in the context of resource extraction – specified that the right to communal property could be restricted for such purposes, as long as concerned communities participated in the planning of such operations, social and environmental impact assessments were undertaken, and communities equitably benefited from the profits generated.[87] So, despite the undeniably innovative reconceptualisation of traditional property rights, the long-standing tradition of constructing a balancing act between corporate interests – constructed as majoritarian development imperative – and indigenous interest – constructed as minoritarian and conservatory – persists. In sum, despite the doctrinal developments designed to capture the harm done to local communities and nature by the extraction of mineral resources, more often than not economic interests take the front seat, which is why in parallel with the environmentalisation of human rights, attempts to infuse economic law regimes – particularly the regime governing the protection of foreign investment with human rights – have been pursued. These efforts are the subject of the following section.

B. Bringing Human Rights to Economic Governance

As early as 1998, Baxi diagnosed how the state-centric human rights model of the Universal Declaration of Human Rights had been supplanted by a

[82] Inter-American Court of Human Rights, *Case of the 'Street Children' (Villagran-Morales et al) v Guatemala*, Judgment on Merits of 19 November 1999. See generally: JM Pasqualucci, 'The Right to a Dignified Life (Vida Digna): The Integration of Economic and Social Rights with Civil and Political Rights in the Inter-American Human Rights System' (2008) 31 *Hastings International and Comparative Law Review* 1.

[83] Daes (n 51).

[84] Art 21, American Convention on Human Rights; Art XXIII, American Declaration of the Rights and Duties of Men.

[85] *Case of the Mayagna (Sumo) Awas Tingni Community v Nicaragua* (n 52) para 149. See: *Case of the Yakye Axa Indigenous Community v Paraguay* (n 52) para 137; *Case of the Saramaka People v Suriname* (n 53) para 115.

[86] *Case of the Saramaka People v Suriname* (n 53) para 118.

[87] ibid, para 129.

market-friendly human rights paradigm. Under this new model, the state's role in the equilibrium of the social order was reduced to guaranteeing minimum human rights standards, thereby curtailing its redistributive function in the name of freedom. What made this model of human rights market friendly is that it is not only permissive of, but also supportive of, corporate globalisation, namely by legitimising public deregulation, denationalisation and disinvestment. Yet, as Baxi also notes, 'the program of rolling back the state aims at the same time at vigorous state action when the interests of global capital are at stake'. On this matter he argues that, 're-distribution signifies not the end of the nation state but the end of the redistributionist state'.[88] Today, this observation would likely require another qualifier. The market-friendly liberal human rights paradigm does promote redistribution by the state, namely redistribution from the public to the private and from the masses to the elites. The regime of foreign investment law is a prime example of this distributional dynamic. Arbitral awards reached under the rules of bilateral or multilateral investment treaties have, in the past, worsened rather than ameliorated the pain of plenty.[89] The regime of foreign investment protection as it has emerged since the late 1950s is under immense pressure and is now widely considered to be an illegitimate means of disciplining political economies in the interests of global capital at the expense of local populations.[90] In the context of extractive companies, few disputes have triggered as much public outrage as the fruitless efforts of Ecuador to hold the American transnational oil company Chevron accountable for its gross negligence in the petroleum operations its subsidiary conducted in the Latin American country since the 1960s. These operations have resulted in severe and irreversible harm to nature in indigenous territories and beyond. Following almost two decades of transnational litigation, as well as litigation in various domestic courts, Chevron has not yet been held accountable, with an arbitral award nullifying the decisions by Ecuadorian courts ordering it to pay US$9.51 billion in damages.[91]

In response to outcomes such as this, but also to address the ever-growing number of critics who point out that the regime of foreign investment was favouring corporate interests at the expense of environmental imperatives and human

[88] Baxi (n 27) 163–64. See also: N Bhuta, 'Recovering Social Rights' in Nehal Bhuta (ed), *Human Rights in Transition* (Oxford University Press 2024) 1.

[89] ICSID, *ConocoPhillips Petrozuata et al v Bolivarian Republic of Venezuela*, Award of 3 September 2013, ARB/07/30; ICSID, *Tethyan Copper Company Pty Limited v Islamic Republic of Pakistan*, Award of 12 July 2019, ARB/12/1; ICSID, *Unión Fenosa Gas, SA v Arab Republic of Egypt*, Award of 31 August 2018, ARB/14/4.

[90] See, eg: NM Perrone, *Investment Treaties and the Legal Imagination: How Foreign Investors Play By Their Own Rules* (New York, Oxford University Press, 2021); St John (n 36).

[91] See generally: Business and Human Rights Resource Centre, 'Texaco/Chevron lawsuits (re Ecuador)', 4 March 2022, available at: www.business-humanrights.org/en/latest-news/texacochevron-lawsuits-re-ecuador-1./. See also: L Pellegrini et al, 'International Investment Agreements, Human Rights, and Environmental Justice: The Texaco/Chevron Case From the Ecuadorian Amazon' (2020) 23 *Journal of International Economic Law* 455.

rights,[92] some efforts have been undertaken to include human rights clauses in investment agreements. To this date, only very few such explicit clauses exist and even fewer have already been adopted or ratified. For instance, Article 24 of the 2018 draft Pan-African Investment Code, spells out principles for business ethics that investors should abide by, including the respect for 'internationally recognized human rights'. The much-noted 2016 Morocco–Nigeria BIT, which has not yet been ratified by Nigeria, includes a provision on human rights, but one which is addressed to each State Party, namely that they should 'ensure that their laws, policies and actions are consistent with the international human rights agreements'.[93] The treaty also includes a provision explicitly designed to preserve the regulatory discretion of each party on environmental matters, as well as the right to take non-discriminatory action against companies violating environmental laws and policies as well as prosecutorial action against perpetrators of environmental crimes.[94] The treaty specifies two sets of investor duties, namely the duty to abide by the precautionary principle entailing also the duty to conduct social and environmental impact assessments, as well as the duty not to engage in bribery of public officials.[95] These examples are still rare instances where human rights and environmental provisions have found their way into the text of an international investment agreement.[96] On occasion, investment tribunals have relied on international human rights law as part of the body of law applicable to a dispute. This, however, has not always worked in favour of the host state and its people, as tribunals have also relied on human rights law to find in favour of the foreign investor, as has happened in the case of the Pezgold arbitration.[97]

In sum, there is little evidence yet that the international law of foreign investment can be recalibrated through the explicit inclusion of human rights clauses, or the reliance on human rights treaties in a manner that would address the structural inequality of the resource curse.[98] On the contrary, as Broude and Henckels have shown, investment tribunals interpret investor rights as endowments to put them above human rights claims, which such tribunals often consider to be mere aspirations.[99] In sum, there are very valid concerns, not only whether

[92] See, eg: T Hahn and C Gschwendtner, 'Protest gegen TTIP und Ceta: "Am Montag, liebe SPD, wollen wir Euch kämpfen sehen"' *Süddeutsche Zeitung* (17 September 2016).

[93] Reciprocal Investment Promotion and Protection Agreement between the Government of the Kingdom of Morocco and the Government of the Federal Republic of Nigeria, 3 December 2016, Art 15, para 6.

[94] ibid, Art 13.

[95] ibid, Arts 14 and 17.

[96] M Krajewski, 'A Nightmare or a Noble Dream? Establishing Investor Obligations Through Treaty-Making and Treaty-Application' (2020) 5 *Business and Human Rights Journal* 105.

[97] N Tzouvala, 'Invested in Whiteness: Zimbabwe, the von Pezgold arbitration, and the question of race in international law (2002) 22 *Journal of Law and Political Economy* 226.

[98] D Atanasova, 'Non-economic disciplines still take the back seat: The tale of conflict clauses in investment treaties' (2021) 34 *Leiden Journal of International Law* 155.

[99] T Broude and C Henckels, 'Not all rights are created equal' (2021) 34 *Leiden Journal of International Law* 93.

international arbitration was a suitable forum to address ecological and social justice concerns, but also a sparse uptake of human rights clauses in investment treaties. In contrast, states have in some instances selected to withdraw from treaty regimes containing investment arbitration clauses altogether as has been the case for the Energy Charter Treaty.[100]

In comparison, efforts to seize courts in the home states of the foreign corporation have been more successful. US courts have been seized particularly often, and, as shown in chapter five, this has had some success in connection with international financial institutions. With the United States being the home state of some of the world's largest mineral resources corporations, and the only legal system which provides for corporate criminal liability as well as for civil liability for grave violations of international law under its Alien Tort Statute (ATS), this seemed promising at first.[101] Yet the initial optimism surrounding possibilities of holding extractive corporations accountable under the ATS have dampened over the years due to its restrictive interpretation by the US Supreme Court.[102]

In contrast, British and Dutch courts have shown more willingness to hold parent companies in their jurisdiction accountable for human rights violations caused by their subsidiaries abroad. In the United Kingdom, two landmark judgments, namely the 2019 *Vedanta* and the 2021 *Okpabi* judgments by the British Supreme Court widened British courts' jurisdictional scope on hearing cases regarding parent companies' civil liability for breaching their duty of care towards their subsidiaries.[103] Both cases concerned environmental degradation and destruction caused by the activities of extractive companies, which resulted in the loss of property and livelihood for local populations. Rather than alleging complicity in grave breaches of human rights, as had been the case for the applications filed in the United States, under the ATS claimants in these British cases alleged violations of the parent companies' duty of care towards their subsidiaries, translating human rights violations into violations of domestic tort law.[104]

[100] Italy, France, Germany, Poland and Luxembourg have already withdrawn from this treaty and the Netherlands, Slovenia, Spain, Denmark, Ireland, Portugal and the European Union have announced their intention to withdraw: 'EU withdrawal from the Energy Charter Treat', 8 August 2024, available at: www.europarl.europa.eu/thinktank/en/document/EPRS_BRI(2023)754632.

[101] See also: TL Putnam, *Courts without Borders: Law, Politics, and US Extraterritoriality* (Cambridge, Cambridge University Press, 2016) 202–54.

[102] *Kiobel, individually and on behalf of her late husband Kiobel et al v Royal Dutch Petroleum co et al* (n 13); US Supreme Court, *Joseph Jesner et al v Arab Bank, PLC*, Opinion of 24 April 2018, No 16-499; US Supreme Court, *Neste USA, Inc, v John Doe I et al & Cargill, Inc v John Doe I et al*, Opinion of 17 June 2021, Nos 19–416 and 19–453; See also: United States Court of Appeals, Ninth Circuit, *Bowoto v Chevron Corp*, Opinion of 10 September 2010, No 09-15641.

[103] *Okpabi and others v Royal Dutch Shell Plc and another* (n 63); UK Supreme Court, *Vedanta Resources PLC and another v Lungowe and others*, Judgment of 10 April 2019, [2019] UKSC 20.

[104] E Aristova, 'Okpabi v Shell in the Supreme Court: Limits of civil liability of the UK parent companies for overseas environmental pollution' *Ardea International* (2020), available at: www.ardeainternational.com/thinking/okpabi-v-shell-in-the-supreme-court-limits-of-civil-liability-of-the-uk-parent-companies-for-overseas-environmental-pollution/.

In the Netherlands, too, courts found that the breach of the duty of care by the Nigerian subsidiary of Royal Dutch Shell could be attributed to the parent company.[105] In 2021, Shell settled the law suit by paying US$15 million in damages, which represented a fraction of the estimated costs of rehabilitating ecosystems in the Niger Delta.[106] In addition, the District Court of the Hague rendered another landmark judgment, which was the first to conceptualise of the grave responsibility that mineral resource extraction companies bear for climate change. In 2021, the Court – interpreting the corporate duty of care through the lens of human rights of present and future generations of Dutch people – ordered the Shell corporation to reduce its global carbon dioxide emissions by 45 per cent by 2030 compared with its 2010 levels, and to be carbon neutral by 2050.[107] Whereas this judgment is still under appeal, it does provide an innovative model for reconceiving of ideas of development and modernity in human rights within planetary boundaries.[108]

In any event, extending the corporate duty of care beyond the territorial boundaries of the home state, and to the conduct of its subsidiaries and even down the supply chain, has made its way from jurisprudence to explicit legislation, namely in the form of supply chain laws, as they have been adopted in many jurisdictions in the Global North over the past years. While many of them emphasise labour standards rather than the protection of nature, or the safeguarding of communal property, or resource sovereignty, these laws, while not being apt to prevent the pain of plenty, may come to serve some remedial function.

IV. CONCLUSION

The logic of improvement by modern development remains a serious challenge for addressing the pain of plenty through human rights. It permits for resource extraction to be associated with improved material conditions for some, and better human rights futures for all.[109] Efforts to bring environmental concerns to the field of human rights and human rights concerns to the field of economic governance, despite having gained considerable traction over the past years, have so far fallen short of unlinking extractivist development models from social

[105] The Hague Court of Appeal, *Fields Ayoro Oguru et al v Shell Petroleum NV*, 29 January 2021, 200.126.804; 200.126.834.

[106] 'Nigeria: Shell settles lawsuit in the Netherlands for €15 million over oil spillages in Niger Delta', 11 August 2024, available at: www.business-humanrights.org/en/latest-news/nigeria-shell-settles-lawsuit-in-the-netherlands-for-15-million-over-oil-spillages-in-niger-delta/.

[107] *Vereniging Milieudefensie and others v Royal Dutch Shell* (n 13).

[108] See also: A/75/181/REV.1.

[109] For foundational critiques of the ideas of development and modernity, see: B Latour, *We Have Never Been Modern* (Cambridge, MA, Harvard University Press, 1993); A Escobar, 'Construction Nature: Elements for a Post-Structuralist Political Ecology' (1996) 28 *Futures* 325; JW Moore, *Capitalism in the Web Of Life: Ecology and the Accumulation of Capital* (London, Verso, 2016).

and economic progress. This is in part due to well-established shortcomings of liberal human rights law, such as their focus on individual, rather than communal rights, their state-centricity and their limited enforceability, but even more so due to the inability of human rights as a dominant epistemology for moral values to break down the multiple form of visible and invisible violence associated with the pain of plenty in human rights terms.

Whereas the critique for international law's role in the production of structural inequalities, and structural violence such as the pathology of plenty, had long been limited to economic regimes such as development finance, trade and investment, human rights law too has been subjected to significant critical scrutiny over the last 15 years.[110] Human rights have been described as 'powerless companions' and 'fellow travelers' to neoliberalism.[111] They have been said to have run their course and accused of being 'part of the problem'.[112]

This has not stopped courts and legal experts from recalibrating human rights law as this chapter has shown.[113] Yet, partly in response to such critiques, some scholars have begun to foreground what can be achieved with human rights beyond their strictly legal outcomes.[114] Using ethnographic methodology, and focusing on the authority of human rights as a legal vocabulary, such work sees human rights as a technique to give demands for justice more traction than they would have had if they were not phrased in human rights terms.[115] A different strand of scholarship foregrounds that the incremental change that has been achieved was moved by human rights epistemologies from the Global South,

[110] P Alston, 'The Myopia of the Handmaidens: International Lawyers and Globalization' (1997) 8 *European Journal of International Law* 435; M Sornarajah, *The International Law on Foreign Investment* (Cambridge, Cambridge University Press, 2021); A Anghie, 'International Financial Institutions' in C Reus-Smit (ed), *The Politics of International Law* (New York, Cambridge University Press, 2004); G Marceau, 'WTO Dispute Settlement and Human Rights' (2002) 13 *European Journal of International Law* 753.

[111] S Moyn, 'A Powerless Companion: Human Rights in the Age of Neoliberalism' (2014) 77 *Law and Contemporary Problems* 147; Whyte (n 25).

[112] D Kennedy, 'International Human Rights Movement: Part of the Problem?' (2002) 15 *Harvard Human Rights Journal* 101; R Kapur, *Gender, Alterity and Human Rights: Freedom in a Fishbowl* (Cheltenham, Edward Elgar, 2018).

[113] One concrete example of this pattern is a 2020 thematic report of the Special Rapporteur on the rights to food: United Nations, General Assembly, Special Rapporteur on the rights to food: Report on the right to food in the context of international trade law and policy, A/75/219, 22 July 2020. This report describes the structural inequality of global food systems in human rights terms to then call for systemic change through the abolition of the Agreement of Agriculture and a reversal of global liberal food policy.

[114] The distinction between human rights as language and as a moral code from human rights law as a set of rights and obligations is not uncommon. See, eg: J Tasioulas, 'Saving Human Rights from Human Rights Law' (2019) 52 *Vanderbilt Journal of Transnational Law* 1167.

[115] P Levitt and S Merry, 'Vernacularization on the Ground: Local Uses of Global Women's Rights in Peru, China, India and the United States' (2009) 9 *Global Networks* 441; M Canfield, 'Compromised collaborations: food, fuel, and power in transnational food security governance' (2018) 9(3–4) *Transnational Legal Theory* 1; B Rajagopal, 'Counter-hegemonic International Law: Rethinking Human Rights and Development as a Third World Strategy' in R Falk, B Rajagopal and J Stevens (eds), *International Law and the Third World: Reshaping Justice* (London, Routledge, 2008).

namely Latin America and Africa.[116] This chapter accepts that human rights are widely recognised, even if not always accepted value codes that states have committed to, but it similarly does not deny that the catalogue of contemporary human rights is ill-equipped to make sense of unbounded suffering that is the pain of plenty. As it has attempted to show, despite significant normative and doctrinal progress, human rights law leaves the logic of extractivist capitalism unchallenged.

[116] See, eg: GEK Dzah, *Sustainable Development, International Law, and a Turn to African Legal Cosmologies* (Cambridge, Cambridge University Press, 2024).

8

Conclusion

BY UTILISING CASE studies and examples from both historical and contemporary contexts, this book seeks to illustrate the multifaceted roles of international law in creating, upholding and addressing the 'pathology of plenty'. Rather than serving as a mere legal digest that compiles all applicable laws governing mineral resources in postcolonial countries, this book theorises on the relationship between these laws and their broader implications. In developing its arguments, it makes specific interventions in each chapter, while simultaneously weaving an overarching narrative throughout that offers a theory of the pathology of plenty from an international law perspective.

The 'Pathology of Plenty' (chapter two) provides an overview of resource curse and paradox of plenty theories. In doing so, it highlights two key characteristics of these theories. First, like all theories, they generalise specific insights based on the experiences of particular communities which are shaped by the realities of their time and place. Secondly, they are rooted in disciplinary traditions, offering insights that reflect sensitivities inherent in those fields. Unsurprisingly, political scientists focus on how resource wealth affects power dynamics and governance structures, while economists concentrate on how mineral resources are translated into economic value. As a result, theories written in different disciplinary traditions are complementary rather than contradictory to one another, despite being divided by theoretical orientations, most notably liberalism and Marxism.[1] While liberal theorists have traditionally dominated this space, a growing body of scholarship on the resource curse and the paradox of plenty is informed by historical-materialist traditions or adopts an explicitly postcolonial lens.[2] Conversations about the resource curse and the pathology of

[1] For an overview, see B Smith and D Waldner, *Rethinking the Resource Curse* (Cambridge, Cambridge University Press, 2021). For contemporary Marxist work, see: B Gill, *The Political Ecology of Colonial Capitalism: Race, Nature, and Accumulation* (Manchester, Manchester University Press, 2024); A Buller, *The Value of a Whale: On the Illusions of Green Capitalism* (Manchester, Manchester University Press, 2022). For recent work, drawing on liberal theory, see V McFarland, *Oil Powers: A History of the US–Saudi Alliance* (New York, Columbia University Press, 2020).

[2] For international law scholarship, see C Schwöbel-Patel, 'Real (E)State: Valuing a Nation under Imperial Rentier Capitalism' in I Feichtner and G Gordon (eds), *Constitutions of Value* (London, Routledge, 2023); S Boysen, *Die postkoloniale Konstellation: Natürliche Ressourcen und das Völkerrecht der Moderne* (Tübingen, Mohr Siebeck, 2021); E Cusato, 'International law, the paradox of plenty and the making of resource-driven conflict' (2020) 33 *Leiden Journal of International Law* 649.

plenty are far from monolithic, and the sophistication of this literature cannot be adequately captured here. Yet, it is important to note that the precise effects of natural resources and the value that they represent on the law and political economy of postcolonial states, while having been much studied, still offers more questions than answers to scientific research of all disciplines, including law, and it is against this background that all subsequent chapters are developed.

The 'Foundation of Plenty' (chapter three) examines the application of core international legal principles in relation to the governance of mineral resources during the transitional phase from colonial to postcolonial times. In doing so, it grapples with the potential of sovereignty as an antidote to the imperial and corporate appropriation of colonial resources, viewing sovereignty not only as a political concept but also as an economic one.[3] More specifically, it traces the emergence of the principles of permanent sovereignty over natural resources and the right of peoples to freely dispose of their natural resources, both in general international law and human rights law. By recounting the negotiation processes surrounding these legal principles and situating them within their historical and political contexts, the chapter offers a sobering account of their transformative potential, while acknowledging that conceptually these principles were both innovative and radical at the time. It also highlights the flawed premise underlying all general principles relating to natural resources: the notion that their export value represents a means of development for post-colonial countries. Through this premise, woven into concepts of resource sovereignty and economic self-determination, international law played a role in stabilising property regimes during the transition from imperial to hegemonic times. By revisiting the work of prominent development theorists, the chapter also shows that the premise of generating prosperity through resource wealth was by no means uncontested at the time.

The 'Hope of Plenty' (chapter four) continues narrating the history of decolonisation processes from an international law perspective, focusing specifically on the transformation of petroleum regimes. By contrasting the ways in which Iran sought to overcome the concession regimes established between the Shah of Persia and British businessman William Knox D'Arcy, through renegotiations and domestic measures, with Algeria's efforts to regain sovereignty over its natural resources as part of its independence from France by means of bilateral treaties and general principles of international law, this chapter attempts to relativise the importance some commentators attribute to the role of international law in decolonising mineral resource regimes. At the same time, it points to the Iranian experience to show how the state-centric concept of sovereignty and the peoples-focused and community-focused concept of collective

[3] This is an insight which builds on a lineage of an intellectual tradition of Third World jurists. See M Bedjaoui, *Towards a New International Economic Order* (New York, Holmes and Meier, 1979).

self-determination can be reconciled with one another, namely by democratising mineral resources governance.

The 'Temptation of Plenty' (chapter five) moves from the past to the present. Against the background of the exceptional role of the state, particularly its executive branches, in mineral resources economies that was established in earlier chapters and that is legitimised by international law, this chapter shows the problems associated with the concentration of wealth and power in the entity of the central government. By introducing 'grand theft' as a concept to signify large-scale fraud schemes involving resources revenues, or their promise, this chapter examines how two of the most sophisticated international legal regimes, namely international money-laundering and international anti-corruption schemes, address this issue. It does so by zooming in on two state-owned companies, namely the Venezuelan company PDVSA and the Malaysian company 1MDB and the ways they were used as instruments of grand theft. Rather than focusing on the actors who initiated these schemes, the chapter zooms in on the role of financial institutions. With anti-money-laundering law being premised on their collaboration in combating financial crimes, this chapter examines the incentive structures that international and domestic law offer in three key jurisdictions of global finance, namely the United States, Switzerland and Singapore, to prevent grand theft. It finds that despite the sophisticated nature of anti-money-laundering regimes, incentives to facilitate grand theft often outweigh those to combat it, creating an alignment of interests between rent-seeking government officials and international financial institutions.

The 'Peril of Plenty' (chapter six) is also concerned with the incentives that the interlinkage between mineral resources wealth and state sovereignty creates. It tackles the ways in which international law addresses mineral resources conceived of both as public good under sovereign discretion, and as private property. Focusing on doctrinal developments over time, this chapter sheds light on the ways in which law contains power, in times of armed conflict and belligerent occupation. In doing so, it contributes to ongoing debates about international law's aptitude to address such situations. It shows that while some progress has been made, international law continues to be wedded to power. This means that the question of whether or not international law's protective, punitive and remedial legal norms are ever given any legal meaning hinges on whether or not they are rendered applicable by the victorious, militarily superior, or politically better-connected party to an armed conflict. Emblematic for this dynamic is the Iraqi High Tribunal set up in 2003 to prosecute a series of grave crimes including war crimes and genocidal acts of Iraqi nationals predating the invasion of Iraq by British and American forces and their allies. A scope not only excluding the acts of foreign private and public security forces, but also of the Coalition Provisional Authority and of all local collaborators.[4] The chapter also shows

[4] A Çubukçu, *For the Love of Humanity: The World Tribunal on Iraq* (Philadelphia, PA, University of Pennsylvania Press, 2018).

that international humanitarian law doctrinally offers a higher degree of protection to mineral resources and the value that they generate if they are subject to concessionary rights or contractual rights, as opposed to sovereign rights or communal rights. This work complements the body of work shedding light on the uneven regimes of protection of domestically held property as opposed to foreign-held property.[5]

Finally, 'The Pain of Plenty' (chapter seven) accepts that two doctrinal developments over the last few years, namely the 'greening' of human rights and the incorporation of human rights into economic governance regimes, have been motivated in part by the adverse effects that mineral resource extraction often has on local communities. The chapter takes a step back to understand how mineral resources extraction was first made sense of as an issue for international human rights. It shows that, early on, human rights bought into the same premise as general international law, namely that resource extraction is beneficial to the majority of the population, while bearing the risk of adversely affecting local communities, ie, the minority of the population. This conceptualisation has two consequences. First, even when resource extraction manifestly affects individual or collective rights, these violations are subject to a balancing act against purportedly majoritarian interests. Secondly, both the adverse effects of mineral resources on the political economy of a country, and the ecological harm of mineral resource extraction at a local, regional and planetary scale, are not considered at all. In sum, the chapter concludes that while human rights have been expanding both doctrinally and jurisprudentially, this expansion does very little to address the planned misery of the pathology of plenty.[6]

Overall, the book shows that while the body of international law has expanded in recognition of the adverse effects of resource wealth on the political economy of postcolonial states, this expansion has not been able to undo the foundations of the pathology of plenty. Efforts to prevent certain aspects of the pathology of plenty, such as the use of mineral resources for conflict finance through the Kimberley Process Certification Scheme, or the loss of public revenue generated through resource extraction due to grand theft by the Extractive Industries Transparency Initiative, have had only very limited success.[7] Similarly, efforts to hold individuals responsible for their involvement in grand theft schemes, or in resources pillage in times of armed conflict, have also only had very modest success, much of which was achieved in domestic courts, rather than international ones.[8] Finally, while there have been some landmark cases

[5] K Greenman, 'On War and International Investment Law' (2024) 73 *International & Comparative Law Quarterly* 579.

[6] On the concept of planned misery, see S Marks, 'Human Rights and Root Causes' (2011) 74 *Modern Law Review* 57.

[7] G Carbonnier et al, 'Curbing Illicit Financial Flows in Commodity Trade and Beyond' (2024) 17 *International Development Policy* 1.

[8] E Cusato, *The Ecology of War and Peace: Marginalising Slow and Structural Violence in International Law* (Cambridge, Cambridge University Press, 2021); F Mégret, 'The "elephant in the

offering remedial measures to those harmed by resource extraction, for instance, through the destruction of local eco-systems, or by private or public security forces deployed to suppress opposition to extractive operations and securitise them, these cases have frequently commanded far more public attention than they have offered remedies.[9] In fact, some of the excitement about cases which ultimately ended up being decided unfavourably for affected communities has obscured them, and in the vast majority of cases justice is never served.

In offering a theory of international law's relationship to the pathology of plenty, this book describes law's role both as foundational and facilitative, while acknowledging that a growing conscientiousness for the pathology of plenty is frequently expressed through the adoption of new legal tools, or the recalibration of old ones. This includes the use of the corporate duty of care under domestic tort law, to order a hydrocarbon corporation to reduce greenhouse gas emissions of the corporate conglomerate including its subsidiaries.[10] It also includes the recognition of new norms such as the right to a healthy environment. Remarkably however, this growing consciousness for the constraints of regimes meant to uphold the exploitation of mineral resources has triggered treaty withdrawal, as was the case for the Energy Charter Treaty. Other changes that are – at least in part – due to the recognition of international law's complicity in the pathology of plenty are ongoing in the regime of foreign investment protection, particularly in response to the mobilisation against investor–state dispute settlement clauses.[11] These changes in international law do not, however, seriously question the promise of overall economic and human development through the value that mineral resources represent. The transition away from traditional mineral resources-driven energy consumption towards forms of energy deemed as being more sustainable, has not ameliorated the pathology of plenty, but just produced new forms of exploitation and violence towards peoples and nature in the Global South.[12]

Recent work is therefore taking a broader view on the relationship between law, the extraction of mineral resources and the premise of development. Some, in fact, inspired by Marxist traditions, not only question the substance of law,

room" in debates about universal jurisdiction: diasporas, duties of hospitality, and the constitution of the political' (2015) 6 *Transnational Legal Theory* 89; D Hovell, 'The Authority of Universal Jurisdiction' (2018) 29 *European Journal of International Law* 427.

[9] BS Chimni, 'The International Law of Jurisdiction: A TWAIL Perspective' (2022) 35 *Leiden Journal of International Law* 29; HM Ahmad, 'The Jurisdictional Vacuum: Transnational Corporate Human Rights Claims in Common Law Home States' (2022) 70 *American Journal of Comparative Law* 227.

[10] The Hague District Court, *Vereniging Milieudefensie and others v Royal Dutch Shell*, Judgment of 26 May 2021, C/09/571932 / HA ZA 19-379.

[11] M Sornarajah, *The International Law on Foreign Investment* (Cambridge, Cambridge University Press, 2021).

[12] O Hailes, 'Lithium in International Law: Trade, Investment, and the Pursuit of Supply Chain Justice' (2022) 25 *Journal of International Economic Law* 148; C Storr, '"Space is the only way to go"' in S Chalmers and S Pahuja (eds), *Routledge Handbook of International Law and the Humanities* (London, Routledge, 2021).

but its very form.[13] Such scholarship goes hand-in-hand with the work that associates the expansion of international law with imperial-capitalist expansion.[14] Emblematic for such work and highlighting its relevance for the pathology of plenty is Porras' writing which traces the legal reasoning of colonial appropriation in European *ius gentium* to excavate the origins of international law's commitment to commerce over that to nature. She observes that

> nature became visible to the early modern Europeans who contributed to a new tradition of *ius gentium* (the law of nations) only in the moment that they articulated it as a material-thing subject to appropriation, reducible to property, and capable of entering the stream of commerce, conceptually transforming nature into what we today call natural resource.[15]

In other words, from the outset of imperialism, law was deeply implicated in disciplining and commodifying and owning nature, given it meaning only in relationship to humanity as 'human environment', or in service to it as 'resource'. To conclude, this book wants to point to different directions of contemporary work engaging with how to identify and undo hierarchical constellations in and through international law.

One avenue such work has taken is the exploration of alternative ontologies and epistemologies in international law. Dzah, for example, argues that only by giving meaning to concepts such as 'sustainable development' through African legal epistemologies as expressed, inter alia, in the case law of African courts, can the concept be rescued from its complicity in the exploitation of the African continent.[16] It is therefore not the form of law that he questions, but the way in which law is given meaning by legal interpreters.

Another avenue taken is by scholars associated with the new materialist tradition and inspired by the work of Haraway and Latour who explore the link between law, anthropocentrism and capitalism.[17] Acknowledging that any notion of universality in (international) law was not premised on the human species, but on the fossil-fuel dependent man whose persistent centrality shaped the Anthropocene as we currently understand it, this strand of scholarship imagines international law through feminist, anti-colonial, queer, anti-racist

[13] C Mieville, *Between Equal Rights: A Marxist Theory of International Law* (Leiden, Brill, 2005); M Hardt and A Negri, *Empire* (Cambridge, MA, Harvard University Press, 2001).

[14] M Koskenniemi, *The Gentle Civilizer of Nations: The Rise and Fall of International Law, 1870–1960* (Cambridge, Cambridge University Press, 2002); N Tzouvala, *Capitalism As Civilisation: A History of International Law* (Cambridge, Cambridge University Press, 2020).

[15] I Porras, 'Appropriating Nature: Commerce, Property and the Commodification of Nature in the Law of Nations' in J Dehm and U Natarajan (eds), *Locating Nature: Making and Unmaking International Law* (Cambridge, Cambridge University Press, 2022) 112.

[16] GEK Dzah, *Sustainable Development, International Law, and a Turn to African Legal Cosmologies* (Cambridge, Cambridge University Press, 2024).

[17] B Latour, *We Have Never Been Modern* (Cambridge, MA, Harvard University Press, 1993); D Haraway, 'Anthropocene, Capitalocene, Plantationocene, Chthulucene: Making Kin' (2015) 6(1) *Environmental Humanities* 159.

and anti-ableist lenses.[18] This work accepts the centrality of mineral resources and fossil-fuel driven capitalism in upholding contemporary social and political hierarchies, expressed sometimes in the term 'Capitalocene'.[19]

Finally, proponents of 'Earth Systems Law', inspired by systems theory, point to the fragmentation and (over-)specialisation of law into self-contained systems to call for a radically new way of thinking law, not only on substance, but also in jurisdictional and institutional terms. Drawing on a number of existing paradigms to legal sense-making of nature, such as ecological law, sustainability law, Earth-centred law, Earth jurisprudence and wild law, Anthropocene law, planetary boundaries law and queer and feminist posthumanism, Earth Systems Law attempts to provide an overarching paradigm for such approaches.[20] As such, Earth Systems Law's unifying concern is the foregrounding of humankind through the reduction of nature to the human environment, as well as the dissonance between legal structures and the ways in which humankind is socially and ecologically embedded in its natural surroundings.

In other words, a more profound rethinking of the form and substance of law has begun that no longer seeks to optimise the extraction of mineral resources with the goal of avoiding, or mitigating, the pathology of plenty. Rather, the new frontier for legal sciences in tandem with other disciplines is to imagine a different social and material world. One which is not premised on the exploitation of nature for the benefit of some, at the expense of the majority of humankind that puts the very existence of Earth as we know it at risk. Such a world requires a legal system which does not elevate the interests of capital over that of nature, and which does not exacerbate social hierarchies and inequalities, but is founded on the understanding that only when we value nature not as a resource, but as the most fundamental – yet most fragile – condition of life. Hopefully, this book has highlighted the importance of exploring such new ways of thinking.

[18] A Grear, 'Deconstructing Anthropos: A Critical Legal Reflection on "Anthropocentric" Law and Anthropocene "Humanity"' (2015) 26 *Law and Critique* 225; E Jones, *Feminist Theory and International Law: Posthuman Perspectives* (London, Routledge, 2023).

[19] JW Moore, *Capitalism in the Web of Life: Ecology and the Accumulation of Capital* (London, Verso, 2016); A Mann, *Fossil Capital: The Rise of Steam-Power and the Roots of Global Warming* (London: Verso, 2016).

[20] LJ Kotzé et al, 'Earth System Law: Exploring New Frontiers in Legal Science' (2022) 11 *Earth System Governance* 1.

Bibliography

Abbott, Kenneth W. and Duncan Snidal, 'Hard and Soft Law in International Governance' (2000) 54(3) *International Organization* 421

——, 'Values and Interests: International Legalization in the Fight Against Corruption' (2002) 31(S1) *The Journal of Legal Studies* S141

Abbott, Kenneth W., Robert O. Keohane, Andrew Moravcsik, Anne-Marie Slaughter and Duncan Snidal, 'The Concept of Legalization' (2000) 54(3) *International Organization* 401

Abi-Saab, Georges, 'Le droit au développement' (1988) 44 *Annuaire Suisse de Droit International* 9

——, 'The Newly Independent States and the Rules of International Law: An Outline' (1962) 8 *Howard Law Journal* 95

——, 'The Role of Law in the Process of Development: With Special Reference to the Transfer of Technology to Underdeveloped Countries' in Soraya Antonius, Claire Nader and Antoine Benjamin Zahlan (eds), *Science and Technology in Developing Countries: Proceedings of a Conference held at the American University of Beirut* (Cambridge University Press 1969)

——, 'Whither the International Community?' (1998) 9(2) *European Journal of International Law* 248

Acemoglu, Daron and James Robinson, *Why Nations Fail: The Origins of Power, Prosperity, and Poverty* (Crown Business 2012)

Ackermann, Tobias, *The Effects of Armed Conflict on Investment Treaties* (Cambridge University Press 2022)

Ahmad, Hassan M., 'The Jurisdictional Vacuum: Transnational Corporate Human Rights Claims in Common Law Home States' (2022) 70(2) *The American Journal of Comparative Law* 227

Alston, Philip, 'The Myopia of the Handmaidens: International Lawyers and Globalization' (1997) 8(3) *European Journal of International Law* 435

Anghie, Antony, *Imperialism, Sovereignty and the Making of International Law* (Cambridge University Press 2005)

——, 'International Financial Institutions' in Christian Reus-Smit (ed), *The Politics of International Law* (Cambridge University Press 2004) 217

Arndt, Heinz Wolfgang, *Economic Development: The History of an Idea* (University of Chicago Press 1989)

Atanasova, Dafina, 'Non-Economic Disciplines Still Take the Back Seat: The Tale of Conflict Clauses in Investment Treaties' (2021) 34(1) *Leiden Journal of International Law* 155

Auty, Richard, *Sustaining Development in Mineral Economies: The Resource Curse Thesis* (Routledge 1993)

Auz, Juan, 'Human Rights-Based Climate Litigation: A Latin American Cartography' (2022) 13(1) *Journal of Human Rights and the Environment* 114

Bak McKenna, Miriam, *Reckoning with Empire: Self-Determination in International Law* (Brill 2022)

Bamberg, James, *The History of the British Petroleum Company, Volume II: The Anglo-Iranian Years 1928–1954* (Cambridge University Press 1994)

Baran, Paul A, 'On the Political Economy of Backwardness' (1952) 20(1) *The Manchester School* 66

Bassiouni, MC and EM Wise, *Aut Dedere Aut Judicare: The Duty to Extradite or Prosecute in International Law* (Martinus Nijhoff 1995)

Bavinck, Maarten, Lorenzo Pellegrini and Erik Mostert (eds), *Conflicts over Natural Resources in the Global South: Conceptual Approaches* (CRC Press 2014)

Baxi, Upendra, 'Voices of Suffering and the Future of Human Rights' (1998) 8(2) *Transnational Law & Contemporary Problems* 125

Becker Lorca, Arnulf, *Mestizo International Law* (Cambridge University Press 2014)

Bedjaoui, Mohammed, *Towards a New International Economic Order* (Holmes and Meier 1979)

Bhandar, Brenna, *Colonial Lives of Property: Law, Land, and Racial Regimes of Ownership* (Duke University Press 2018)

Bhuta, Nehal, 'Recovering Social Rights' in Nehal Bhuta (ed), *Human Rights in Transition* (Oxford University Press 2024) 1

Bollecker-Stern, Brigitte, 'The Legal Character of Emerging Norms Relating to the New International Economic Order: Some Comments' in Kamal Hossain (ed), *Legal Aspects of the New International Economic Order* (Frances Pinter 1980) 68

Boon, Kristen E, 'UN Sanctions as Regulation' (2016) 15(3) *Chinese Journal of International Law* 543

Bothe, Michael and others, 'International Law Protecting the Environment During Armed Conflict: Gaps and Opportunities' (2010) 92(879) *International Review of the Red Cross* 569

Boyd, David R, *The Environmental Rights Revolution: A Global Study of Constitutions, Human Rights, and the Environment* (UBC Press 2011)

Boysen, Sigrid, *Die Postkoloniale Konstellation: Natürliche Ressourcen und das Völkerrecht der Moderne* (Mohr Siebeck 2021)

Brand, Ulrich, Kristina Dietz and Miriam Lang, 'Neo-Extractivism in Latin America. One Side of a New Phase of Global Capitalist Dynamics' (2016) 11(2) *Ciencia Política* 125

Broude, Tomer and Caroline Henckels, 'Not All Rights Are Created Equal: A Loss–Gain Frame of Investor Rights and Human Rights' (2021) 34(1) *Leiden Journal of International Law* 93

Brower, Charles N and John B Tepe, 'The Charter of Economic Rights and Duties of States: Reflection or Rejection of International Law?' (1975) 9(2) *The International Lawyer* 295

Brownlie, Ian, *Loaves and Fishes: Access to Natural Resources and International Law* (London School of Economics and Political Science 1978)

——, 'The Legal Status of Natural Resources in International Law (Some Aspects)' in *Collected Courses of the Hague Academy of International Law* (Brill 1979)

Buller, Adrianne, *The Value of a Whale: On the Illusions of Green Capitalism* (Manchester University Press 2022)

Byrne, Jeffrey James, *Mecca of Revolution: Algeria, Decolonization, and the Third World Order* (Oxford University Press 2016)

Calder, Jack, 'Resource Tax Administration: Functions, Procedures and Institutions' in Daniel Philip, Michael Keen and Charles McPherson (eds), *The Taxation of Petroleum and Minerals: Principles, Problems and Practice* (Routledge 2010) 340

Canfield, Matthew, 'Compromised Collaborations: Food, Fuel, and Power in Transnational Food Security Governance' (2018) 9(3–4) *Transnational Legal Theory* 272

Carbonnier, Gilles, Fritz Brugger, Elisabeth Bürgi Bonanomi, Fred M. Dzanku and Stabandith Insisienmay, 'Curbing Illicit Financial Flows in Commodity Trade and Beyond' (2024) 17 *International Development Policy* 1

Cardoso, Eliana A. and Albert Fishlow, 'The Macroeconomics of the Brazilian External Debt' in Jeffrey D. Sachs (ed), *Developing Country Debt and the World Economy* (University of Chicago Press 1989) 81

Carlston, Kenneth S., 'Concession Agreements and Nationalization' (1958) 52(2) *American Journal of International Law* 260

Cassese, Antonio, *Self-Determination of Peoples: A Legal Reappraisal* (Cambridge University Press 1995)

Chatterjee, Partha, 'The Legacy of Bandung' in Luis Eslava, Michael Fakhri and Vasuki Nesiah (eds), *Bandung, Global History, and International Law: Critical Pasts and Pending Futures* (Cambridge University Press 2017) 657

Chatterjee, Shanker K., 'The Charter of Economic Rights and Duties of States: An Evaluation after 15 Years' (1991) 40(3) *International and Comparative Law Quarterly* 669

Chi, Manjiao, 'Resource Sovereignty in the WTO Dispute Settlement: Implications in China – Raw Materials and China – Rare Earths' (2015) 12(1) *Manchester Journal of International Economic Law* 2

Chimni, Bhupinder S., 'The International Law of Jurisdiction: A TWAIL Perspective' (2022) 35(1) *Leiden Journal of International Law* 29

Clagett, Brice M. and O. Thomas Johnson, 'May Israel as a Belligerent Occupant Lawfully Exploit Previously Unexploited Oil Resources of the Gulf of Suez?' (1978) 72(3) *American Journal of International Law* 558

Collier, Paul, *The Bottom Billion: Why the Poorest Countries Are Failing and What Can Be Done About It* (Oxford University Press 2007)

Collier, Paul and Anke Hoefler, 'The Political Economy of Secession' in E. F. Babbitt and Hurst Hannum (eds), *Negotiating Self-Determination* (Development Research Group, World Bank 2006) 37

Cooper, Richard N., *The Economics of Interdependence: Economic Policy in the Atlantic Community* (Columbia University Press 1968)

Crow, Kevin, 'Bandung's Fate' in Ingo Venzke and Kevin Heller (eds), *Contingency in International Law* (Oxford University Press 2021) 441

Cusato, Eliana, *The Ecology of War and Peace: Marginalising Slow and Structural Violence in International Law* (Cambridge University Press 2021)

——, 'International Law, the Paradox of Plenty and the Making of Resource-Driven Conflict' (2020) 33(3) *Leiden Journal of International Law* 649

Cutler, Claire, *Private Power and Global Authority: Transnational Merchant Law in the Global Political Economy* (Cambridge University Press 2003)

Çubukçu, Ayça, *For the Love of Humanity: The World Tribunal on Iraq* (University of Pennsylvania Press 2018)

Dam-de Jong, Daniëlla, *International Law and Governance of Natural Resources in Conflict and Post-Conflict Situations* (Cambridge University Press 2015)

——, 'UN Natural Resources Sanctions Regimes: Incorporating Market-Based Responses to Address Market-Driven Problems' in Larissa Van den Herik (ed), *Research Handbook on UN Sanctions and International Law* (Edward Elgar 2017) 147

Davis, Kevin E., 'Corruption as a Violation of International Human Rights: A Reply to Anne Peters' (2018) 29(4) *European Journal of International Law* 1289

——, *Between Impunity and Imperialism: The Regulation of Transnational Bribery* (Oxford University Press 2019)

Davis, Mike, *Late Victorian Holocausts: El Niño Famines and the Making of the Third World* (Verso 2002)

Dehm, Julia, 'The Temporalities of Environmental Human Rights' in Kathryn McNeilly and Ben Warwick (eds), *The Times and Temporalities of International Human Rights Law* (Hart Publishing 2022) 33

Dhooge, Lucien J., 'Aguinda v Chevrontexaco: Mandatory Grounds for the Non-Recognition of Foreign Judgments for Environmental Injury in the United States' (2009) 19(1) *Journal of Transnational Law & Policy* 1

Dietrich, Christopher, *Oil Revolution* (Cambridge University Press 2017)

——, 'Mossadegh Madness: Oil and Sovereignty in the Anticolonial Community' (2015) 6(1) *Humanity* 63

Droege, Cordula and Marie-Louise Tougas, 'The Protection of the Natural Environment in Armed Conflict – Existing Rules and Need for Further Legal Protection' (2013) 82(1) *Nordic Journal of International Law* 21

Dupuy, Pierre-Marie and Jorge E. Viñuales, *International Environmental Law* (2nd edn, Cambridge University Press 2018)

Dzah, Godwin Eli Kwadzo, *Sustainable Development, International Law, and a Turn to African Legal Cosmologies* (Cambridge University Press 2024)

Ermacora, Felix, 'Ursprung und Wesen des Selbstbestimmungsrechts der Völker und seine Entwicklung bis zum Zweiten Weltkrieg' in Kurt Rabl (ed), (1964) 50

Escobar, Arturo, 'Construction Nature: Elements for a Post-Structuralist Political Ecology' (1996) 28(4) *Futures* 325

Fakhri, Michael, *Sugar and the Making of International Trade Law* (Cambridge University Press 2017)

Falk, Richard, 'Environmental Warfare and Ecocide – Facts, Appraisal, and Proposals' (1973) 4(1) *Bulletin of Peace Proposals* 80

——, 'The Inadequacy of the Existing Legal Approach to Environmental Protection in Wartime' in Jay E. Austin and Carl E. Bruch (eds), *The Environmental Consequences of War* (Cambridge University Press 2000) 137

Fisch, Jörg, 'State Power and the Will of the People' in Bardo Fassbender and Anne Peters (eds), *The Oxford Handbook of the History of International Law* (Oxford University Press 2012) 30

Franck, Thomas, 'The Emerging Right to Democratic Governance' (1992) 86(1) *American Journal of International Law* 46

Frank, Andre Gunder, *Latin America: Underdevelopment or Revolution* (Monthly Review Press 1971)

Garavini, Giuliano, 'From Boumedienomics to Reaganomics: Algeria, OPEC, and the International Struggle for Economic Equality' (2015) 6(1) *Humanity* 79

Gathii, James Thuo, 'Corruption and Donor Reforms: Expanding the Promises and Possibilities of the Rule of Law as an Anti-Corruption Strategy in Kenya' (1999) 14(2) *Connecticut Journal of International Law* 407

——, 'Africa and the Radical Origins of the Right to Development' (2020) 1(1) *TWAIL Review* 28

——, 'Promise of International Law: A Third World View' (2020) 114 *Proceedings of the ASIL Annual Meeting* 165

Getachew, Adom, *Worldmaking after Empire: The Rise and Fall of Self-Determination* (Princeton University Press 2019)

Gibb, Herman and Keri Grace O'Leary, 'Mercury Exposure and Health Impacts among Individuals in the Artisanal and Small-Scale Gold Mining Community: A Comprehensive Review' (2014) 122(7) *Environmental Health Perspectives* 667

Gilbert, Jérémie, *Natural Resources and Human Rights: An Appraisal* (Oxford University Press 2018)

Gill, Bikrum, *The Political Ecology of Colonial Capitalism: Race, Nature, and Accumulation* (Manchester University Press 2024)

Grear, Anna, 'Deconstructing Anthropos: A Critical Legal Reflection on "Anthropocentric" Law and Anthropocene "Humanity"' (2015) 26(3) *Law and Critique* 225

Greenman, Kathryn, 'On War and International Investment Law' (2024) 73(3) *International and Comparative Law Quarterly* 579

Gu, Bin, 'Mineral Export Restraints and Sustainable Development – Are Rare Earths Testing the WTO's Loopholes?' (2011) 14(4) *Journal of International Economic Law* 765

Gylfason, Thorvaldur, 'Natural Resources, Education, and Economic Development' (2001) 45(4–6) *European Economic Review* 847

Haight, George W., 'The New International Economic Order and the Charter of Economic Rights and Duties of States' (1975) 9(4) *The International Lawyer* 591

Hailes, Oliver, 'Lithium in International Law: Trade, Investment, and the Pursuit of Supply Chain Justice' (2022) 25(1) *Journal of International Economic Law* 148

Haller, Tobias (ed), *Fossil Fuels, Oil Companies, and Indigenous Peoples: Strategies of Multinational Oil Companies, States, and Ethnic Minorities – Impact on Environment, Livelihoods, and Cultural Change* (LIT Verlag Münster 2007)

Haraway, Donna, 'Anthropocene, Capitalocene, Plantationocene, Chthulucene: Making Kin' (2015) 6(1) *Environmental Humanities* 159

Hardt, Michael and Antonio Negri, *Empire* (Harvard University Press 2001)

Harris, Pamela Beth, 'The Humanitarian God in the Political Marketplace' (2016) 7(2) *Humanity* 325

Hasan, Aiah, 'The Algerian Problem' (presented at the Afro-Asian Peoples' Solidarity Conference, Cairo, 1957)

Haslam, Paul A. and Pablo Heidrich (eds), *The Political Economy of Natural Resources and Development: From Neoliberalism to Resource Nationalism* (Routledge 2016)

Hendrix, Cullen S. and Marcus Noland, *Confronting the Curse: The Economics and Geopolitics of Natural Resource Governance* (Columbia University Press 2014)

Heri, Corina, 'Climate Change before the European Court of Human Rights: Capturing Risk, Ill-Treatment and Vulnerability' (2022) 33(3) *European Journal of International Law* 925

Higgins, Rosalyn, *Themes and Theories: Selected Essays, Speeches, and Writings in International Law* (Oxford University Press 2009)

——, 'Natural Resources in the Case Law of the International Court' in Alan Boyle and David Freestone (eds), *International Law and Sustainable Development: Past Achievements and Future Challenges* (Oxford University Press 1998) 87

Hilferding, Rudolf, *Das Finanzkapital: Eine Studie über die jüngste Entwicklung des Kapitalismus* (Wiener Volksbuchhandlung 1910)

Hopgood, Stephen, *The Endtimes of Human Rights* (Cornell University Press 2013)

Hosman, Laura, 'Dividing the Oils: Dynamic Bargaining as Policy Formation in the Nigerian Petroleum Industry' (2009) 26(5) *The Review of Policy Research* 609

Hovell, Devika, 'The Authority of Universal Jurisdiction' (2018) 29(2) *European Journal of International Law* 427

Hummel, Joseph, 'Diamonds Are Smuggler's Best Friend: Regulation, Economics, and Enforcement in the Global Effort to Curb the Trade in Conflict Diamonds' (2007) 41(4) *The International Lawyer* 1145

Humphreys, Macartan and Martin E. Sandbu, 'What is the Problem with Natural Resource Wealth?' in Macartan Humphreys, Jeffrey D. Sachs and Joseph E. Stiglitz (eds), *Escaping the Resource Curse* (Columbia University Press 2007) 1

Husted, Bryan W., 'Wealth, Culture, and Corruption' (1999) 30(2) *Journal of International Business Studies* 339

Hyde, James N., 'Permanent Sovereignty over Natural Wealth and Resources' (1956) 50(4) *American Journal of International Law* 854

IGLP, 'The Role of Law in Global Value Chains: A Research Manifesto' (2016) 4(1) *London Review of International Law* 57

Ivory, Radha, *Corruption, Asset Recovery, and the Protection of Property in Public International Law: The Human Rights of Bad Guys* (2nd edn, Cambridge University Press 2016)

Ivory, Radha and Tina Søreide, 'The International Endorsement of Corporate Settlements in Foreign Bribery Cases' (2020) 69(4) *International and Comparative Law Quarterly* 945

Johnson, David, 'How to Evaluate the Fiscal Terms of Oil Contracts' in Macartan Humphreys, Jeffrey D. Sachs and Joseph E. Stiglitz (eds), *Escaping the Resource Curse* (Columbia University Press 2007) 53

Jones, Emily, *Feminist Theory and International Law: Posthuman Perspectives* (Routledge 2023)

Jones Luong, Pauline and Erika Weinthal, *Oil Is Not a Curse: Ownership Structure and Institutions in Soviet Successor States* (Cambridge University Press 2010)

Kara, Siddarth, *Cobalt Red: How the Blood of the Congo Powers Our Lives* (St. Martin's Press 2023)

Kapur, Ratna, *Gender, Alterity and Human Rights: Freedom in a Fishbowl* (Edward Elgar 2018)

Karl, Terry Lynn, 'The Case for a Transparent Fiscal Social Contract' in Macartan Humphreys, Jeffrey D. Sachs and Joseph E. Stiglitz (eds), *Escaping the Resource Curse* (Columbia University Press 2007) 256

——, *The Paradox of Plenty: Oil Booms and Petro-States* (University of California Press 1997)

Kennedy, David, *On Law and War* (Princeton University Press 2006)

——, 'International Human Rights Movement: Part of the Problem?' (2002) 15 *Harvard Human Rights Journal* 101

——, 'The International Anti-Corruption Campaign' (1999) 14(2) *Connecticut Journal of International Law* 455

Keohane, Robert O. and Joseph S. Nye, 'The Club Model of Multilateral Cooperation and Problems of Democratic Legitimacy' in Robert O. Keohane (ed), *Power and Governance in a Partially Globalized World* (Routledge 2002) 219

Kimberling, Judith, 'Indigenous Peoples and the Oil Frontier in Amazonia: The Case of Ecuador, Chevrontexaco, and Aguinda v. Texaco' (2006) 38(3) *New York University Journal of International Law and Politics* 413

Klein, Naomi, *The Shock Doctrine: The Rise of Disaster Capitalism* (Macmillan 2007)

Knop, Karen, 'Statehood: Territory, People, Government' in James Crawford and Martti Koskenniemi (eds), *The Cambridge Companion to International Law* (Cambridge University Press 2012) 95

Kohen, Marcelo (ed), *Secession: International Law Perspectives* (Cambridge University Press 2006)

——, 'Titles and Effectivités in Territorial Disputes' in Marcelo Kohen and Mamadou Hébié (eds), *Research Handbook on Territorial Disputes in International Law* (Edward Elgar 2018) 145

——, 'Uti Possidetis, Prescription et Pratique Subsequente à un Traité dans l'Affaire de l'Ile de Kasikili/Sedudu Devant la Cour Internationale de Justice' (2000) 43 *German Yearbook of International Law* 253

Koskenniemi, Martti, *The Gentle Civilizer of Nations: The Rise and Fall of International Law, 1870–1960* (Cambridge University Press 2002)

——, 'Empire and International Law: The Real Spanish Contribution' (2011) 61(1) *University of Toronto Law Journal* 1

——, 'National Self-Determination Today: Problems of Legal Theory and Practice' (1994) 43(1) *International and Comparative Law Quarterly* 241

——, '"The Lady Doth Protest Too Much": Kosovo, and the Turn to Ethics in International Law' (2002) 65(2) *The Modern Law Review* 159

Kotzé, Louis J. and others, 'Earth System Law: Exploring New Frontiers in Legal Science' (2022) 11 *Earth System Governance* 1

Krajewski, Markus, 'A Nightmare or a Noble Dream? Establishing Investor Obligations Through Treaty-Making and Treaty-Application' (2020) 5(1) *Business and Human Rights Journal* 105

Krisch, Nico, 'The Decay of Consent: International Law in an Age of Global Public Goods' (2014) 108(1) *The American Journal of International Law* 1

Kulamadayil, Lys, 'Grand Theft in International Law' (2022) 10(3) *London Review of International Law* 427

——, 'Placed in Between: The Natural Environment in International Law' (2022) 13(4) *Transnational Legal Theory* 466

——, 'When International Law Distracts: Reconsidering Anti-Corruption Law' (2018) 7(3) *ESIL Reflections* 1

Latour, Bruno, *We Have Never Been Modern* (Harvard University Press 1993)

Le Billon, Philippe, *Wars of Plunder: Conflicts, Profits and the Politics of Resources* (Hurst 2012)

—— (ed), *The Geopolitics of Resource Wars* (Routledge 2017)

Leite, Carlos and Jens Weidmann, 'Does Mother Nature Corrupt? Natural Resources, Corruption, and Economic Growth' (1999) *IMF Working Paper*

Leiter, Andrea, 'Protecting Concessionary Rights: General Principles and the Making of International Investment Law' (2022) 35(1) *Leiden Journal of International Law* 55

Lenin, Vladimir, *Imperialism: The Highest Stage of Capitalism* (Resistance Books 1999)

——, *The Right of Nations to Self-Determination* (Collected Works vol 20, 3rd edn, Progress Publishers 1977)

Levitt, Peggy and Sally Merry, 'Vernacularization on the Ground: Local Uses of Global Women's Rights in Peru, China, India and the United States' (2009) 9(4) *Global Networks* 441

Lindgren, Tim, 'Ecocide, Genocide and the Disregard of Alternative Life-Systems' (2018) 22(4) *The International Journal of Human Rights* 525

Lüth, Felix, 'Corporate Non-Prosecution Agreements as Transnational Human Problems: Transnational Law and the Study of Domestic Criminal Justice Reforms in a Globalised World' (2021) 12(2) *Transnational Legal Theory* 315

Macklem, Patrick, 'Human Rights in International Law: Three Generations or One?' (2015) 3(1) *London Review of International Law* 61

Mahdavy, Hossein, 'The Pattern and Problems of Economic Development in Rentier States: The Case of Iran' in M. A. Cook (ed), *Studies in the Economic History of the Middle East* (Oxford University Press 1970) 428

Mann, Andreas, *Fossil Capital: The Rise of Steam-Power and the Roots of Global Warming* (Versio 2016)

Mann, F. A., 'Outlines of a History of Expropriation' (1959) 75 *Law Quarterly Review*

Marchal, Jules, *Forced Labor in the Gold & Copper Mines: A History of Congo under Belgian Rule, 1910–1945* (Per Ankh Publishers 2005)

——, *Lord Leverhulme's Ghosts: Colonial Exploitation in the Congo* (Verso 2017)

Marceau, Gabrielle, 'WTO Dispute Settlement and Human Rights' (2002) 13(4) *European Journal of International Law* 753

Marks, Susan, *The Riddle of All Constitutions: International Law, Democracy, and the Critique of Ideology* (Oxford University Press 2000)

——, 'Human Rights and Root Causes' (2011) 74(1) *Modern Law Review* 57

McCreary, Tyler and Vanessa Lamb, 'Reflections on a Political Ecology of Sovereignty: Engaging International Law and "the Map"' in Julia Dehm and Usha Natarajan (eds), *Locating Nature: Making and Unmaking International Law* (Cambridge University Press 2022) 134

McFarland, Victor, 'The New International Economic Order, Interdependence, and Globalization' (2015) 6(1) *Humanity* 217

——, *Oil Powers: A History of the U.S.-Saudi Alliance* (Columbia University Press 2020)

McGregor, Katharine and Vannessa Hearman, 'Challenging the Lifeline of Imperialism' in Luis Eslava, Michael Fakhri and Vasuki Nesiah (eds), *Bandung, Global History, and International Law: Critical Pasts and Pending Futures* (Cambridge University Press 2017) 161

McNeilly, Kathryn, 'Are Rights Out of Time? International Human Rights Law, Temporality, and Radical Social Change' (2018) 28(6) *Social & Legal Studies* 817

Megret, Frédéric, 'From "Savages" to "Unlawful Combatants": A Postcolonial Look at International Humanitarian Law's "Other"' in Anne Oxford (ed), *International Law and Its "Others"* (Cambridge University Press 2006) 265

Mégret, Frédéric, 'The "Elephant in the Room" in Debates about Universal Jurisdiction: Diasporas, Duties of Hospitality, and the Constitution of the Political' (2015) 6(1) *Transnational Legal Theory* 89

Menaldo, Victor, *The Institutions Curse: Natural Resources, Politics, and Development* (Cambridge University Press 2016)

Mieville, China, *Between Equal Rights: A Marxist Theory of International Law* (Brill 2005)

Mingst, Karen A., 'Cooperation or Illusion: An Examination of the Intergovernmental Council of Copper Exporting Countries' (1976) 30(2) *International Organization* 263

Mitchell, Timothy, *Carbon Democracy: Political Power in the Age of Oil* (Verso 2011)

Moore, Jason W., *Capitalism in the Web of Life: Ecology and the Accumulation of Capital* (Verso 2016)

Morgera, Elisa and Kati Kulovesi (eds), *Research Handbook on International Law and Natural Resources* (Edward Elgar 2016)

Moyn, Samuel, *Not Enough: Human Rights in an Unequal World* (Harvard University Press 2018)

——, *The Last Utopia: Human Rights in History* (Harvard University Press 2010)

——, 'A Powerless Companion: Human Rights in the Age of Neoliberalism' (2014) 77(4) *Law and Contemporary Problems*

Mutua, Makau W., 'Why Redraw the Map of Africa: A Moral and Legal Inquiry' (1994) 16 *Michigan Journal of International Law* 1113

Myrdal, Gunnar, *Economic Theory and Under-Developed Regions* (Harper & Row 1957)

Nadakavukaren Schefer, Krista, 'Causation in the Corruption – Human Rights Relationship' (2010) 1(4) *RW Rechtswissenschaft* 397

Natarajan, Usha, 'Who Do We Think We Are?: Human Rights in a Time of Ecological Change' in Julia Dehm and Usha Natarajan (eds), *Locating Nature: Making and Unmaking International Law* (Cambridge University Press 2022) 200

Nesiah, Vasuki, 'Placing International Law: White Spaces on a Map' (2003) 16(1) *Leiden Journal of International Law* 1

Nixon, Rob, *Slow Violence and the Environmentalism of the Poor* (Harvard University Press 2011)

Okafor, Obiora Chinedu, 'Newness, Imperialism, and International Legal Reform in Our Time: A TWAIL Perspective' (2005) 43(1&2) *Osgoode Hall Law Journal* 171

Okowa, Phoebe, 'Natural Resources in Situations of Armed Conflict: Is There a Coherent Framework for Protection?' (2007) 9(3) *International Community Law Review* 237

——, 'Sovereignty Contests and the Protection of Natural Resources in Conflict Zones' (2013) 66(1) *Current Legal Problems* 33

Özsu, Umut, 'Determining New Selves: Mohammed Bedjaoui on Algeria, Western Sahara, and Post-Classical International Law' in Jochen von Bernstorff and Philipp Dann (eds), *The Battle for International Law in the Decolonization Era* (Oxford University Press 2019) 311

——, 'Organizing Internationally: Georges Abi-Saab, the Congo Crisis and the Decolonization of the United Nations' (2020) 31(2) *European Journal of International Law* 601

Pahuja, Sundhya, *Decolonising International Law: Development, Economic Growth and the Politics of Universality* (Cambridge University Press 2011)

Pahuja, Sundhya and Cait Storr, 'Rethinking Iran and International Law: The Anglo-Iranian Oil Company Case Revisited' in James Crawford, Abdul Koroma, Said Mahmoudi and Alain Pellet (eds), *The International Legal Order: Current Needs and Possible Responses* (Brill | Nijhoff 2017) 53

Pasqualucci, Jo M., 'The Right to a Dignified Life (Vida Digna): The Integration of Economic and Social Rights with Civil and Political Rights in the Inter-American Human Rights System' (2008) 31(1) *Hastings International and Comparative Law Review* 1

Pellegrini, Lorenzo, Murat Arsel, Martí Orta-Martínez and Carlos F. Mena, 'International Investment Agreements, Human Rights, and Environmental Justice: The Texaco/Chevron Case from the Ecuadorian Amazon' (2020) 23(2) *Journal of International Economic Law* 455

Pentassuglia, Gaetano, 'Towards a Jurisprudential Articulation of Indigenous Land Rights' (2011) 22(1) *European Journal of International Law* 165

Pertile, Marco, *La Relazione tra Risorse Naturali e Conflitti Armati nel Diritto Internazionale* (CEDAM 2013)

Peters, Anne, 'Corruption as a Violation of International Human Rights' (2019) 29(4) *European Journal of International Law* 1251

Petersmann, Marie-Catherine, *When Environmental Protection and Human Rights Collide: The Politics of Conflict Management by Regional Courts* (Cambridge University Press 2022)

Pistor, Katharina, *The Code of Capital: How the Law Creates Wealth and Inequality* (Princeton University Press 2019)

Pogge, Thomas, 'The Role of International Law in Reproducing Massive Poverty' in Samantha Besson and John Tasioulas (eds), *The Philosophy of International Law* (Oxford University Press 2010) 417

Pomerance, Michla, 'The United States and Self-Determination: Perspectives on the Wilsonian Conception' (1976) 70(1) *American Journal of International Law* 1

Porras, Ileana, 'Appropriating Nature: Commerce, Property and the Commodification of Nature in the Law of Nations' in Julia Dehm and Usha Natarajan (eds), *Locating Nature: Making and Unmaking International Law* (Cambridge University Press 2022) 111

Prashad, Vijay, *The Darker Nations: A People's History of the Third World* (The New Press 2008)

——, *The Poorer Nations: A Possible History of the Global South* (2nd edn, Verso 2014)

Putnam, Tonya L., 'Courts Without Borders: Domestic Sources of U.S. Extraterritoriality in the Regulatory Sphere' (2009) 63(3) *International Organization* 459

Radon, Jenik and George Soros, 'How to Negotiate an Oil Agreement' in Macartan Humphreys, Jeffrey D. Sachs and Joseph E. Stiglitz (eds), *Escaping the Resource Curse* (Columbia University Press 2007) 89

Rajagopal, Balakrishnan, 'Corruption, Legitimacy and Human Rights: The Dialectic of the Relationship' (1999) 14(2) *Connecticut Journal of International Law* 495

——, 'Counter-Hegemonic International Law: Rethinking Human Rights and Development as a Third World Strategy' in Richard Falk, Balakrishnan Rajagopal and Jacqueline Stevens (eds), *International Law and the Third World – Reshaping Justice* (Routledge 2008) 63

Rajkovic, Nikolas M., 'The Visual Conquest of International Law: Brute Boundaries, the Map, and the Legacy of Cartogenesis' (2018) 31(2) *Leiden Journal of International Law* 267

Randeria, Shalini, 'The State of Globalization: Legal Plurality, Overlapping Sovereignties and Ambiguous Alliances Between Civil Society and the Cunning State in India' (2007) 24(1)

Redslob, Robert, *Völkerrechtliche Ideen der Französischen Revolution* (Mohr Siebeck 1916)

Ross, Michael L., *The Oil Curse: How Petroleum Wealth Shapes the Development of Nations* (Princeton University Press 2012)

Rose-Ackerman, Susan, 'International Actors and the Promises and Pitfalls of Anti-Corruption Reform' (2012) 34(3) *University of Pennsylvania Journal of International Law* 447

——, 'Political Corruption and Democracy' (1999) 14(2) *Connecticut Journal of International Law* 363

Rostow, Walt Whitman, *The Stages of Economic Growth: A Non-Communist Manifesto* (Cambridge University Press 1960)

Rueskamp, Hella, John Ariki, Klaus Stieglitz and Christoph Treskatis, 'Effect of Oil Exploration and Production on the Salinity of a Marginally Permeable Aquifer System in the Thar Jath-, Mala- and Unity Oilfields, Southern Sudan' (2014) 1(1) *Zentralblatt für Geologie und Paläontologie*

Ruggie, John Gerard, *Just Business: Multinational Corporations and Human Rights* (W. W. Norton & Company 2013)

Ryngaert, Cedric, *Jurisdiction in International Law* (2nd edn, Oxford University Press 2015)

Sachs, Jeffrey D., 'Government, Geography, and Growth: The True Drivers of Economic Development' (2012) 142–150

——, 'How to Handle the Macroeconomics of Oil Wealth' in Macartan Humphreys, Jeffrey D. Sachs and Joseph E. Stiglitz (eds), *Escaping the Resource Curse* (Columbia University Press 2007) 173

Sachs, Jeffrey D. and Andrew M. Warner, 'The Big Push, Natural Resource Booms and Growth' (1999) 59(1) *Journal of Development Economics* 43

——, 'The Curse of Natural Resources' (2001) 45(4–6) *European Economic Review* 827

Sandholtz, Wayne, *Prohibiting Plunder: How Norms Change* (Oxford University Press 2007)

Schachter, Oscar, *Sharing the World's Resources* (Columbia University Press 1972)

——, 'Invisible College of International Lawyers' (1977) 72(2) *Northwestern University Law Review* 217

Schrijver, Nico, *Sovereignty over Natural Resources: Balancing Rights and Duties* (Cambridge University Press 1997)

Schwöbel-Patel, Christine, 'Real (E)State' in Isabel Feichtner and Geoff Gordon (eds), *Constitutions of Value* (Routledge 2023) 68

Shafer, Michael, *Winners and Losers: How Sectors Shape the Developmental Prospects of States* (Cornell University Press 1994)

Sharman, Jason Campbell, *The Despot's Guide to Wealth Management: On the International Campaign Against Grand Corruption* (Cornell University Press 2017)

Silverstein, Ken, *The Secret World of Oil* (Verso Books 2015)

Simpson, Gerry, *Great Powers and Outlaw States: Unequal Sovereigns in the International Legal Order* (Cambridge University Press 2004)

Singer, Hans W., 'Economic Progress in Underdeveloped Countries' (1949) 16(1) *Social Research* 1

——, 'The Distribution of Gains Between Investing and Borrowing Countries' (1950) 40(2) *The American Economic Review* 473

Singh, Anup, 'Report by Dr. Anup Singh (India)' in *Afro-Asian Peoples Solidarity Conference, Cairo, 1957–1958*, ed. Afro-Asian Peoples Solidarity Conference (Moscow Foreign Languages Publishing House 1958)

Sornarajah, M., *The International Law on Foreign Investment* (5th edn, Cambridge University Press 2021)

Sparks, Tom, *Self-Determination in the International Legal System: Whose Claim, to What Right?* (Hart Publishing 2023)

St John, Taylor, *The Rise of Investor-State Arbitration: Politics, Law, and Unintended Consequences* (Oxford University Press 2018)

Stephens, Beth, 'Translating *Filartiga*: A Comparative and International Law Analysis of Domestic Remedies for International Human Rights Violations' (2002) 27(1) *Yale Journal of International Law* 1

Stessens, Guy, *Money Laundering: A New International Law Enforcement Model* (Cambridge University Press 2000)

Stiglitz, Joseph E., 'What is the Role of the State?' in Macartan Humphreys, Jeffrey D. Sachs and Joseph E. Stiglitz (eds), *Escaping the Resource Curse* (Columbia University Press 2007) 23

Storr, Cait, '"Space is the Only Way to Go"' in Shane Chalmers and Sundhya Pahuja (eds), *Routledge Handbook of International Law and the Humanities* (Routledge 2021)

Tasioulas, John, 'Saving Human Rights from Human Rights Law' (2019) 52(5) *Vanderbilt Journal of Transnational Law* 1167

Taylor, Mark, *War Economies and International Law* (Cambridge University Press 2021)

Teubner, Günther, 'Globale Bukowina, Zur Emergenz eines transnationalen Rechtspluralismus' (1996) 15 *Rechtshistorisches Journal* 255

——, 'Globale Zivilverfassungen: Alternativen zur staatszentrierten Verfassungstheorie' in Marcelo Neves and Rüdiger Voigt (eds), *Die Staaten der Weltgesellschaft: Niklas Luhmanns Staatsverständnis* (Nomos 2007) 115

Thomas, Chantal, 'Does the Good Governance Policy of the International Financial Institutions Privilege Markets at the Expense of Democracy' (1999) 14(2) *Connecticut Journal of International Law* 551

Tourme-Jouannet, Emmanuelle, *What Is a Fair International Society? International Law Between Development and Recognition* (Hart Publishing 2013)

Tunkin, Grigoriĭ Ivanovich, *Theory of International Law* (Harvard University Press 1974)

Tzouvala, Ntina, *Capitalism As Civilisation: A History of International Law* (Cambridge University Press 2020)

——, 'Invested in Whiteness: Zimbabwe, the von Pezold Arbitration, and the Question of Race in International Law' (2022) 2(2) *Journal of Law and Political Economy* 226

Veltmeyer, Henry and James F. Petras, 'Introduction' in Henry Veltmeyer and James F. Petras (eds), *The New Extractivism: A Post-Neoliberal Development Model or Imperialism of the Twenty-First Century?* (Zed Books 2014) 1

Venables, Anthony J. and Paul Collier, *Plundered Nations? Successes and Failures in Natural Resource Extraction* (Palgrave 2011)

Venzke, Ingo, 'The Law of the Global Economy and the Spectre of Inequality' (2021) 9(1) *London Review of International Law* 111

——, 'What If? Counterfactual (Hi)Stories of International Law' (2018) 8(2) *Asian Journal of International Law* 403

——, 'Possibilities of the Past: Histories of the NIEO and the Travails of Critique' (2017) 20(3) *Journal of the History of International Law* 263

Viñuales, Jorge E., 'International Investment Law and Natural Resource Governance' in Elisa Morgera and Kati Kulovesi (eds), *Research Handbook on International Law and Natural Resources* (Edward Elgar 2016) 26

Vitalis, Robert, 'The Midnight Ride of Kwame Nkrumah and Other Fables of Bandung (Ban-doong)' (2013) 4(2) *Humanity* 261

von Bogdandy, Armin, Matthias Goldmann and Ingo Venzke, 'From Public International to International Public Law: Translating World Public Opinion into International Public Authority' (2017) 28(1) *European Journal of International Law* 115

Watts, Michael, *Curse of the Black Gold: 50 Years of Oil in the Niger Delta* (Powerhouse Books 2008)

——, 'Resource Curse? Governmentality, Oil and Power in the Niger Delta, Nigeria' (2004) 9(1) *Geopolitics* 50

Webb, Philippa, 'The United Nations Convention Against Corruption: Global Achievement or Missed Opportunity?' (2005) 8(1) *Journal of International Economic Law* 191

Wenar, Leif, *Blood Oil: Tyrants, Violence, and the Rules That Run the World* (Oxford University Press 2016)

White, Gillian, 'New International Economic Order' (1976) 16(2) *Virginia Journal of International Law* 323

Whyte, Jessica, *The Morals of the Market: Human Rights and the Rise of Neoliberalism* (Verso 2019)

Williams, Patricia J., 'Alchemical Notes: Reconstructing Ideals from Deconstructed Rights' (1987) 22 *Harvard Civil Rights–Civil Liberties Law Review* 401

Wright, Tom and Bradley Hope, *Billion Dollar Whale: The Man Who Fooled Wall Street, Hollywood, and the World* (Hachette Books 2018)

Zerk, Jennifer A., *Multinationals and Corporate Social Responsibility: Limitations and Opportunities in International Law* (Cambridge University Press 2006)

Index

www.ingramcontent.com/pod-product-compliance
Ingram Content Group UK Ltd.
Pitfield, Milton Keynes, MK11 3LW, UK
UKHW020843290926
15470UKWH00004B/1521

9 781509 969623